REAGANOMICS

REAGANOMICS

Supply-Side Economics
In Action

BRUCE R. BARTLETT

Foreword by U.S. Rep. Jack Kemp

QUILL

New York   1982

Library of Congress Cataloging in Publication Data.

Bartlett, Bruce R., 1951-
  Reaganomics: supply-side economics in action.

  Originally published: Westport, Conn.: Arlington House, c1981.
  Includes bibliographical references and index.
  1. United States — Economic policy — 1981-
2. Supply-side economics — United States. I. Title.
[HC106.8.B37   1982]   338.973   82-472
ISBN 0-688-01182-9 (pbk.)   AACR2

Printed in the United States of America

First Quill Edition

1 2 3 4 5 6 7 8 9 10

Contents

Foreword, Representative Jack Kemp   vii
Acknowledgments   viii
Preface   ix

1 / Supply-Side Economics   1
2 / Taxes and Revenues   14
3 / The Cost of Progressive Tax Rates   27
4 / The Income-Transfer Wedge   41
5 / Taxation and Regional Growth and Decline   54
6 / Inflation and Taxation   70
7 / Econometrics and Politics   83
8 / The Mellon Tax Cuts   97
9 / The Rediscovery of Incentive, 1946–1954   106
10 / The Kennedy Tax Cuts   114
11 / The Kemp-Roth Revolution   125
12 / Proposition 13 and Its Aftermath   139
13 / The Capital Gains Tax Cut   150
14 / The Balanced Budget Question   159

15 / *The High Cost of Jimmy Carter*   167
16 / *Taxes in Great Britain*   182
17 / *Supply-Side Economics Abroad*   191

18 / *Economic Policies for the Eighties and Beyond*   204
Epilogue   211

Appendix A / Excerpts from President Calvin Coolidge's
   Speech to the National Republican Club, New York,
   February 12, 1924   224
Appendix B / 1976 Congressional Research Service Re-
   port on the Revenue Impact of Tax Reductions   226
Appendix C / The Revenue Act of 1964 and Its Effects   228
Appendix D / Federal Government Receipts, 1963–68   230
Appendix E / Congressman Jack Kemp's Speech to the
   Republican National Convention, August 17, 1976   231
Appendix F / How a Family of Four with the Median
   Income Fared During the Carter Administration   234
Appendix G / Estimated Increased Social Security and
   Inflation Tax Burden on Individuals in 1981   235
Index   236

Foreword

Bruce Bartlett has written a brilliant exposition of supply-side economics, which will be an important addition to economic literature for years to come.

I am sure that he had no idea when he joined my congressional staff in January, 1977 that he was joining a movement as well. He has been an important participant and ally in the political and economic revolution which has been taking place in America and which culminated in the election of Ronald Reagan as President of the United States.

As a member of the congressional staff and in his many published articles Bruce has made invaluable contributions to supply-side economic thought and to the political success of the tax reduction movement in America. His book will undoubtedly serve as an important guide for President Reagan and the Congress, as we work together to put America on a new economic course, one that will bring sustained prosperity to all Americans without inflation. I will continue to rely on his advice and counsel in years to come and I hope that *Reganomics* receives the widest possible distribution.

CONGRESSMAN JACK F. KEMP

Acknowledgments

My greatest intellectual debt is to Jack Kemp, who first introduced me to supply-side economics when I went to work for him in January 1977. One of the very first things he asked me when we were introduced was, "Are you a supply-side fiscalist?" Not having any idea what the term meant, I naturally said yes. It must have been the right answer, because I got the job as his staff economist.

Soon thereafter, I learned what supply-side economics is really all about. Through Kemp I soon came to know all the intellectual leaders of supply-side economics, including Arthur Laffer, Jude Wanniski, Paul Craig Roberts, Norman Ture and Steve Entin. Others who, in one way or another, also helped me develop the thinking that went into this book include Randall Teague, Stuart Sweet, Robert Ferguson, Janet Olson, Bruce Thompson, Dave Smick, George Gilder, Peter Brimelow, and Mark Policinski.

In closing, I would like to mention one other intellectual debt, and that is to the *Wall Street Journal*. The *Journal*, particularly its editorial page, under the leadership of Robert Bartley, is one of the most intellectually stimulating publications in America. Moreover, it has been the vanguard of neoconservatism and supply-side economics. This book probably could not have been written without the *Journal*, a fact amply demonstrated in the footnotes.

Preface

The present book was conceived and written prior to the 1980 election. However, I feel it is entirely appropriate to call the book *Reaganomics*. Early in the presidential campaign Ronald Reagan established himself as a forceful and eloquent spokesman for supply-side economics. He alone, of all the major candidates of either major party, voiced his strong support for the Kemp-Roth tax rate reduction bill. Even after achieving the Republican presidential nomination in August, when many of his economic and political advisors were urging him to backtrack on his support for Kemp-Roth, he continued his unequivocal support for a 30 percent across-the-board tax rate reduction. There is no doubt in my mind that Reagan's support for tax reduction to get our economy moving again by stimulating work, investment and production incentives—supply-side economics—was a significant factor in his landslide victory.

Since Ronald Reagan took office, I have had no reason to doubt that my judgment was correct: he is a supply-sider through and through. Time and time again Reagan has rejected efforts by his advisors to drop or tone down his supply-side policies.

For this edition, a new epilogue has been included which discusses Reagan's economic policies since taking office. Although it is too early to say with certainty that his program is working, I am confident that time will demonstrate the wisdom of his policies.

1

Supply-Side Economics

I N MANY RESPECTS, SUPPLY-SIDE ECONOMICS IS NOTHING MORE than classical economics rediscovered. More particularly, it is Say's law of markets rediscovered. The essence of Say's law, named for the great French economist Jean Baptiste Say, is that goods are ultimately paid for with other goods. Thus it is production which limits the satisfaction of human wants, not the ability to consume, which, in the aggregate, is unlimited. Consequently, Say argued that

> the encouragement of mere consumption is no benefit to commerce; for the difficulty lies in supplying the means, not in stimulating the desire of consumption; and we have seen that production alone furnishes those means. Thus, it is the aim of good government to stimulate production, of bad government to encourage consumption.[1]

Similarly, John Stuart Mill said:

> What a country wants to make it richer, is never consumption, but production. Where there is the latter, we may be sure that there is no want of the former. To produce, implies that the producer desires to consume; why else should he give himself useless labour? He may not wish to consume what he himself produces, but his motive for producing and selling is the desire to buy. Therefore, if the producers generally produce and sell more and more, they certainly also buy more and

more. Each may not want more of what he himself produces, but each wants more of what some other produces; and, by producing what the other wants, hopes to obtain what the other produces. There will never, therefore, be a greater quantity produced, of commodities in general, than there are consumers for. But there may be, and always are, abundance of persons who have the inclination to become consumers of some commodity, but are unable to satisfy their wish, because they have not the means of producing either that, or anything to give in exchange for it. The legislator, therefore, needs not give himself any concern about consumption. There will always be consumption for everything which can be produced, until the wants of all who possess the means of producing are completely satisfied, and then production will not increase any farther. The legislator has to look solely to two points: that no obstacle shall exist to prevent those who have the means of producing, from employing those means as they find most for their interest; and that those who have not at present the means of producing, to the extent of their desire to consume, shall have every facility afforded their acquiring the means, that, becoming producers, they may be enabled to consume.[2]

This doctrine was essentially accepted by all economists until the Great Depression, when it came under heavy attack from John Maynard Keynes, who in fact misunderstood and misrepresented the basis of Say's law. In particular he turned Say's law into a simple statement that "supply creates its own demand" and said that this is "equivalent to the proposition that there is no obstacle to full employment." In defense of this proposition, Keynes quoted John Stuart Mill out of context, implying that Say's law holds that there can never be an oversupply of any product, when it only states that there cannot be a general oversupply of all goods.[3]

In his *General Theory of Employment, Interest and Money*, Keynes succeeded in arguing that the cause of the Great Depression was underconsumption and that government policy ought to be directed toward stimulating demand, via budget deficits and easy money. Keynes' theory soon became the new economic orthodoxy, largely because his policy prescriptions coincided with the politics of the times. As Joseph Schumpeter said of *The General Theory*, "whatever its merit as a piece of analysis may be, there cannot be any doubt that it owed its victorious career primarily to the fact that its argument implemented some of the strongest political preferences of a large number of modern economists."[4]

In fact, there was a serious problem with the demand side of the economy in the 1930s, but it had nothing to do with the Keynesian view. It related to the Federal Reserve Board's tragic blunder of causing the U.S. money stock to decline by over a third between 1929 and 1932. When the rigidities of the economy prevented prices and wages from falling to an equilibrium level consistent with the existing money stock, the depression ensued.[5] The great error of economists and policymakers was the acceptance of Keynesian demand-management theories as the basis for a general economic program, rather than being applicable—if at all—to just the conditions of a deflationary depression.

By the end of World War II Keynesian economics had virtually total allegiance of the younger members of the economics profession. By the 1960s they were the full professors at most universities, their influence so pervasive that Milton Friedman, the preeminent monetarist, remarked in 1965, "We are all Keynesians now."[6] But the heavily Keynesian economic policies of the 1960s and 1970s were sowing the seeds of their own destruction.

In a real sense, Keynesian economics died during the recession of 1974–75. In 1975 the unemployment rate hit its highest level since the depression—8.5 percent—despite a $45 billion federal budget deficit (at that time, the largest since World War II) and a soaring inflation rate. According to conventional Keynesian theory this could not happen. The Phillips Curve, a basic Keynesian component, states that there is an inverse relationship between inflation and unemployment—the higher one is, the lower the other should be.[7] Thus, the Keynesians were completely baffled about what policy prescription to offer for the situation. Normally, unemployment calls for a budget deficit, while inflation calls for a budget surplus. Since they already had the largest peacetime deficit in American history, they could hardly call for more deficit spending. And a reduction in the deficit to battle inflation would exacerbate the already bad unemployment situation. The Keynesians were therefore left without anything to offer to rectify the situation. Soon, many were proclaiming the death of Keynesian economics.[8]

The question thus arose, What will take the place of Keynesian economics? Irving Kristol was first to draw attention to supply-side economics as a replacement for the discredited Keynesian school:

> In response to this crisis in the theory of economic policy, a "new" economics is beginning to emerge. . . . Its focus is on economic growth, rather than on economic equilibrium or disequilibrium, and it sees such growth arising from a free response (e.g., investment, hard work, etc.) to the economic incentives of a free market.
>
> It does retain the Keynesian macroeconomic apparatus for diagnostic purposes, but its inclination is "conservative" rather than "liberal"— i.e., it believes that only the private sector can bring us sustained economic growth, and that whatever tasks one might wish to assign to the public sector, economic growth cannot be one of them.
>
> This "new" economics is sometimes described, rather cumbersomely,

as "supply-side fiscal policy". . . . It arises in opposition to the Keynesian notion that an increase in demand, by itself, will increase supply and therefore accelerate economic growth. The "new" economics asserts that an increase in demand, where the natural incentives to economic growth are stifled, will result simply in inflation. It is only an increase in *productivity,* which converts latent into actual demand by bringing commodities (old and new) to market at prices people can afford, that generates economic growth.[9]

The serious decline in productivity growth in the U.S., which was only just becoming apparent in 1977, fueled the development of supply-side approaches to the economy. Table 1 summarizes the problem.

The Joint Economic Committee of the U.S. Congress was instrumental in pointing to the decline in productivity growth in the U.S. and its impact on inflation and the standard of living. As the committee chairman, Senator Lloyd Bentsen of Texas, said in the committee's mid-year report in 1979, "productivity is the linchpin of economic progress in the 1980s." More important, the committee report made clear that the way to stimulate productivity lay not in conventional Keynesian economics but in supply-side policies:

> In brief, the solution to our long-run stagflation problem does not lie in short-run policy initiatives designed to maintain aggregate spending far below our Nation's productive potential. Rather, the solution lies in the adoption of longer run policies aimed at expanding the supply side of the economy; that is, at expanding our Nation's productive potential in a manner that raises dramatically the growth of American productivity. . . . Only by understanding our productivity problems will we be able to develop solutions to the stagflation that dominates the economic outlook in the forseeable future.[10]

To most Keynesian economists, the drop in productivity growth is a mystery.[11] Most monetarists are also baffled by the slowdown.[12] It is the economists whose primary focus is on the supply side of the economy who believe that they have an explanation and solution for the productivity decline. Beryl Sprinkel, chief economist for the Harris Bank, offers this supply-side explanation for the problem:

> In my opinion, the reason for the poor performance of our economy has been the growing burden of government. The tax burden at all levels of government in 1966 was 33 percent of national income. This past fiscal year the tax burden rose to a record 39.2 percent of national income. Although voters perceive taxes paid as the cost of government, the real economic cost is represented by the share of national income

TABLE 1

The Productivity Problem

	Relative Productivity*	Average Annual Percent Change in Productivity†			
		1950-67	1967-72	1972-77	1950-77
Japan	62.2	7.4	9.2	3.5	7.0
West Germany	79.1	5.0	4.8	3.5	4.7
Italy	54.3	5.3	5.0	1.0	4.4
France	84.7	4.7	4.5	3.1	4.3
Canada	91.6	2.5	2.8	0.8	2.3
United Kingdom	55.1	2.2	3.0	1.2	2.2
United States	100.0	2.4	1.1	0.6	1.8

*Measured by real gross domestic product per employed civilian, using international price weights, relative to the United States.

†Measured by growth in real domestic product per employed civilian, using own country's price weights.

SOURCE: *Joint Economic Report, 1979*, p. 58.

devoted to government outlays. This figure rose from 34 percent of national income in fiscal 1966 to 41 percent last year. Over the same time frame Federal expenditures rose from 22.6 percent of national income to 27.8 percent. Government has grown relative to the total economy and also relative to capital spending. The sharp increase in government has discouraged savings and investment and expenditures on research and development, and has also been accompanied by massive increases in government regulation. All of these developments limit the potential of our economy for further growth.[13]

The difference between the supply-side economists and the Keynesians is most graphically shown by their contrary attitudes toward taxation. To the Keynesians, rising taxes hurt the economy only because they cut down on consumer purchasing power. More-

over, to the Keynesians, all tax cuts are the same. It makes no difference whether you have a tax rebate, a tax cut only for those with low
incomes, a tax cut only for those with high incomes, a corporate tax
cut, whether you cut average tax rates or marginal tax rates, or
whether you cut taxes for individuals or businesses. No matter how
you do it only one thing counts: the aggregate size of the tax cut. This
alone determines how much fiscal stimulus there will be to aggregate
demand.[14] Consequently, it makes no difference to the Keynesians
whether you cut taxes or increase government spending by the same
amount. The effects will be identical. As David Ott and Attiat Ott
said in the standard work, *Federal Budget Policy:*

> Changes in certain types of government expenditures have the same
> effect on GNP as tax changes in that they change private disposable
> income without changing government purchases of goods and services.
> . . . Reductions in transfer payments or (net) interest payments are
> comparable to increases in taxes, since they also reduce private dispos-
> able income. Increases in transfer payments or (net) interest payments
> have the same effect as tax cuts; that is, they increase private disposable
> income.[15]

By contrast, to the supply-side fiscalists, the "new" economists, it
makes all the difference in the world whether you cut taxes or increase spending, and there are vast differences between the effects
of various kinds of tax cuts. They would say that tax rebates and
increases in spending only stimulate inflation and do nothing for
supply, because they must be financed either through borrowing—
which "crowds out" private borrowers and raises interest rates—or
by increasing the quantity of money through monetization of the
debt.[16]

Thus the supply-side economists argue that tax cuts should be
structured so as to give the maximum stimulus to investment, savings, and work incentive. This means a preference for marginal tax
rate reductions, since they increase the tradeoff between work and
leisure, investment and consumption. (The marginal tax is that imposed on each additional dollar earned.) Similarly, they favor reductions in the corporate tax rate, which affect the rate of return,
rather than investment tax credits, which primarily affect cash
flow.[17]

Needless to say, the new economists are pitted squarely against the
prevailing liberal orthodoxy, which says that taxes should be increased for corporations and high-income individuals and cut only
for those with low incomes. But the new economists have been gaining powerful allies in Washington and may end up doing an end run

around the economics profession the same way that Friedman and the monetarists did.[18]

Supply-side economics got a big boost in 1977 when Martin Feldstein became president of the National Bureau of Economic Research (NBER). Feldstein, a professor of economics at Harvard, has been for many years doing enormously important work on national health insurance (his dissertation topic at Oxford), social security, saving and capital investment, and the effect of inflation on the tax system. Through his own work and work commissioned by the NBER he has made politicians and economists rethink many of their ideas about the economy.[19] For example, at an NBER conference on taxation in 1975 Prof. Michael Boskin of Stanford presented a paper which radically altered the conventional view of taxation and saving. Conventional wisdom, as embodied in "Denison's law," was that national saving stays roughly at 16 percent of GNP regardless of what tax rates are.[20] But Boskin showed that saving is in fact highly responsive to changes in tax rates.[21]

In addition to Feldstein and the NBER, the major intellectual influence on supply-side thinking has been the work of the Joint Economic Committee (JEC). The JEC was created by the Employment Act of 1946 to make a continuing study of the U.S. economy and report to Congress on its findings. Considering the fact that the Employment Act of 1946 was, in many respects, the zenith of Keynesian thinking, and considering the magnitude of the differences that traditionally have divided the members of the JEC, it is extremely interesting that the committee's first unanimous annual report in 20 years was based essentially on supply-side thinking. As Chairman Bentsen stated in his introduction to this 1979 report:

> To post–World War II economists, the basic economic problem was to insure an adequate level of demand. Insufficient demand was the main economic problem of the depression era. Excessive demand was the main economic culprit during World War II. So it was not surprising that economists were preoccupied for almost 30 years with the problem of maintaining an adequate level of demand in the economy. The Arab oil embargo and the subsequent behavior of the OPEC cartel suddenly and dramatically began to force the attention of the country and its economic experts on the supply side of the economy.
> The Report emphasizes the need to stimulate job-creating new investment. It recommends consideration of incentives to promote industrial research and development. It calls for a more rational and effective Federal regulatory system. . . . All of these recommendations are designed to advance the theory that expanding the capacity of the economy to produce goods and services efficiently is the most effective policy to combat the major economic ill of our time—stagflation.[22]

In its 1980 annual report, the Joint Economic Committee again affirmed its support of supply-side approaches to our nation's economic problems. Quoting Senator Bentsen once more:

The 1980 annual report signals the start of a new era of economic thinking. The past has been dominated by economists who focused almost exclusively on the demand side of the economy and who, as a result, were trapped into believing that there is an inevitable tradeoff between unemployment and inflation. America does not have to fight inflation during the 1980s by periodically pulling up the drawbridge with recessions that doom millions of Americans to unemployment.

The Committee's 1980 report says that steady economic growth, created by productivity gains and accompanied by a stable fiscal policy and a gradual reduction in the growth of the money supply over a period of years, can reduce inflation significantly during the 1980s without increasing unemployment. To achieve this goal, the Committee recommends a comprehensive set of policies designed to enhance the productive side, the supply side of the economy. . . .

The Committee recommends that fully one-half of the next tax cut be directed to enhancing saving and investment in the economy. Traditionally, tax cuts have been viewed solely as countercyclical devices designed to shore up the demand side of the economy. The Joint Economic Committee is now on record in support of the view that tax policy can and should be directed toward improving the productivity performance of the economy over the long term and need not be enacted only to counter a recession.[23]

The Joint Economic Committee reports endorsing supply-side economics received wide notice, encouraging serious academic research on the subject and spurring the committee to further its work in this area.[24] The result was that even members of the Carter Administration began talking about supply-side economics. Treasury Secretary Michael Blumenthal, for example, testified before the JEC on July 11, 1979, as follows:

For decades we have operated on a consensus—that the major economic policy concern of governments should be to manage aggregate demand to smooth out swings in the business cycle and assure steady increases in income and employment. The supply side of the equation was largely neglected, assumed to take care of itself and respond to changing demands.

This assumption no longer holds. The supply side is not responding. Productivity is lagging badly—in the U.S. productivity growth in the past five years has only been about half of what it was in the 1950s and 1960s. Government spending has taken a growing share of income, and has shifted away from capital construction and defense toward income transfers. Effective tax rates have escalated sharply. Tax structures and levels are such to stultify innovation and risk taking. Industry is bound in a shifting web of regulations. Indexation, formal and informal, tends to fix relative prices and weaken incentives for movement of resources between industries and sectors.

We need, in short, to reorient economic policy to concentrate more heavily on the supply side, to reduce rigidities and inefficiencies that create supply constraints throughout the economy. This task involves rebuilding our capital stock, reinvigorating productivity growth, reducing structural unemployment—all on top of creating a new base for the energy needs of the economy.[25]

Perhaps even more amazingly, the Brookings Institution—a bastion of Keynesian economics—is now talking about supply-side economics.[26] This raises a problem. How much of this talk about supply-side economics expresses sincere and correct statements of supply-side principles, and how much is just talk? The danger is that, as supply-side economics becomes more politically popular, it may become perverted into a kind of conservative Keynesianism. This problem is exacerbated by theoretical and political differences within the supply-side camp, i.e., between "conservative" and "radical" supply-siders.

The principal issues at hand are whether or not a tax cut *per se* is inflationary and whether a tax cut must be accompanied by a dollar-for-dollar cut in government spending to be effective. Those who argue against tax cuts because they are inflationary or who demand matching spending cuts are not true supply-siders. They are in fact conservative Keynesians, for it is only in the Keynesian model that tax cuts are assumed to stimulate demand and therefore inflation. In the supply-side model the critical question is, *How* are taxes being cut? A tax cut which merely reduces government revenue, government spending staying the same, might be inflationary because it would probably require monetization of the increased debt. But a reduction in tax rates—in particular, marginal tax rates—does more than just increase individual disposable incomes. It alters relative prices, changing the tradeoff between work and leisure, savings and consumption. Whether such a tax cut would be inflationary in the short run will depends on how much additional production and saving it generates and how the government finances its short-run deficit.

Even some self-professed supply-siders fail to see this difference and oppose any tax cut without a corresponding spending reduction. Martin Feldstein, for example, recently said, "Although I support a supply-side approach to unemployment and productivity, I am convinced that inflation will be tamed only by appropriate limits to demand."[27] Dr. Michael Evans, who built a supply-side econometric model for the Senate Finance Committee, has made much the same point, saying the Kemp-Roth 30 percent tax rate reduction would be highly inflationary.[28] And the Federal Reserve Bank of Minneapolis has argued that since the real burden of government is what it spends, a tax cut merely shifts government finances from taxes to borrowing. Insofar as the increased deficit is inflationary, it may actually increase the tax burden in the long run, by pushing people up into higher tax brackets.[29]

Unfortunately, all of this criticism misses the point, which is that cutting tax rates does much more than reduce government revenue. It eliminates disincentives. As Paul Craig Roberts recently argued:

> The total resources claimed by government *is* a better measure of the tax burden than tax revenues alone. But some economists let this adding up of concrete resources blind them to another measure of the real tax burden—*the production that is lost to disincentives.* It is difficult to see the production that doesn't take place because the government has made it unprofitable, but it is nevertheless a part of the tax burden.
>
> From the viewpoint of this more complete measure of the tax burden, a tax cut can be real even if it is not matched dollar for dollar with a spending cut. That's because a reduction in marginal tax rates changes relative prices. It causes people to shift into work out of leisure and into investment out of current consumption. These shifts occur even if people expect that in the future taxes might be raised to pay off any government debt incurred by cutting tax rates. In the meantime, however, the additional work and investment expands the tax base; to make good on the deficit, future tax rates would not have to be raised as much as they were cut—if they need to be raised at all.[30]

The theoretical support for Roberts' argument can be found in the work of Sir John Hicks, among others. In *Value and Capital* Hicks pointed out that price changes involve income and substitution effects. Thus a drop in the price of a commodity makes the consumer better off. It raises his real income in terms of goods. On the other hand, it changes relative prices, causing a substitution effect in which the consumer will substitute the commodity whose price has fallen for other commodities. Since the buyer's income gain is exactly offset by the seller's loss, the income effects are cancelled, leaving the substitution effect.[31]

So too with changes in tax rates. A reduction in tax rates may reduce government revenue, requiring it to borrow more from the public, but the income gain of the taxpayer whose rate is cut is exactly offset by another whose savings went into government debt instead of being consumed or invested in some other way. Again, the income effects cancel out leaving the substitution effect. (If the government had inflated the currency instead of borrowing the money it would have produced the same effect, the currency expansion being forced saving or a tax on cash balances.) The substitution effect will cause people to substitute work for leisure and saving for consumption.

Another line of argument is that, since inflation is fundamentally caused by an increase in the quantity of money in excess of the growth of goods and services, any tax cut which causes more goods and services to be produced will be anti-inflationary so long as the money supply is tightly controlled. This is essentially the view of the Joint Economic Committee, which has published two papers showing how tax cuts can reduce inflation.[32] Conversely, there is now growing doubt that the traditional Keynesian cure for inflation—a recession—will work, because it leads to a decline in the production of goods and services while the money stock remains unchanged.[33]

In the end, the political process will decide whether an anti-inflationary tax cut is possible. The fact is that the Congress just does not like the Keynesian cure for inflation—unemployment, declining economic growth, etc. Despite opposition to a supply-side tax cut, the political appeal is enormous. It holds forth the promise that inflation can be reduced without running the country through a wringer and allows politicians to give the people tax cuts without fearing additional inflation.[34] If such a tax cut is enacted and works, supply-side economics may suddenly find itself the new economic orthodoxy.

Notes

1. Jean Baptiste Say, *A Treatise on Political Economy* (1832), reprinted in Henry Hazlitt, ed., *The Critics of Keynesian Economics* (Princeton, NJ: Van Nostrand, 1960), pp. 20–21. On the history of Say's law, see Thomas Sowell, *Say's Law: An Historical Analysis* (Princeton, NJ: Princeton University Press, 1972).

2. John Stuart Mill, *Essays on Some Unsettled Questions of Political Economy* (1844), reprinted in Hazlitt, *Critics,* p. 26.

3. John Maynard Keynes, *The General Theory of Employment Interest and Money* (New York: Harcourt, Brace & Co., 1936), pp. 18, 26; Benjamin M. Anderson, *Economics and The Public Interest* (Princeton, NJ: Van Nostrand, 1949), pp. 390–93; W.H. Hutt, *A Rehabilitation of Say's Law* (Athens, OH: Ohio University Press, 1974), pp. 24–29.

4. Joseph Schumpeter, *History of Economic Analysis* (New York: Oxford University Press, 1954), p. 1121n; see also Bruce Bartlett, *The Keynesian Revolution Revisited* (Greenwich, CN: Committee for Monetary Research and Education, Monetary Tract No. 20, October 1977).

5. Milton Friedman and Anna Schwartz, *A Monetary History of the United States, 1867–1960* (Princeton, NJ: Princeton University Press, 1963), pp. 209–419.

6. Similarly, in 1971 President Richard Nixon said, "I am now a Keynesian."

7. A.W. Phillips, "The Relationship Between Unemployment and the Rate of Change of Money Wage Rates in the United Kingdom, 1861–1957," *Economica* (November 1958), pp. 283–99.

8. Editorial, "Keynes Is Dead," *Wall Street Journal* (January 31, 1977); "Is Keynes Dead?" *Newsweek* (June 20, 1977), pp. 74–75.

9. Irving Kristol, "Toward a 'New' Economics?" *Wall Street Journal* (May 9, 1977).

10. U.S. Congress, Joint Economic Committee, *Midyear Review of the Economy: The Outlook for 1979,* Joint Committee Print, 96th Cong., 1st sess. (Washington: U.S. Government Printing Office, 1979), pp. 28–29.

11. Edward F. Denison, *Accounting for Slower Economic Growth: The United States in the 1970s* (Washington: The Brookings Institution, 1979); J.R. Norsworthy, Michael J. Harper, and Kent Kunze, "The Slowdown in Productivity Growth: Analysis of Some Contributing Factors," *Brookings Papers on Economic Activity* (2:1979), pp. 387–421.

12. John A. Tatom, "The Productivity Problem," *Federal Reserve Bank of St. Louis Review* (September 1979), pp. 3–16.

13. U.S. House of Representatives, Committee on Ways and Means, *Economists' Comments on H.R. 8333 and S. 1860,* Committee Print, 95th Cong., 2nd sess. (Washington: U.S. Government Printing Office, 1978), pp. 85–86.

14. Paul Craig Roberts, "The Breakdown of the Keynesian Model," *The Public Interest* (Summer 1978), pp. 20–33.

15. David J. Ott and Attiat F. Ott, *Federal Budget Policy* (Washington: The Brookings Institution, 1977), pp. 83–84.

16. See Keith M. Carlson and Roger W. Spencer, "Crowding Out and Its Critics," *Federal Reserve Bank of St. Louis Review* (December 1975), pp. 2–17; Charlotte E. Ruebling, "Financing Government Through Monetary Expansion and Inflation," *Federal Reserve Bank of St Louis Review* (February 1975), pp. 15–23.

17. See Arthur B. Laffer, "An Equilibrium Rational Macroeconomic Framework," in Nake M. Kamrany and Richard H. Day, eds., *Economic Issues of the Eighties* (Baltimore, MD: The Johns Hopkins University Press, 1979), pp. 44–57; Paul Craig Roberts, "The Economic Case for Kemp-Roth," *Wall Street Journal* (August 1, 1978).

18. "The New Economists," *Newsweek* (June 26, 1978), pp. 59–60; Walter Guzzardi, Jr., "The New Down-to-Earth Economics," *Fortune* (December 31, 1978), pp. 72–79; "To Set the Economy Right," *Time* (August 27, 1979), pp. 24–35; "Why Supply-Side Economics Is Suddenly Popular," *Business Week* (September 17, 1979), pp. 116–18.

19. Space limitations forbid any meaningful listing of Feldstein's amazingly prolific output; for a summary of his views and work see A.F. Ehrbar, "Martin Feldstein's Electric-Blue Economic Prescriptions," *Fortune* (February 27, 1978), pp. 54–58; Ann Crittenden, "Feldstein: The Bull in a Data

Shop," *New York Times* (May 20, 1979); Soma Golden, "Superstar of the New Economists," *New York Times Magazine* (March 23, 1980), pp. 30–33, 91–95.

20. Edward F. Denison, "A Note on Private Saving," *Review of Economics and Statistics* (August 1958), pp. 261–67; see also Paul A. David and John L. Scadding, "Private Savings: Ultrarationality, Aggregation, and 'Denison's Law,' " *Journal of Political Economy* (March-April 1974), pt. 1, pp. 225–49.

21. Michael J. Boskin, "Taxation, Saving, and the Rate of Interest," *Journal of Political Economy* (April 1978), pt. 2, pp. S3–S27.

22. Congress of the United States, Joint Economic Committee, *Joint Economic Report, 1979,* Senate Report No. 96–44, 96th Cong., 1st sess. (Washington: U.S. Government Printing Office, 1979), p. 3.

23. Congress of the United States, Joint Economic Committee, *Joint Economic Report, 1980,* Senate Report No. 96–618, 96th Cong., 2d sess. (Washington: U.S. Government Printing Office, 1980), p. 1.

24. Paul Craig Roberts, "A New Economic Era," *Wall Street Journal* (March 22, 1979); Editorial, "The Economy in the 1980s," *Wall Street Journal* (August 15, 1979); Steven Rattner, "Joint Economic Panel's New Thrust," *New York Times* (February 18, 1980); John M. Berry, "Hill Economic Committee Breaks With Carter, Seeks Tax Cut," *Washington Post* (February 29, 1980); Robert E. Keleher, *Supply-Side Effects of Fiscal Policy: Some Preliminary Hypotheses* (Federal Reserve Bank of Atlanta, Research Paper No. 9, June 1979).

25. U.S. Congress, *The 1979 Midyear Review of the Economy: Hearings Before the Joint Economic Committee,* 96th Cong., 1st sess. (Washington: U.S. Government Printing Office, 1979), pp. 388–89.

26. Barry P. Bosworth, "Economic Policy," in Joseph A. Pechman, ed., *Setting National Priorities: Agenda for the 1980s* (Washington: The Brookings Institution, 1980), pp. 35–70.

27. Martin Feldstein, "Inflation and Supply Side Economics," *Wall Street Journal* (May 20, 1980).

28. Michael K. Evans, "The Reagan-Kemp Inflation Plan," *Industry Week* (April 28, 1980), p. 84.

29. *Federal Reserve Bank of Minneapolis 1979 Annual Report.*

30. Paul Craig Roberts, "Caricatures of Tax-Cutting," *Wall Street Journal* (April 24, 1980). This point is also strongly emphasized by Dr. Norman Ture in testimony before the Joint Economic Committee on May 21, 1980.

31. J.R. Hicks, *Value and Capital* (London: Oxford University Press, 1946), pp. 31–37.

32. U.S. Congress, Joint Economic Committee, *Tax Policy and Core Inflation* by Otto Eckstein, Joint Committee Print, 96th Cong., 2d sess. (Washington: U.S. Government Printing Office, 1980); idem, *Productivity and Inflation* by William Freund and Paul Manchester, Joint Committee Print, 96th Cong., 2d sess. (Washington: U.S. Government Printing Office, 1980).

33. Art Pine, "Industry Cutbacks May Feed Inflation," *Washington Post* (May 12, 1980).

34. Judith Miller, "Budget Debate: Cutting Taxes To Stop Inflation," *New York Times* (March 9, 1980); Editorial, "Feast of the Tax-Cut Free Lunch," *New York Times* (February 24, 1980).

2

Taxes and Revenues

MOST PUBLIC DISCUSSION OF THE "LAFFER CURVE" HAS focused on its implication that a cut in tax rates will increase tax revenue.[1] But it also implies that at some point an increase in tax rates will begin to reduce the tax base, as the sources of tax revenue —wages, profits, interest, etc.—begin to dry up. Thus, tax revenue will fall; perhaps not in absolute terms, but below what a lower tax rate which did not erode the tax base would have achieved. Consequently, what the Laffer Curve is really saying is that there are always two tax rates which will bring in the same revenue: a high tax rate on a small base and a lower tax rate on a large tax base. There is nothing particularly startling about this proposition; it is simple price theory applied to tax rates and revenues rather than prices for goods and services. Another way of putting it would be to say that the Laffer Curve demonstrates the law of diminishing returns with respect to tax rates.[2]

The earliest known reference to what could be called the Laffer Curve comes from the Moslem philosopher Ibn Khaldun (1332–1406), who observed that "at the beginning of the dynasty, taxation yields a large revenue from small assessments. At the end of the dynasty, taxation yields a small revenue from large assessments."[3]

14

Similarly, the soldier-engineer-economist Vauban stressed the importance of moderate taxation during the early eighteenth century. Of Vauban, Joseph Schumpeter wrote in his *History of Economic Analysis:* "With Gladstonian vision he realized that fiscal measures affect the economic organism's right to its cells and that the method of raising a given amount of revenue may make all of the difference between paralysis and prosperity."[4]

The same principle is involved in discussions of a revenue tariff. In the *Wealth of Nations* (1776), Adam Smith noted that tariff rates in England were so high in many cases that they were only encouraging smuggling and reducing revenue below what lower rates would bring in:

> The high duties which have been imposed upon the importation of many different sorts of foreign goods, in order to discourage their consumption in Great Britain, have in many cases served only to encourage smuggling; and in all cases have reduced the revenue of the customs below what more moderate duties would have afforded. The saying of Dr. Swift, that in the arithmetic of the customs two and two, instead of making four, make sometimes only one, holds perfectly true with regard to such heavy duties, which never could have been imposed, had not the mercantile system taught us, in many cases, to employ taxation as an instrument, not of revenue, but of monopoly.[5]

It should be emphasized that it is the tax or tariff *rate* which is critical, not its overall burden. As Henry George put it in *Progress and Poverty* (1879):

> The mode of taxation is, in fact, quite as important as the amount. As a small burden badly placed may distress a horse that could carry with ease a much larger one properly adjusted, so a people may be impoverished and their power of producing wealth destroyed by taxation, which, if levied another way, could be borne with ease.[6]

In the nineteenth century many public finance theorists suggested that tax rates could not be increased beyond a certain point. Justi said 25 percent was the maximum. Hock said 15 percent was the upper limit. Leroy-Beaulieu thought that when taxes reached 15 to 16 percent of national income they could not be increased. Bastable also thought there was a limit to taxation, but that it varied from country to country and with circumstances.[7]

Throughout the public finance literature one often finds the goals of social reformers and proper fiscal policy to be in conflict. It may be socially desirable to have those with large incomes pay a larger proportion of their income in tax than those with modest incomes, but if the tax rate is too high, its effect will be to shift the burden of the tax onto those who were not intended to be so burdened. This point was made by Prof. Edwin Cannan in response to the proposition that the tax which would raise the most revenue while burdening the fewest people would be a tax of 100 percent on all incomes above £50,000. "But," said Cannan, "the given income would not remain. The persons with more than £50,000 a year would not continue to have more than £50,000 a year, at any rate within the purview of the state, and next year the limit might have to be reduced to £40,000 a year, and so on. . . ."[8]

In *Human Action,* Ludwig von Mises also pointed out how the fiscal and nonfiscal objectives of taxation do not agree with each other:

> Consider, for instance, excise duties on liquor. If one considers them as a source of government revenue, the more money they yield the better they appear. Of course, as the duty must enhance the price of the beverage, it restricts sales and consumption. It is necessary to find out by testing under what rate of duty the yield becomes the highest. But if one looks at liquor taxes as a means of reducing the consumption of liquor as much as possible, the rate is better the higher it is. Pushed beyond a certain limit, the tax makes consumption drop considerably, and also the revenue concomitantly. If the tax fully attains its non-fiscal objective of weaning people entirely from drinking alcoholic beverages, the revenue is zero. It no longer serves any fiscal purpose; its effects are merely prohibitive. The same is valid not only with regard to all kinds of indirect taxation but no less for direct taxation. Discriminating taxes levied upon corporations and big business would, if raised above a certain limit, result in the total disappearance of corporations and big business. Capital levies, inheritance and estate taxes, and income taxes are similarly self-defeating if carried to extremes.[9]

The estate tax is a good example of what Mises is talking about. Although regarded by most economists as an ideal sort of tax, because presumably it has no effect on economic incentives, in fact it has substantial economic effects.[10] As Prof. Richard Posner points out, "Since the accumulation of a substantial estate is one of the motivations that drive people to work hard, a death tax is indirectly a tax on work."[11] Moreover, because it is a direct tax on saving, it ultimately has important negative effects on the nation's accumulation of capital.[12]

Interestingly, for a tax which is supposed to inflict such little pain, people have devoted a great deal of ingenuity to getting around it.[13] As a result, the estate and gift tax is an almost insignificant source of tax revenue, raising a mere 1.2 percent of federal revenue in 1979. Indeed, although the tax was supposedly toughened in 1976, estate tax revenues in 1979 were no higher in real terms (adjusted for inflation) than they were in 1964. For these reasons, many people now believe that the estate tax should simply be abolished—a move taken by Canada a few years ago with no apparent adverse effects.[14]

The resourcefulness that taxpayers show in escaping income taxes is equally impressive. Prior to passage of the Tax Reform Act of 1976, tax shelters ran the gamut from real estate, oil and gas, cattle, equipment leasing and agriculture to such exotic investments as catfish farming, chinchilla breeding, movies and making master records. But Congress and the IRS became quite disenchanted with business deals that were set up for only one purpose: to pass on deductions and write-offs to the taxpayer. Although the Tax Reform Act eliminated many tax shelters, there are still enormous opportunities to escape taxation legally. So long as such basic features of the tax code as the investment tax credit, preferential treatment of capital gains, and tax-exempt municipal bonds remain, there will always be ways to reduce one's tax liability. And there are always investment advisors around ready to lead one through the tax code maze in order to find a program which fits individual circumstances. For example, table 1 recently appeared in a newspaper ad extolling the virtues of tax-free municipal bonds.

Ultimately, of course, one can just drop out of the tax-economy and earn his income in the so-called underground economy. Indeed, so many people have done so that the U.S. now has a thriving underground economy, which is out of reach of the tax collectors and government regulators. Although much of the underground economy is made up of outright criminal activity, most of it is comprised of activities such as the following: (1) owners, managers or employees of a small business skimming cash receipts off the top, thereby receiving undeclared, untaxed income; (2) employees paid to work "off the books," free from taxation; and (3) businesses which pay suppliers in cash or barter for supplies in order to appear smaller than they really are, thus permitting additional cash skimming without alerting the tax authorities.[15]

The beauty of the system is that everyone gains and only the Internal Revenue Service loses. Since it is not uncommon for even a moderately paid worker to be in the 50 percent marginal tax bracket (so that each additional dollar earned is taxed 50 percent), it would clearly be to a worker's benefit to accept a 10, 20, or 30 percent reduction in pay provided that he is paid cash "off the books." It is a well-known fact that in many parts of the country

TABLE 1

For New York City Residents

Joint Return Taxable Income	Federal N.Y.C. & N.Y.S. Taxes	A Tax Exempt Rate of 6.25%	6.50%	6.75%	7.00%
		Is Approximately Equivalent to a Taxable Rate of			
$ 16,000–20,000	38%	10.08%	10.48%	10.88%	11.29%
20,000–24,000	42%	10.78%	11.21%	11.63%	12.07%
24,000–28,000	48%	12.01%	12.50%	12.98%	13.46%
28,000–32,000	51%	12.75%	13.26%	13.77%	14.28%
32,000–36,000	53%	13.29%	13.82%	14.36%	14.89%
36,000–40,000	56%	14.20%	14.77%	15.34%	15.90%
40,000–44,000	58%	14.88%	15.47%	16.07%	16.66%
44,000–52,000	60%	15.62%	16.25%	16.87%	17.50%
52,000–64,000	62%	16.45%	17.10%	17.76%	18.42%
64,000–76,000	64%	17.36%	18.05%	18.75%	19.44%
76,000–88,000	66%	18.38%	19.11%	19.85%	20.58%
88,000–100,000	68%	19.53%	20.31%	21.09%	21.87%
100,000–200,000	69%	20.16%	20.96%	21.77%	22.58%
over $200,000	76%	26.04%	27.08%	28.12%	29.16%

workers simply refuse to work overtime unless it is "off the books," because the additional income would push them into a higher tax bracket.

Recently, Professor Peter Gutmann of Baruch College made estimates of the size of the subterranean economy. What drew Gutmann's attention to its size was his discovery that the amount of cash in circulation has increased enormously since World War II. In 1941 there was only about $219 of currency per $1,000 of demand deposits (checking accounts and the like) in the U.S. By 1976 this figure had grown to $344 per $1,000. This amounts to $380 in currency for every person in the U.S., or $1,522 for a family of four. Gutmann concluded that this growth in currency was necessary to lubricate the subterranean economy. On this basis he estimated that the subterranean economy may account for more than $200 billion in gross national product which is totally excluded from the GNP statistics (see table 2).[16] Gutmann laid the blame for growth of this underground economy squarely on government:

> The subterranean economy, like black markets throughout the world, was created by government rules and restrictions. It is a creature of the income tax, of other taxes, of limitations on the legal employment of certain groups and of prohibitions on certain activities. It exists because it provides goods and services that are either unavailable elsewhere or obtainable only at higher prices. It also provides employment for those unemployable in the legal economy; employment for those—like the retired who draw social security, or illegal aliens without residence status—whose freedom to work is restricted; and incentive to do additional work for those who would not do so if they were taxed.[17]

The existence of the subterranean economy is enormously important for a variety of reasons. First, it mitigates the harmful effects of high marginal tax rates, encouraging work and production which otherwise would not exist. Secondly, it is essential to the survival of small business in America. Large businesses need controls and records to operate efficiently, but small businesses, especially sole proprietorships, do not. Thus small businesses which operate partially in the subterranean economy can save business taxes, income taxes on employers and employees, social security taxes, sales taxes, pension and health costs, and the cost of government regulation. "In short," as Gutmann says, "the existence of the subterranean economy is very important for the maintenance, health, and prosperity of small business."[18]

Another factor which is extremely important is that the subterranean economy severely distorts our national economic statistics, which may be responsible for producing inappropriate government policies. A prime example is the distortion of the official unemployment rate. Since the official unemployment rate is based on survey data, it is highly unlikely that those working in the subterranean economy are counted as employed for statistical purposes. Thus Gutmann estimates that the official unemployment rate may be overstated by as much as 1.5 percentage points. Consequently, it is not surprising that a recent study of 60 unemployed youth in Boston discovered that more than half were partially employed in the subterranean economy while officially unemployed. According to the interviewer:

> More than half of the youngsters interviewed said that they had engaged in illegal activity during the course of the survey week. These

TABLE 2

GROSS NATIONAL PRODUCT

	BILLIONS OF DOLLARS		PERCENT CHANGE	
	Official	Underground*	Official	Underground
1948	259.1	17.8	11.3	6.5
1949	258.0	15.9	−0.4	−10.6
1950	286.2	13.4	10.9	−15.7
1951	330.2	14.5	15.4	8.2
1952	347.2	15.9	5.1	9.7
1953	366.1	17.1	5.5	7.5
1954	366.3	13.3	0.0	−22.2
1955	399.3	13.7	9.0	3.0
1956	420.7	14.7	5.4	7.3
1957	442.8	16.7	5.2	13.6
1958	448.9	13.6	1.4	−18.5
1959	486.5	14.2	8.4	4.4
1960	506.0	14.4	4.0	1.4
1961	523.3	13.6	3.4	−5.6
1962	563.8	17.3	7.7	27.2
1963	594.7	21.9	5.5	26.6
1964	635.7	25.0	6.9	14.2
1965	688.1	29.2	8.2	16.8
1966	753.0	38.1	9.4	30.5
1967	796.3	37.8	5.8	−0.1
1968	868.5	39.9	9.1	5.6
1969	935.5	50.7	7.7	27.1
1970	982.4	56.5	5.0	11.4
1971	1,063.4	63.1	8.2	11.7
1972	1,171.1	67.2	10.1	6.5
1973	1,306.6	83.5	11.6	24.3
1974	1,412.9	113.7	8.1	36.2
1975	1,528.8	145.6	8.2	28.1
1976	1,700.1	181.3	11.2	24.5
1977	1,887.2	212.8	11.0	17.4
1978	2,107.6	264.5	11.7	24.3

*Computed by the Congressional Research Service using methodology developed by Peter Gutmann.

SOURCE: Reported GNP is from the U.S. Department of Commerce, Bureau of Economic Analysis. Underground GNP is calculated from data published by the U.S. Department of Commerce, Bureau of Economic Analysis and Board of Governors of the Federal Reserve System.

youths sold marijuana frequently, and some reported that robbery, pickpocketing, burglary and breaking and entering took up most of their time the week prior to the survey week.[19]

Thus, although these youths were unemployed in the conventional sense, they were in fact "employed" in the subterranean economy. If this is true generally, it might mean that black youth unemployment—at least in the inner city—is substantially overe-stimated.[20]

Gutmann's work caused a great stir. The Internal Revenue Service immediately launched an investigation of the underground econ-omy. The IRS report indicates that in 1976 individuals failed to re-port about $13 to 17 billion in income taxes on about $75 to 100 billion of unreported income from legal sources. Another $6 to 9 billion of taxes was not paid on $25 to 35 billion of unreported indi-vidual income from criminal activities in narcotics, illegal gambling, and prostitution.[21]

Subsequent analysis was almost unanimous that the IRS study sig-nificantly understated the problem. The General Accounting Office pointed out that some significant types of illegal activity were ig-nored by the IRS, including kickbacks from corporations; arson for profit; smuggling of goods other than drugs; bootlegging of ciga-rettes, films, tapes, records, and pornography; protection rackets; embezzlements; and theft. The GAO pointed out that some esti-mates of white-collar crime in general were as high as $40 billion annually.[22]

Professor Robert Eisner of Northwestern also thought the IRS esti-mates to be low, and mentioned shoplifting, overstated deductions on income tax returns, moonlighting and self-employment in general as other sources of lost tax revenue.[23] Meanwhile, another study by Edgar Feige put the underground economy at $542 billion, based on the ratio of total checking and cash transactions in the economy to GNP. Since the ratio has increased dramatically since 1939, Feige attributes the reason to growth of the underground economy.[24]

A poll done by the Roper Organization further amplifies the extent of the underground economy. Based on survey data, Roper es-timated untaxed barter transactions to be between $1.65 billion and $4.125 billion annually. Thirteen percent of the population reported having participated in bartering. Eleven percent reported having been solicited cash transactions, which presumably were not re-ported to the IRS. Such transactions amount to between $1.153 bil-lion and $2.882 billion annually. The poll also found tax cheating in general to be widespread.[25]

The growth of the subterranean economy is not unique to the United States. It is a worldwide phenomenon. In 1978 the Organiza-tion for Economic Cooperation and Development reported that 3 to 5 percent of the total labor force in Western Europe worked off the books and paid no taxes.[26] In Italy, estimates of the underground economy are anywhere from 10 to 30 percent of reported GNP, with perhaps a third of the labor force involved.[27] In Great Britain, the "black economy" is estimated to cost the Treasury between £3 billion and £5 billion per year.[28] Sweden is also suffering from an increase in tax cheating resulting from the heaviest tax burden in the world. Thus Gunnar Myrdal, one of the fathers of the Swedish welfare state, recently said:

> The Swedish honesty has been a pride for me and my generation. Now I have the feeling that we are becoming a people of hustlers as a result of bad laws. Of all the deficiencies of our income tax system, for me the most serious is that the laws directly invite us to tax evasion and tax cheating.[29]

Most discussions about the growth of tax cheating and the underground economy usually end up with a call for stricter enforcement. However, a better alternative would be to cut tax rates sufficiently to make the profit from cheating so small that it virtually disappears. As Peter Passell recently wrote in the *New York Times,* "With Federal tax rates, say, one-third lower, the incentive to break the law would be much diminished. Revenues lost thereby would, at least in part, be made up at the expense of the subterranean economy."[30]

Specifically, it has been suggested that cigarette bootlegging—a billion dollar business—would be significantly curtailed if cigarette taxes were lowered. In endorsing a reduction in New York State's 21 cents per pack cigarette tax by 9 cents the *New York Times* said:

> Since the state's present taxes took effect in 1972, revenue from cigarette taxes has dropped far below estimates even though smoking has not. The difference is so great that a reduction in the tax rate to put the smugglers out of business would probably produce greater income for the state. It is estimated that a 9-cent reduction in the tax would take the profit out of smuggling and stimulate the growth of normal, taxpaying patterns of distribution.[31]

New York rejected the suggestion and instead called for imposition of a national cigarette tax, with revenues rebated to the states. The assumption is that people will continue to smoke as much as they do now, but because the tax is national it can no longer be avoided. Hence, the state will get all the revenue it thinks it should be getting now. Unfortunately, even if there were a national cigarette tax there is no guarantee that smuggling would not continue or that the present level of smoking will continue. Ultimately, lowering the tax rate is the only way of getting significant revenue.

The same could be said for the underground economy in general. Increased enforcement can never hope to do any more than touch the surface of the underground economy so long as the incentive to avoid paying taxes is so great. As the *Wall Street Journal* put it:

The answer to the underground economy, and really the only answer, is to get government out of all the things that waste money—manipulating the energy markets, employing people in meaningless jobs on "public service" doles, handing out money to various "poverty" lobbies that perpetuate dependency, funneling vast sums into housing subsidies that mainly serve to benefit builders and construction unions, maintaining a vast army of regulators who mainly serve to gum up normal commerce.

These things can all be done with the proper leadership in Washington. If they are not done, the nation's honest working people are going to become more and more demoralized and the underground economy will continue to grow. The solution is not more vigorous taxation, but precisely the opposite.[32]

In conclusion, there is ample demonstration that high tax rates can be counterproductive in terms of raising revenue. If rates get too high people will find ways to earn nontaxable income, whether by using tax shelters contained in the tax code or by dropping out of the tax economy altogether and earning their income in the underground economy. Policymakers should keep in mind that when one's marginal tax rate is above 50 percent it becomes more profitable to save a dollar in taxes than to earn an additional dollar of income. Hence, those in high tax brackets can well afford the time, effort, and legal help necessary to arrange their affairs so as to pay as little tax as possible.

The real problem, however, is that all this effort is not costless. The nation loses more than just tax revenue when so much of its citizens' time is occupied by efforts to save taxes. All of the money spent on tax lawyers and accountants and the time individuals spend on their own tax-related financial affairs is pure, deadweight loss to the economy. This would all be saved if tax rates were much lower. The misdirection of capital caused by the tax code would also cease. People would take their money out of exotic—and often totally uneconomic—tax shelter investments and out of more conventional investments which are only worthwhile because of tax considerations, and put their money where it will do the economy and themselves more good. And the underground economy would substantially disappear. Of course, criminal activity, like drug smuggling, would remain, but it would no longer be as worthwhile to run the risk of being caught skimming profits or working off the books. Most people are honest and they would just as soon work honestly—if the tax penalty does not force them to do otherwise.

For all these reasons, it is not unrealistic to assume that a reduction in tax rates might increase tax revenue even in the short run. An elimination of the underground economy, for example, all other things being equal, would immediately increase federal tax revenues by as much as $40 billion. Of course, in the long run, a lower tax burden will strengthen the economic base of the country and raise the same tax revenue from lower tax rates than would be necessary if the economy had not grown as fast. It is worth keeping in mind that if the U.S. economy had grown each year since 1950 just 1.5 percent faster than it did—a rate which would still be much less than that experienced by Japan and West Germany—the U.S. economy would be one-third larger. This is equivalent to more than $1 trillion in GNP and sufficient to raise average family income to well over $20,000, provide full employment, and produce $200 billion in tax revenue.

We can't turn back the clock, but it is never too late to stop making mistakes and get the country back on a growth track. The first step might usefully be an across the board reduction in tax rates.

Notes

1. On the "Laffer Curve," see Jude Wanniski, *The Way the World Works* (New York: Basic Books, 1978), pp. 97–115; "The Tax Revolt's Guru," *Newsweek* (June 26, 1978), pp. 24–25; Richard Reeves, "Eureka! Guru in California," *Esquire* (July 18, 1978), pp. 6–8; Alfred Malabre, Jr., "Arthur Laffer's Influence Climbs a Rising Curve, Although Many Other Economists Flunk His Ideas," *Wall Street Journal* (December 1, 1978); Editorial, "Riding the Laffer Curve," *New York Times* (June 19, 1978).

2. On the law of diminishing returns, see Thomas Sowell, *Classical Economics Reconsidered* (Princeton, NJ: Princeton University Press, 1974), pp. 74–77; George Stigler, *The Theory of Price* (New York: Macmillan, 1952), pp. 111–32.

3. Ibn Khaldun, *The Mugaddimah,* quoted in the *Wall Street Journal* (September 29, 1978).

4. Joseph Schumpeter, *History of Economic Analysis* (New York: Oxford University Press, 1954), p. 204.

5. Adam Smith, *The Wealth of Nations* (New York: Random House, 1937), pp. 832–33.

6. Henry George, *Progress and Poverty* (New York: Robert Schalkenbach Foundation, 1975; originally published in 1879), p. 409.

7. C.F. Bastable, *Public Finance* (London: Macmillan, 1903), pp. 136–37.

8. Edwin Cannan, "Equity and Economy in Taxation," *The Economic Journal* 11 (December 1901), p. 473.

9. Ludwig von Mises, *Human Action* (New Haven, CT: Yale University Press, 1949), p. 733.

10. See, for example, George F. Break and Joseph A. Pechman, *Federal Tax Reform: The Impossible Dream?* (Washington: The Brookings Institution, 1975), p. 111.

11. Richard A. Posner, *Economic Analysis of Law* (Boston: Little, Brown, 1972), p. 244.

12. See Glenn E. Hoover, "The Economic Effects of Inheritance Taxes," *American Economic Review* (March 1927), pp. 38–49; Carl S. Shoup, *Federal Estate and Gift Taxes* (Washington: The Brookings Institution, 1966), pp. 86–99; C. Lowell Harriss, "Revising Estate Taxation," *Tax Review* (April 1971); Richard E. Wagner, *Inheritance and the State* (Washington: American Enterprise Institute, 1977), pp. 11–19.

13. George Cooper, *A Voluntary Tax? New Perspectives on Sophisticated Estate Tax Avoidance* (Washington: The Brookings Institution, 1979).

14. See the *Congressional Record* (July 2, 1980), p. S 9340 (daily ed.).

15. See "The Underground Economy: How 20 Million Americans Cheat Uncle Sam Out of Billions in Taxes," *U.S. News and World Report* (October 22, 1979), pp. 49–52; Terri Schultz, "The Untaxed Millions," *New York Times Magazine* (March 16, 1980), pp. 42–60; Jerry Flint, "Unreported Work May Cost U.S. Billions in Taxes and Impair Plans," *New York Times* (January 15, 1978); "The Fast Growth of the Underground Economy," *Business Week* (March 13, 1978), pp. 73–77; Irwin Ross, "Why the Underground Economy Is Booming," *Fortune* (October 9, 1978), pp. 92–98; Richard Reeves, "Underground Economics," *Esquire* (May 22, 1979); "How Tax Cheaters Get Away With Billions," *U.S. News and World Report* (March 27, 1978), pp. 102–5; "The Barter Boom," *Newsweek* (June 26, 1978), pp. 63–64; Denise Kalette, "Western Entrepreneurs Barter Goods and Services," *Washington Post* (November 6, 1978).

16. Peter M. Gutmann, "The Subterranean Economy," *Financial Analysts Journal* (November/December 1977), pp. 26–27, 34.

17. Ibid., p. 26.

18. Peter M. Gutmann, "The Subterranean Economy," *Taxing & Spending* (April 1979), p. 6.

19. John Herbers, "Change in Society Holding Black Youth in Jobless Web," *New York Times* (March 11, 1979).

20. Peter M. Gutmann, "Are the Unemployed, Unemployed?" *Financial Analysts Journal* (September/October 1978), pp. 26–29; idem, "The Grand Unemployment Illusion," *Journal of the Institute for Socioeconomic Studies* 4(Summer 1979), pp. 20–29.

21. *Estimates of Income Unreported on Individual Income Tax Returns* (Washington: Department of the Treasury, Internal Revenue Service, Publication 1104).

22. Congress of the United States, *Subterranean or Underground Economy: Hearings Before a Subcommittee of the Committee on Government Operations, House of Representatives* 96th Cong., 1st sess. (Washington: U.S. Government Printing Office, 1979), p. 65.

23. Congress of the United States, *Underground Economy: Hearings Before the Subcommittee on Oversight of the Committee on Ways and Means, House of Representatives* 96th Cong., 1st sess. (Washington: U.S. Government Printing Office, 1980), pp. 136–47.

24. Edgard Feige, "How Big Is the Irregular Economy?" *Challenge* (November/December 1979), pp. 5–13.

25. The Roper Organization, *Third Annual Tax Study* (Kansas City, MO: Public Affairs Dept., H&R Block, Inc., July 1979), pp. 61–70.

26. Jonathan Kendell, "West Europe Trying to Curb Moonlighters," *New York Times* (October 16, 1978).

27. Hobart Rowan, "Italy's Underground Economy Thriving," *Washington Post* (September 30, 1979); see also Jonathan Spivak, "Italy Booms Despite 'Crisis,'" *Wall Street Journal* (July 18, 1979).

28. "Exploring the Underground Economy," *The Economist* (September 22, 1979), pp. 106–7; Robert Prinsky, "Income-Tax Cheating Is On the Rise in Britain as Prices Outstrip Pay," *Wall Street Journal* (October 10, 1977).

29. Quoted in the *Wall Street Journal* (January 29, 1979); see also Robert Bartley, "A Conversation With Gunnar Myrdal," *Wall Street Journal* (February 14, 1979).

30. Peter Passell, "The Underground Economy," *New York Times* (April 15, 1978).

31. Editorial, "Taxing Cigarettes Less to Take In More," *New York Times* (June 24, 1977); see also "Tobacco Industry in a Drive Asking 9¢-a-Pack Tax Cut in New York City," *New York Times* (May 9, 1977); Advisory Commission on Intergovernmental Relations, *Cigarette Bootlegging: A State AND Federal Responsibility* (Washington: U.S. Government Printing Office, 1977).

32. Editorial, "Notes From the Underground," *Wall Street Journal* (April 8, 1980).

3

The Cost of Progressive Tax Rates

INCOME REDISTRIBUTION AND PROGRESSIVE TAXATION ARE VIRTU-
ally synonymous. Although there are numerous economic arguments in favor of progressivity, based on ability to pay, equal sacrifice, the diminishing marginal utility of money, etc., in the end,
equity is the only justification worth seriously considering.[1] As H. C.
Simons wrote, "The case for drastic progression in taxation must be
rested on the case against inequality—on the ethical or aesthetic
judgement that the prevailing distribution of wealth and income
reveals a degree (and/or kind) of inequality which is distinctly evil
or unlovely."[2]

The problem is, as Friedrich Hayek has noted, "that all arguments
in support of progression can be used to justify any degree of progression."[3] As a result, many economists over the years have warned
against the adoption of progressive tax rates. In 1863 Prof. J. R.
McCulloch said:

> The moment you abandon, in the framing of such taxes, the cardinal
> principle of exacting from all individuals the same proportion of their
> income or property, you are at sea without a rudder or compass, and
> there is no amount of injustice or folly you may not commit.[4]

More recently, Prof. Harley L. Lutz of Princeton wrote:

> Since there is no standard whereby a choice can be made among
> progressive rate scales, it follows that one scale is just as good as any
> other as an application of the principle. A progression that rises to a tax
> rate of 100 per cent on all income in excess of $25,000, or even in excess
> of $5,000, is quite as defensible in terms of the vague and half-baked
> theory on which the entire system rests as one that imposes a top rate
> of 5 per cent on all income in excess of $1,000,000.[5]

In the United States, marginal income tax rates now go up to 70
percent on taxable incomes above $108,300 for a single individual,
with a 50 percent maximum on "earned" income. Of course, average
or effective tax rates vary quite widely, depending upon the source
of one's income or one's ability to manipulate the tax code. Although
much publicity is given to those few wealthy individuals who manage
to escape paying any tax at all, such individuals represent a very tiny
proportion of all wealthy individuals, most of whom pay substantial
income taxes (see table 1).

TABLE 1

FEDERAL INCOME TAXES OF HIGH INCOME RETURNS, EXPANDED INCOME IN
EXCESS OF $200,000 (1976)

	Number	Average Income	Average Total Tax	Average Tax Rate
All returns over $200,000	53,587	$414,000	$145,000	35.0%
Nontaxable returns	89	350,000	0	0

SOURCE: Department of the Treasury, Office of Tax Analysis.

So-called tax reformers frequently charge that the U.S. tax system
is not progressive at all, because tax deductions, tax shelters, and
highly regressive social security, state and local taxes offset the nominal progressivity of the federal income tax. Thus, a recent study
declared that "the tax system is virtually proportional for the vast
majority of families in the United States."[6] However, more recent
work by Prof. Edgar Browning and William Johnson shows that the
U.S. tax system is highly progressive, that those with incomes above
$100,000 pay an average tax rate of 48 percent, compared to 21
percent for those earning between $10,000 and $15,000. Moreover,
the Browning-Johnson data indicate that *all* taxpayers face very high
average marginal tax rates, ranging from 27.4 percent on the lowest
20 percent of income classes to 47.4 percent for the highest 10
percent of income classes (see tables 2 and 3).

Most people believe that progressive tax rates are desirable because they allow those with lower incomes to pay less tax. In fact, the main purpose of progressive tax rates is to make tolerable high tax rates on *everyone*. Historically, tax systems come into being during wartime. The enormous war-spawned revenue demands of government can only be met by unprecedented tax rates on all citizens. In

TABLE 2

AVERAGE TAX RATES BY TYPE OF TAX BY INCOME CLASS* (1976)

INCOME CLASS ($000)	AVERAGE TAX RATES				
	Sales & Excise	Payroll	Income	Property & Corporate	Combined
0–5	2.3%	3.3%	.7%	5.5%	11.7%
5–10	3.0	4.7	2.4	4.4	14.5
10–15	4.3	7.3	5.3	4.2	21.0
15–20	5.0	8.4	8.0	4.0	25.3
20–25	5.2	8.2	9.9	3.9	27.1
25–30	5.3	7.7	11.2	4.5	28.8
30–40	5.3	7.1	12.6	5.4	30.4
40–50	5.4	5.9	13.8	7.8	32.9
50–100	5.5	3.7	14.4	13.5	37.0
100+	5.6	1.1	12.4	28.9	48.0

TABLE 3

DISTRIBUTION OF TAXES PAID AND MARGINAL RATE BY DECILE (1976)

DECILE	SHARE OF TOTAL TAXES PAID					MARGINAL TAX RATE TOTAL
	Sales & Excise	Payroll	Income	Property & Corporate	Total	
1	0.7%	0.8%	0.1%	1.0%	0.6%	—
2	1.6	2.0	0.6	1.7	1.4	27.4%
3	3.0	3.8	1.3	2.5	2.5	25.4
4	4.7	6.3	2.7	3.2	3.9	29.2
5	6.6	9.1	4.5	3.7	5.6	31.3
6	8.6	11.6	6.9	4.3	7.5	31.9
7	10.6	13.5	9.6	5.0	9.4	34.4
8	13.1	15.7	13.3	6.5	11.9	36.4
9	16.9	18.2	19.1	10.6	16.2	47.4
10	34.2	19.0	42.0	61.5	40.9	

*The Browning and Johnson data presented in tables 2 and 3 use estimates of income before taxes but include in-kind government transfers (i.e., food stamps), imputed rental income for owner-occupied housing and accrued capital gains. It is also assumed that the U.S. economy is sufficiently competitive that the tax burden, for the most part, is not shifted from where it is imposed initially. According to this study, using alternative "noncompetitive" assumptions does not result in significant changes in distribution. For a detailed explanation of the tax incidence assumptions see "Source," chapter 2.

SOURCE: Edgar K. Browning and William R. Johnson, *The Distribution of the Tax Burden* (Washington: American Enterprise Institute, 1979).

order to elicit the necessary sacrifice without a steep drop-off in work effort, government must put higher tax rates on the well to do. As the tax burden continues to rise and relief is granted to those in the lower tax brackets through higher exemptions, still higher tax rates on the rich are required in order to bring in the same revenue.

When peace comes, governments are reluctant to give up the revenue, using it to buy votes from the lower classes.[7] But the upper classes have more opportunities for escaping high tax rates than do the lower classes; if necessary, a wealthy person can simply stop earning income and live on his wealth, whereas a poorer individual must work to live. Thus Hayek argues that progressive tax rates ultimately cause the poor to pay far more taxes than they would otherwise:

> The illusion that by some means of progressive taxation the burden can be shifted substantially onto the shoulders of the wealthy has been the chief reason why taxation has increased as fast as it has done and that, under the influence of this illusion, the masses have come to accept a much heavier load than they would have done otherwise. The only major result of the policy has been the severe limitation of the incomes that could be earned by the most successful and thereby gratification of the envy of the less well off.[8]

Society unfortunately loses a great deal more than tax revenue when high marginal tax rates prevent entrepreneurs from accumulating wealth. It loses inventiveness, innovation, risk-taking and originality in its business enterprises. Such qualities historically are more highly developed in individual proprietorships and small businesses hoping to become big businesses than in large corporations, which tend to be more concerned about protecting their positions than in taking risks on untested ideas. Thus, even today the largest proportion of important new inventions are still the result of individuals working virtually alone, rather than by big corporate laboratories.[9] Yet tax policies which discourage the accumulation of wealth discourage individual inventiveness. Lord Robbins comments:

> The fact that it has become so difficult to accumulate even a comparatively small fortune must have the most profound effects on the organization of business; and it is by no means clear to me that these results are in the social interest. Must not the inevitable consequences of all this be that it will become more and more difficult for innovation to develop save within the ambit of established corporate enterprise, and that more and more of what accumulation takes place will take place within the large concerns which—largely as a result of individual enterprise in the past—managed to get started before the ice age descended?[10]

Indeed, the present tax climate severely retards competition and creates monopolies and quasi monopolies, by making it so difficult for new enterprises to challenge the established order. New firms can no longer grow large, as the Ford Motor Company did, by just plowing the profits back into the company year after year, because taxes will seize such a large share. Thus, as Ludwig von Mises notes, society not only loses the value that would have been created by the firms that were prevented from growing, but also the value that would have been created by large firms concerned about competition from newcomers:

> Every ingenious man is free to start new business projects. He may be poor, his funds may be modest and most of them may be borrowed. But if he fills the wants of consumers in the best and cheapest way, he will succeed by means of "excessive" profits. He ploughs back the greater part of his profits into his business, thus making it grow rapidly. It is the activity of such enterprising parvenus that provides the market economy with its "dynamism." These nouveaux riches are the harbingers of economic improvement. Their threatening competition forces the old firms and big corporations either to adjust their conduct to the best possible service to the public or go out of business.
>
> But today taxes often absorb the greater part of the newcomer's "excessive" profits. He cannot accumulate capital; he cannot expand his own business; he will never become big business and a match for the vested interests. The old firms do not need to fear his competition; they are sheltered by the tax collector. They may with impunity indulge in routine, they may defy the wishes of the public and become conservative. It is true, the income tax prevents them, too, from accumulating any capital. They are virtually privileged by the tax system. In this sense progressive taxation checks economic progress and makes for rigidity.[11]

This suppression of competition and stifling of innovation caused by the progressive tax system is, perhaps, its single most detrimental effect on the economy in the long run. It probably explains the growing lack of investment opportunity which troubled Schumpeter.[12] It also explains why politicians seeking to bolster the economy from the effects of the many shackles they themselves have imposed will fail if they only consider tax incentives for business and ignore the individual. The fact is that the individual entrepreneur is still the basic motivating force in the economy, not just in terms of new inventions, as noted earlier, but in terms of meeting all of the consumer's wants. Any measures which suppress entrepreneurship will ultimately cause the economy to stagnate.[13]

Of course, circumstances make a great deal of difference in how harmful a given tax or tax burden is to the economy. In times of war, national crisis or patriotic fervor people will accept tax burdens which would cause all production to cease under normal circumstances.[14] Related to this point is the idea that people will suffer different tax burdens depending on what the revenue is to be used for. If people thought they would directly benefit in some way from the raising of additional revenue, because it went to build roads or other capital improvements from which everyone benefits, the majority probably would be willing to shoulder a heavier burden than if they thought the money was going for some less desirable purpose, such as income redistribution.[15]

In any case, the type of income which is being taxed makes a great deal of difference in determining the capacity of that income to be taxed. Even a small tax burden on entrepreneurial profit would be quite destructive, whereas a tax on monopoly profits or ground rents might be much higher without adverse consequences. In the case of wage income, many believe that anything above what is necessary for subsistance can be taxed away with impunity. But as Schumpeter points out, "the possible tax yield is limited not only by the size of the taxable object less the subsistence minimum of the taxable subject, but also by the nature of the driving forces of the free economy."[16] Similarly, Sir Josiah Stamp said, "But taxation is not merely a stationary or static problem, the cutting up of an existing cake—it is a moving and dynamic problem. We have to ask not only how little we can leave him with, but also, how much reduction will he stand before he slackens in work and abstinence? How long will he come up smiling to be taxed this way?"[17]

To this proposition people like Frank H. Knight argued that taxes have an income effect; that is, insofar as they deny workers their income, those workers must work more in order to have the same disposable income.[18] If this were always true it would mean that there is effectively no limit to the taxable capacity of labor short of a 100 percent tax rate. However, this argument was refuted by Lionel Robbins, who pointed out:

Professor Knight's argument assumes that the prices of the commodities constituting real income are unaltered. This is presumably true so far as money prices are concerned. But the relevant conception in this connection is not *money price* but *effort price*, and a change in the rate at which money income can be earned, money prices remaining constant, *constitutes* a change in the effort price of commodities. *The money price is the same but the effort price is diminished.* And, that being the case, the question whether more or less effort is expended is obviously still an open one. It depends on the elasticity of demand for income in terms of effort.[19] (Emphasis in original.)

There was almost no discussion of the problem of taxable capacity during the 1930s, but with the outbreak of World War II and the enormous increase in revenue demands by governments everywhere, economists again took up the issue. While it is recognized that people will probably be willing to carry a heavier burden of taxation in wartime than they would in peacetime, they are still going to look for ways to minimize the tax as best they can.

In 1941, income tax rates in the United States were increased substantially; the bottom rate went from 4 to 10 percent, and rates on all other income classes increased a similar amount. In 1942 the bottom rate was dramatically increased still further, to 19 percent, with the top rate raised from 81 to 88 percent, which began at $200,000 of taxable income. Again in 1944 tax rates were increased, to 23 percent at the bottom and 94 percent at the top. Thus, in 1939 the highest marginal tax rate for someone with an income of $10,000 per year was 10 percent; by 1944 it had quadrupled.[20]

TABLE 4

COMPARISON OF AVERAGE AND MARGINAL TAX RATES AT VARIOUS INCOME
LEVELS (1944)*

	U.S.		BRITAIN	
INCOME	Average	Marginal	Average	Marginal
$1,000	1.2%	2.7%	0.0%	0.0%
2,000	4.8	20.7	13	37
3,000	10.1	20.7	23	45
4,000	12.7	22.5	28	45
5,000	14.7	22.5	35	45
7,500	16.9	33.0	37	45
10,000	19.0	37.0	39	62.5

*Family of three.

SOURCE: Tibor Scitovsky, Edward Shaw and Lorie Tarshis, *Mobilizing Resources for War* (New York: McGraw-Hill, 1951), p. 68.

As early as 1942, Prof. Martin Bronfenbrenner argued that the United States was already close to the point of diminishing returns in federal taxation, and that Britain had probably already reached it.[21] A study of war finance in 1943 by Prof. Carl Shoup tried to sort out the economic effects of existing tax rates. Shoup found that "the heavier the tax rate immediately above and below the margin of the worker's income, and the lighter the tax rate on the earnings up to somewhere near the margin, the greater is the work-restricting effect of the tax and the smaller its work-inducing effect."[22] He also found that rationing had the effect of increasing marginal tax rates, because it benefits those with a low time preference while hurting those with a high time preference.[23] In other words, the lower one's income the less it costs to have goods rationed; the higher one's income the more it costs. Thus, if one is restricted to a limited amount of goods to purchase, he has less incentive to earn more income, because there is nothing to buy with it.

By the end of the war, it was generally agreed that an increase in the average rate of taxation and a reduction in the marginal rate would tend to stimulate work effort, while a reduction in the average rate and an increase in the marginal rate would probably discourage work effort.[24] Hence, if one were only interested in stimulating work effort, without regard to fairness or equity, the ideal tax would probably be a head tax—with everyone obliged to pay a certain sum such as $1,000 per year. Then the average tax rate would be quite high, but the marginal rate would be zero.[25]

With the end of war, the discussion about an economic limit on taxation took quite a different turn. Inspired by two articles by Prof. Colin Clark, the question was whether a high level of taxation was inflationary. Clark put forth the proposition that when taxation exceeded 25 percent of national income any further increases would be strongly inflationary.[26]

Clark came in for a heavy attack. Joseph Pechman and Thomas Mayer said that Clark's analysis could not be correct because "it is generally accepted that an increase in government expenditures will tend to increase national income in money terms, even if it is balanced by an equal increase in taxes."[27] On the other hand, Benjamin Higgins argued that any increase in taxes would almost certainly be deflationary, not inflationary.[28] Richard Goode found Clark's data to be insufficient to prove his case.[29] Only Dan Throop Smith found Clark's argument to be plausible, although he did not endorse it.[30]

The discussion about Clark's thesis—and indeed, the whole question of economic limits to taxation—soon died out, although some economists still do argue that taxes can have a "cost-push" effect on inflation.[31]

In recent years, economists have returned to the question of the disincentive effects of taxation. Throughout most of the 1950s and 1960s it was generally held that the disincentive effects of taxation on labor supply were negligible, because people had little freedom to vary their hours of work in response to taxes and because the income effect cancelled out the substitution effect. In other words, although taxes make leisure relatively less costly, people must still work harder to maintain the same net income level.[32] The Congressional Budget Office still holds this view.[33]

However, there is now important work which implies that the

effects of high tax rates on labor supply and saving are much greater than previously believed. The effect of high tax rates on saving is most easily shown by an example:

Consider an economy in which there are no taxes and suppose that one has $1,000. One can either save it or spend it. If the rate of interest is 5 percent, then saving the $1,000 is equivalent to buying an income of $50 per year. Thus, the cost of consuming the $1,000 is $50 per year, and the cost of having $50 per year is $1,000 of foregone consumption. Now suppose a 50 percent tax is imposed. Afterwards it requires $2,000 of pretax income to buy the same consumer goods—the tax has doubled the cost of consumption. But to have $50 a year of after-tax income one now must get $100 of pretax income. If the market rate of interest is the same, this means that $2,000 must be saved. But to save $2,000 one must have a pretax income of $4,000—the tax has quadrupled the cost of saving. It is now twice as costly to save as consume.[34]

Consequently, it is now estimated that present high tax rates are having a significant effect on the savings rate.[35] Since ultimately capital can be created only by foregone consumption, the decline in personal saving which has developed in recent years must reduce the growth of GNP and the standard of living for all Americans. Recent data suggests that the price we have paid is already quite high (see tables 5, 6 and 7).

Arnold Harberger estimated in 1963, that, in terms of labor supply, when tax rates went from 20 percent at the bottom to 91 percent at the top, such marginal tax rates were reducing work effort by 2.5 percent in the lower brackets to more than 11 percent in the upper brackets. This says, in effect, that if it were possible to extract out of

TABLE 5

SAVING AS A PERCENTAGE OF
DISPOSABLE PERSONAL
INCOME

Year	Percent
1971	7.7
1972	6.2
1973	7.8
1974	7.3
1975	7.7
1976	5.8
1977	5.0
1978	4.9
1979	4.5

SOURCE: Department of Commerce, Bureau of Economic Analysis.

TABLE 6
GROWTH RATE OF FIXED BUSINESS CAPITAL PER EMPLOYED WORKER IN PRIVATE BUSINESS (1947–78)

	1946–1966	1966–1973	1973–1978	1973–1974	1974–1975	1975–1976	1976–1977	1977–1978
Total Gross	2.0%	1.8%	1.0%	1.6%	6.1%	−0.6%	−1.0%	−1.3%
Plant	1.1	1.0	0.2	0.7	5.3	−1.2	−1.9	−2.0
Equipment	4.0	3.0	2.0	2.9	7.1	0.2	0.2	−0.3
Total Net	2.5	2.1	0.5	1.5	5.2	−1.2	−1.3	−1.5
Plant	1.9	1.5	−0.2	0.7	4.6	−1.8	−2.3	−2.3
Equipment	3.8	3.1	1.6	2.8	6.1	−0.5	0.2	−0.5

SOURCE: *Statistical Abstract of the United States, 1979*, p. 559.

each income class the same tax as was in fact obtained, but in such a way that tax incentives did not distort the choice between labor and leisure at the margin, there would be 11 percent more work out of the top income brackets and 2.5 percent more work out of people in the lower brackets. These figures do not imply that top-bracket people work less than low-bracket people, but only that they work 11 or so percent less than they would in the absence of the income tax incentive for leisure.[36]

More recent evidence derived from the negative income tax experiments conducted by the federal government also indicate a significant negative labor response to high de facto tax rates. An analysis of data from the New Jersey–Pennsylvania experiment, for example, found that white males participating in the experiment reduced

TABLE 7

ANNUAL GROWTH IN GNP PER EMPLOYED WORKER IN
MAJOR INDUSTRIALIZED COUNTRIES (1963–79)

	1963–1973	1973–1979
Japan	8.7%	3.4%
West Germany	4.6	3.2
France	4.6	2.7
Italy	5.4	1.6
Canada	2.4	0.4
United Kingdom	3.0	0.3
United States	1.9	0.1

SOURCE: *Economic Report of the President, 1980*, p. 85.

their work effort by five to seven hours per week on average. This data is particularly significant because male heads of households were previously thought to be the group least likely to reduce their work effort in response to high tax rates.[37] Data from the Seattle and Denver income maintenance experiments found that husbands reduced their hours worked by 5 percent, wives 22 percent, and female heads of households 11 percent.[38] Based on such evidence, Jerry Hausman of M.I.T. recently concluded:

> The progressivity of taxation may be leading to substantial deadweight loss due to the tax induced distortion. . . . For the mean individual who earns $5 per hour we find the deadweight loss to be $378 which is 4.6% of his net income and 21.9% of tax revenues collected from him. To see the effect of progressivity of the income tax, we repeat the calculations for the mean individual who earns $10 per hour. The deadweight loss now rises to $2,995 which is 19.2% of net income or 71% of tax revenues. . . . For the $5 per hour individual deadweight loss for a proportional tax is $246 or 42.9% less than for the progressive tax case. For the $10 per hour individual deadweight loss for a proportional tax is $1,270 which is 85.5% less than for the progressive tax. . . .
>
> The finding of a significant income effect and concomitant welfare cost for male heads of households is contrary to the received knowledge in the field, e.g., Pechman [*Federal Tax Policy*]. But the finding only appears when progressivity of the income tax is accounted for. Since most previous studies did not attempt to model the tax system, their estimates might be interpreted "as if" a proportional tax system existed so that they could not find the income effect found here. To the extent that our findings are substantiated in future research, the previous presumption that the efficiency effect of a progressive income tax system is quite small or zero needs to be revised.[39]

Other studies have shown that taxes have important long-term considerations for individuals quite apart from hours worked. For example, the decision to retire sooner rather than later can be strongly affected by one's tax bracket. It has also been found that the quality of one's work effort is affected by tax rates. Lastly, many individuals make career choices and human capital decisions (such as how much education to get) based partly on tax considerations.[40]

In the early 1950s Professors Walter Blum and Harry Kalven of the University of Chicago Law School undertook an impartial examination of progressive taxation and concluded, "The case for progression, after a long critical look, thus turns out to be stubborn but uneasy."[41] It is, perhaps, an indication of changing times that a prominent economist, Dr. Norman Ture, recently said of progressive taxation, "For the economist qua economist, the case is not uneasy; it is virtually nonexistent."[42]

Notes

1. For a summary of economic theories in support of progressivity, see Elmer Fagan, "Recent and Contemporary Theories of Progressive Taxation," *Journal of Political Economy* 46 (August 1938), pp. 457–98.

2. H.C. Simons, *Personal Income Taxation* (Chicago: University of Chicago Press, 1938), pp. 18–19.

3. F. A. Hayek, *The Constitution of Liberty* (Chicago: University of Chicago Press, 1960), p. 313.

4. J. R. McCulloch, *A Treatise on the Principles and Practical Influence of Taxation and the Funding System* (London: Scottish Academic Press, 1975), p. 147.

5. Harley L. Lutz, *Guideposts to a Free Economy* (New York: McGraw-Hill, 1945), p. 75.

6. Joseph A. Pechman and Benjamin Okner, *Who Bears the Tax Burden?* (Washington: The Brookings Institution, 1974), p. 64.

7. Bertrand de Jouvenel, *The Ethics of Redistribution* (London: Cambridge University Press, 1951), p. 76.

8. Hayek, *Constitution*, p. 311; see also Friedrich Hayek, "The Case Against Progressive Income Taxes," *The Freeman* (December 28, 1953), pp. 229–32; idem, "Progressive Taxation Reconsidered," in Mary Sennholz, ed., *On Freedom and Free Enterprise* (Princeton: D. Van Nostrand, 1956), pp. 265–84.

9. See John Jewkes, David Sawers, and Richard Stillerman, *The Sources of Invention*, 2nd ed. (New York: W. W. Norton, 1969).

10. Lionel (Lord) Robbins, "Notes on Public Finance," *Lloyds Bank Review* (October 1955), p. 10; see also Jewkes, et al, *Sources of Invention*, pp. 192–93.

11. Ludwig von Mises, *Human Action* (New Haven: Yale University Press, 1949), pp. 804–5.

12. Joseph A. Schumpeter, *Capitalism, Socialism and Democracy*, 3rd ed. (New York: Harper & Row, 1950), pp. 111–20.

13. See Israel M. Kirzner, *Competition and Entrepreneurship* (Chicago: University of Chicago Press, 1973); idem, *Perception, Opportunity, and Profit* (Chicago: University of Chicago Press, 1979); Jonathan Hughes, "Entrepreneurial Activity and American Economic Progress," *Journal of Libertarian Studies* 3 (Winter 1979), pp. 361–70.

14. Joseph A. Schumpeter, "The Crisis of the Tax State," *International Economics Papers* (4: 1954), p. 20. This is a transcript of a lecture originally given in 1918.

15. Sir Josiah Stamp, *Wealth and Taxable Capacity* (London: P.S. King & Son, Ltd., 1922), pp. 118–19.

16. Schumpeter, "Tax State," pp. 22–23.

17. Stamp, *Taxable Capacity*, pp. 114–15.

18. Frank H. Knight, *Risk, Uncertainty and Profit* (Chicago: University of Chicago Press, 1971; originally published in 1921), p. 117.

19. Lionel Robbins, "On the Elasticity of Demand for Income in Terms of Effort," *Economica* 10 (June 1930), p. 127.

20. Tax Foundation, *Facts and Figures on Government Finance* (Washington: Tax Foundation, 1979), pp. 102–3.

21. Martin Bronfenbrenner, "Diminishing Returns in Federal Taxation?" *Journal of Political Economy* (1942), p. 717.

22. Carl Shoup, "Problems in War Finance," *American Economic Review* 34 (March 1943), p. 76.

23. Ibid., p. 78; see also F. W. Paish, "Economic Incentive in Wartime," *Economica* (August 1941), pp. 239–48.

24. Gershon Cooper, "Taxation and Incentive in Mobilization," *Quarterly Journal of Economics* 66 (February 1952), pp. 43–66; see also Richard A. Musgrave, *The Theory of Public Finance* (New York: McGraw-Hill, 1959), pp. 232–56.

25. Tibor Scitovsky, Edward Shaw and Lorie Tarshis, *Mobilizing Resources for War* (New York: McGraw-Hill, 1951), p. 67; see also Shoup, "War Finance," p. 76.

26. Colin Clark, "Public Finance and Changes in the Value of Money," *The Economic Journal* 60 (December 1945), pp. 371–89; idem, "The Danger Point in Taxes," *Harper's* (December 1950), pp. 67–69.

27. Joseph A. Pechman and Thomas Mayer, "Mr. Colin Clark on the Limits of Taxation," *Review of Economics and Statistics* 34(1952), p. 242.

28. Benjamin Higgins, "A Note on Taxation and Inflation," *Canadian Journal of Economics and Political Science* 19(August 1953), pp. 392–402.

29. Richard Goode, "An Economic Limit on Taxes: Some Recent Discussions," *National Tax Journal* 5 (3: 1952), pp. 227–33.

30. Dan Throop Smith, "Note on Inflationary Consequences of High Taxation," *Review of Economics and Statistics* 34 (1952), pp. 243–47.

31. "Inflation Is Now Too Serious A Matter to Leave to the Economists," *Forbes* (November 15, 1976), pp. 121–41; John H. Hotson, *Inflation & the Rise of the Government Sector: A Survey of Alternative Approaches* (Waterloo, Ontario, Canada: University of Waterloo Economic Series #100); C. Northcote Parkinson, *The Law and the Profits* (Boston: Houghton Mifflin, 1960), pp. 89–90.

32. Richard Goode, "The Income Tax and the Supply of Labor," *Journal of Political Economy* 58 (October 1949), pp. 428–37; idem, *The Individual Income Tax* (Washington: Brookings, 1976), pp. 52–56; George F. Break, "Income Taxes, Wage Rates, and the Incentive to Supply Labor Services," *National Tax Journal* 6 (December 1953), pp. 333–52; idem, "The Incidence and Economic Effects of Taxation," in *The Economics of Public Finance* (Washington: Brookings, 1974), pp. 180–91; Joseph A. Pechman, *Federal Tax Policy* 3rd ed. (Washington: Brookings, 1977), pp. 68–69; Marvin Kosters, "Effects of an Income Tax on Labor Supply," in Arnold Harberger and Martin J. Bailey, eds., *The Taxation of Income from Capital* (Washington: Brookings, 1969), pp. 301–24.

33. Congress of the United States, Congressional Budget Office, *Understanding Fiscal Policy* (Washington: U.S. Government Printing Office, 1978), p. 7.

34. Norman B. Ture and B. Kenneth Sanden, *The Effects of Tax Policy on Capital Formation* (New York: Financial Executives Research Foundation, 1977), pp. 60–61.

35. Michael J. Boskin, "Taxation, Saving, and the Rate of Interest," *Journal of Political Economy* 86 (April 1978), Pt. 2, pp. S3–S27.

36. Arnold C. Harberger, *Taxation and Welfare* (Boston: Little, Brown, 1974), pp. 45–46.

37. John F. Cogan, *Negative Income Taxation and Labor Supply: New Evidence from the New Jersey-Pennsylvania Experiment* (Santa Monica, CA: The Rand Corporation, 1978).

38. Congress of the United States, *Materials Related to Welfare Research and Experimentation: Assembled by the Staff of the Committee on Finance for the Use of the Subcommittee on Public Assistance, Committee on Finance, United States Senate,* Committee Print, 95th Cong., 2nd sess. (Washington: U.S. Government Printing Office, 1978), pp. 114–18.

39. J. A. Hausman, "The Effect of Taxes on Labor Supply," a paper presented to the Brookings Conference on Taxation, October 18–19, 1979, pp. 43–44.

40. Harvey S. Rosen, "What Is Labor Supply and Do Taxes Affect It?" *American Economic Review, Papers and Proceedings* 70 (May 1980), pp. 171–76.

41. Walter J. Blum and Harry Kalven, *The Uneasy Case for Progressive Taxation* (Chicago: University of Chicago Press, 1953), p. 103.

42. Norman Ture, "Comment," in Colin D. Campbell, ed., *Income Redistribution* (Washington: American Enterprise Institute, 1977), p. 162.

4

The Income-Transfer Wedge

INCOME TRANSFERS—WELFARE, SOCIAL SECURITY, UNEMPLOY-ment compensation, and the like—have effects on individual incentive almost identical to those caused by high marginal tax rates. This results from the reduction in the tradeoff between work and leisure caused by benefit levels which are not substantially below the net income an individual would get from work and from explicit de facto tax rates caused by means tests, which reduce benefits as one earns other income. Thus, the system encourages those who are working to stop and discourages those who are not working from doing so. It is only by understanding the tax effects of income transfers that we can ever hope to develop a social welfare system which aids the truly needy while providing the maximum incentive to work.

There is no question that for a significant portion of the U.S. population the wedge between what they could earn by working and what they could receive in welfare benefits is quite small. As former Congresswoman Martha Griffiths of Michigan noted in the foreword to a comprehensive study of social welfare in the U.S. by the Joint Economic Committee:

Some years ago, I received a letter from a woman in my district who earned $5,300 gross per year. She outlined her taxes, her take-home pay and her problems. The next day I received a call from a woman living in a far better area of my district whose home had been purchased under section 235 and who was drawing, she said, $750 per month, untaxed, in AFDC [Aid for Families with Dependent Children, the principal Federal welfare program] money, including $200 per month for a housekeeper. My "tired lady," earning $5,300, was paying taxes to help support a woman at a $750 rate per month. I seethed. There are no jobs of which I am aware that increase your pay because you have children.[1]

Nevertheless, in many cases, those on welfare can and do receive total benefit levels which exceed the net incomes of many who work. As one can see from table 1, maximum federal welfare benefits can go as high as $8,748 per year for a family of four. And remember that, since welfare benefits are tax-free, a working family would have to earn 30 to 40 percent more to have the same disposable income.

Similarly, many economists now believe that unemployment compensation benefits are so high that they lead to a higher unemployment rate. The economists argue that unemployment benefits reduce the incentive for workers to take new jobs, that workers are encouraged to take seasonal jobs knowing that unemployment benefits will tide them over nonwork periods, and that employers are encouraged to lay off workers during slow periods rather than keeping them on because they know that the workers can receive unemployment compensation. The effect is to permanently increase the measured rate of unemployment by more than a full percentage point and increase cyclical swings in the unemployment rate.

The U.S. General Accounting Office (GAO) recently issued a report confirming this view. It charged that unemployment compensation benefits are too high, thereby causing unemployed workers to stay unemployed longer even though jobs similar to their last ones may be available, exhaust their unemployment benefits before taking another job, and quit jobs more frequently.

The GAO points out that although benefit levels have been fixed at approximately 50 percent of a worker's gross pay, up to state-set maximums, the increase in taxes since 1935 has widened the gap between gross and net (after tax) income. Consequently, most unemployment insurance recipients now replace at least 60 percent of their prior net wages during unemployment. Nearly 25 percent of recipients in a sample studied by the GAO replaced over 75 percent of their prior net income and 7 percent replaced over 100 percent.[2] These figures are consistent with an earlier study done by Mathematica Policy Research, summarized in table 2.

TABLE 1

MAXIMUM POTENTIAL BENEFITS, AFDC AND FOOD STAMPS FOR A 4-PERSON
FAMILY (July 1979)

	Maximum AFDC Grant[1]	Food Stamp Benefits[2]	COMBINED BENEFITS	
			Monthly	Yearly
Alabama	$148	$204	$352	$4,224
Alaska	450	237	687	8,244
Arizona	240[3]	180	420	5,040
Arkansas	188	196	384	4,608
California	487	106	593	7,116
Colorado	327[4]	154	481	5,772[5]
Connecticut	517[3]	97	614	7,368
Delaware	287	166	453	5,436
District of Columbia	349	148	497	5,964
Florida	230	183	413	4,956
Georgia	170	201	371	4,452
Hawaii	546	183	729	8,748
Idaho	421	126	547	6,564
Illinois	350[3]	147	497	5,964
Indiana	275[6]	170	445	5,340
Iowa	419	127	546	6,552
Kansas	375[3]	140	515	6,180
Kentucky	235	182	417	5,004
Louisiana	187[3]	196	383	4,596
Maine	332	153	485	5,820
Maryland	294	164	458	5,496
Massachusetts	420[7]	126	546	6,552
Michigan[3][8]	505[9]	101	606	7,272
(Detroit)	(470)[9]	(111)	(581)	(6,972)
Minnesota	454	116	570	6,840
Mississippi	120	204	324	3,888
Missouri	270	171	441	5,292
Montana	331	153	484	5,808
Nebraska	370	141	511	6,132
Nevada	297	163	460	5,520
New Hampshire	367[7]	142	509	6,108
New Jersey	386	137	523	6,276
New Mexico	242	180	422	5,064
New York[3][10]	536	92	628	7,536
(New York City)	(476)	(110)	(586)	(7,032)
North Carolina	210	189	399	4,788
North Dakota	370	141	511	6,132
Ohio	327	154	481	5,772
Oklahoma	349	148	497	5,964
Oregon	463[11]	113	576	6,912
Pennsylvania	373[3][12]	141	514	6,168
Rhode Island	359[4][13]	145	504	6,048[5]
South Carolina	142	204	346	4,152
South Dakota	340	150	490	5,880

TABLE 1 (Continued)

MAXIMUM POTENTIAL BENEFITS, AFDC AND FOOD STAMPS FOR A 4-PERSON
FAMILY (July 1979)

	Maximum AFDC Grant[1]	Food Stamp Benefits[2]	COMBINED BENEFITS	
			Monthly	Yearly
Tennessee	148	204	352	4,224
Texas	140	204	344	4,128
Utah	389	136	525	6,300
Vermont	524[3]	95	619	7,428
Virginia	335[14]	152	487	5,844
Washington	483[3]	108	591	7,092
West Virginia	249[3]	178	427	5,124
Wisconsin	458[3]	115	573	6,876
Wyoming	340	150	490	5,880
Guam	306	270	576	6,912
Puerto Rico	57	190	247	2,964
Virgin Islands	205	228	433	5,196
Median State (AFDC grant)	340	150	490	5,880

[1]As of July 1979 unless otherwise indicated. Maximum paid to a family with zero countable income.

[2]Food stamp benefits assume deductions of $160 monthly (maximum allowable in July-December 1979; $70 standard allowance plus $90 deduction for excess shelter costs and/or dependent care) in the 48 contiguous states and D.C. In the remaining five jurisdictions these maximum deductions were assumed: Alaska, $280; Hawaii, $230; Guam, $250; Puerto Rico, $75; and Virgin Islands, $125. If only the $70 standard deduction were assumed, food stamp benefits would drop by $27 monthly in the 48 contiguous States and D.C. Maximum food stamp benefits in the last half of 1979 were $204 monthly for a family of 4 except in these five jurisdictions, where they were as follows: Alaska, $288; Hawaii, $277; Guam, $286; Puerto Rico, $190; and Virgin Islands, $251.

[3]Highest of area standards within the state.

[4]Higher in winter. Winter AFDC maximum benefits are $347 in Colorado and $518 in Rhode Island.

[5]Annual total does not reflect higher winter benefits.

[6]Indiana's maximum AFDC payment rose to $315 on Jan. 1, 1980.

[7]As of August 1979.

[8]Washtenaw County (Ann Arbor).

[9]Effective in October 1979 Michigan payments rose to a maximum of $531 in Ann Arbor and $501 in Detroit.

[10]Suffolk County.

[11]Oregon payment is for a mother and three children, aged 7-12. The state varies payments by age of child.

[12]Pennsylvania's maximum AFDC payment rose to $395 on Jan. 1, 1980.

[13]Figure reflects November 1979 increase retroactive to July 1979.

[14]Fairfax and Arlington Counties supplement these benefits.

SOURCE: Congressional Research Service.

As one can see from the table, a significantly higher percentage of unemployment insurance recipients replace more than 50 percent of their previous income when contrasted to net income than when contrasted to gross income. One should keep in mind also that unemployed workers not only save taxes they would otherwise have paid but work-related expenses, such as travel and child care expenses, as well. Moreover, unemployment insurance recipients are more likely to have other income today than in earlier years. For example, 8 percent of recipients in the GAO sample had retirement income which they could continue to receive on top of their unemployment benefits. Many also had spouses or children who continued to work and provide family income. It can be assumed that many also took the opportunity to do work which was not charged against their benefits, such as home repairs or temporary jobs.

When a worker can replace 60 percent or more of his previous net income, save on many expenses, continue to draw outside income, and possibly still have a wife or husband working at the same time, the financial incentive to work is obviously reduced significantly. Prof. Martin Feldstein of Harvard makes the following illustrative point:

TABLE 2

DISTRIBUTION OF RECIPIENTS AND
PERCENTAGE OF WAGES REPLACED BY
UNEMPLOYMENT INSURANCE BENEFITS

PERCENTAGE OF WAGES REPLACED	PERCENT OF RECIPIENTS	
	Gross Wages	Net Wages
White		
0–20	6.7	5.3
20–40	32.6	19.3
40–50	27.5	16.3
50–60	21.5	18.8
60–80	9.5	27.8
80+	2.4	12.4
0–50	66.8	40.9
50+	33.4	59.0
Nonwhite		
0–20	4.5	2.2
20–40	36.1	16.6
40–50	29.4	20.2
50–60	19.1	20.9
60–80	8.6	27.9
80+	2.3	12.3
0–50	70.0	39.0
50+	30.0	61.1

SOURCE: *A Longitudinal Study of Unemployment Insurance Exhaustees,* Mathematica Policy Research Project No. 76-01, pp. 74–79, cited in Congressional Budget Office, *Unemployment Compensation: A Background Report* (December 8, 1978), pp. 29–32.

To understand the adverse incentive effects of unemployment benefits, it is useful to think of unemployment compensation as imposing a very high rate of tax on the income that the individual would earn if he were not unemployed. Two different tax rates can be distinguished. The *net tax rate* is the ratio of the unemployment compensation to the net earnings that an individual would receive if he were employed. It measures the extent to which unemployment compensation replaces prospective net earnings. The *gross tax rate* is the ratio of unemployment compensation plus taxes (federal and state income taxes and the social security tax) to the *gross* wage that an individual would earn if he were employed. The gross tax rate therefore measures the wedge between the individual's marginal social product and the additional net income that he would receive if he worked.[3]

Feldstein calculated that the net tax rate for an unemployed individual earning $6,000 per year with an employed wife earning $4,200 per year would be 83 percent. In other words, in this case, unemployment compensation would replace 83 percent of the net wages he would have received had he worked. The gross tax rate was 87 percent. The implied tax rates would be even higher if the wife lost her job and the husband continued to work. In this case the net tax rate rises to 88 percent and the gross tax rate to 91 percent. Feldstein concluded that the effects of such a situation are clearly negative:

These high marginal tax rates obviously provide very strong adverse incentives. For those who are already unemployed, it greatly reduces and often eliminates the cost of increasing the period of unemployment. More generally, for all types of unsteady work—seasonal, cyclical and casual—it raises the net wage to the employee relative to the cost to the employer. This encourages employers and employees to organize production in ways that increase the level of unemployment by making the seasonal and cyclical variations in unemployment too large and by making casual and temporary jobs too common.[4]

High marginal tax rates are also evident in the case of welfare recipients. To see how these high marginal tax rates develop (the tax on each additional dollar earned), suppose that a family of four in Los Angeles attempted to earn some money on top of welfare in order to better itself and ultimately get off welfare altogether. If this family is currently receiving all the benefits to which it is entitled under present law, its welfare income amounts to about $718.33 per month. But each dollar earned on top of this reduces part of these benefits. Thus if the family earns $100 per month on top of welfare, its disposable monthly income will not increase by $100. Because taxes must be paid on that $100 and because some welfare benefits are reduced, this family's spendable monthly income only rises to $759.43—an increase of $41.10. This translates into an effective marginal tax rate on that $100 of gross income of 58.9 percent.

Suppose this same family has reached a point where it is making $400 per month in gross income on top of welfare. Its spendable monthly income will only increase to $815.80 per month—a mere $97.47 more than it would have under welfare alone. This translates into better than a 75 percent average tax rate on the family's earned income. And the marginal tax rate is even higher. If this family were to earn as much as an additional $300 per month, bringing its gross earned income up to $700, its spendable income would actually drop! From the $815.80 the family had to spend while earning $400 in addition to welfare, its spendable income would drop to $794.58 when it earned $700 in addition to welfare. In other words, the actual taxes which must be paid combined with a reduction in welfare benefits has imposed an effective marginal tax rate in excess of 100 percent on this poor family.

Table 3 demonstrates how the welfare system conspires to impose confiscatory tax rates on the poorest members of society, thus robbing them of any incentive to improve themselves and ultimately get off welfare.[5]

These high de facto tax rates are not exceptional. Similarly high tax

TABLE 3

The Effects of Income and Taxes on Family Spendable Income from Wages and Welfare Benefits*

Monthly Gross Wages†	Net Family Spendable Income	Increase in Spendable Income	*De Facto* Marginal Tax Rate
$ 0	$718.33	n.a.‡	n.a.
100	759.43	$41.10	58.9%
200	780.53	21.10	78.9
300	810.57	30.04	70.0
400	815.80	5.23	94.5
500	794.58	−21.22	121.2
600	794.58	0	100.0
700	794.58	0	100.0
800	809.92	15.34	84.7
900	832.49	22.57	77.4
1000	858.58	26.09	73.9

*Applies to a family of four in Los Angeles, one member of which is unemployed or disabled.
†Including employment taxes paid by employer.
‡Not applicable

SOURCE: Arthur B. Laffer and Christopher Petruzzi of the University of Southern California and the H. C. Wainwright Company.

TABLE 4

EFFECTS OF THE EARNINGS LIMITATION, SOCIAL SECURITY, AND FEDERAL
INCOME TAXES ON SPENDABLE INCOME OF SOCIAL SECURITY
RECIPIENTS

Monthly Gross Wages	Net Spendable Income	Increase in Spendable Income	De Facto Marginal Tax Rate
$ 0	$298.00	—	—
100	391.87	$93.87	6.13%
200	485.74	93.87	6.13
300	579.61	93.87	6.13
400	654.81	75.20	24.80
500	683.68	28.87	71.13
600	710.14	26.46	73.54
700	736.01	25.87	74.13
800	760.96	24.95	75.05
900	785.33	24.37	75.63
1,000	822.70	37.37	62.63

rates exist through the spectrum of income transfers wherever there is a means test or earnings test. Table 4 estimates the de facto tax rates on a social security recipient resulting from the earnings test, based on 1979 social security and income tax laws.

The principal argument against lifting the social security earnings limitation is, of course, that it will cost the government money. It is estimated that elimination of the earnings limitation will cost $2.1 billion on a static basis. While this may be true it ignores the economic benefits which will come from the skills of older Americans presently discouraged from working, and it ignores the revenue which will be generated by those people who will work who otherwise would not. The latest estimate from the Social Security Administration of what the revenue feedback would be ranges from 16 percent of increased expenditures in combined social security and federal income tax revenue, to 79 percent of expenditures, assuming that 10 percent more people age 65 to 69 stay in the work force. But based on the work of Professors Boskin and Pellechio, it is quite probable that a 10 percent increase in labor force participation by workers over age 65 is conservative, given elimination of the earnings test. According to Boskin, a decrease in the explicit tax rate on earnings from one-half to one-third would reduce the annual probability of work by about 50 percent, while Pellechio found that elimination of the earnings test would increase labor supplied by 151 annual hours and payroll tax revenues by $31 per individual.[6]

A solution to the problem of high tax rates on welfare recipients would be to take away less of each dollar that is earned. Unfortunately, this would mean extending benefits upward to families with relatively high incomes. It is estimated that if it were decided that each family of four were to receive a basic income of $6,000 and lose only an average of 25 percent of each dollar earned above this level, then the "break-even" point would be an annual income of $24,000. Under such a system there would certainly be an increase in the incentive for welfare recipients to earn income, but more than two-thirds of all American families would qualify for some sort of cash payment.[7] Secretary of HEW Joseph Califano commented on this dilemma during testimony regarding President Carter's welfare reform plan:

> The system of "benefit reduction rates" is designed to address a fundamental problem: if cash benefits are reduced at too steep a rate as earnings increase there will be no incentive for work.
>
> For example, if the cash benefit is reduced by $1 for every $1 earned, there is obviously no work incentive whatsoever.
>
> If the cash grant is reduced 90 cents for every $1 earned, there may be no incentive, because travel costs and other expenses of going to work will mean there is still little or no real improvement in the individual's financial condition as the result of employment.
>
> But, there is also a problem at the other extreme. If the cash benefit is reduced only 25 cents for every $1 earned, there is a good incentive to work, but families will continue to receive cash assistance at income levels that seem too high to many taxpayers.[8]

Thus you are left with only two ways of encouraging welfare recipients to work: you can either cut benefits or increase them to include those with higher incomes. There is not much middle ground that can be carved out of this, and obviously there are heavy political obstacles to either approach. One that has received the most attention in recent years is the guaranteed minimum wage, or negative income tax, approach. The idea is simply to place an income floor under everyone which would ensure a minimum standard of living and nothing more. The problem, unfortunately, is that for people with no marketable skills the work opportunities that exist are so dismal that they prefer staying on welfare even if the marginal tax barrier did not exist. This fact has recently been confirmed by the so-called Seattle-Denver income maintenance experiment and was reported by its director, Mr. Robert Spiegelman, in testimony before Senator Moynihan's welfare subcommittee. Mr. Spiegelman said that the experiment developed the following conclusions:

(1) People work less in general. A national minimum income program guaranteeing all needy families support at 100 percent of the poverty-line level and reducing the welfare benefit by 50 cents for each dollar earned if the recipient worked would result in husbands in welfare families working 6.2 percent fewer hours, wives 22.7 per-

cent fewer, and female heads of families 12 percent less. Such a program would cost in excess of $40 billion more than the present system.

(2) Minorities tended to work even less. On a long-range basis, white husbands worked 96 hours less per year than if they weren't given a guaranteed income, black husbands worked 230 hours less, and Hispanic husbands 204 hours less.

(3) The system encouraged family breakups. White families suffered breakups from 18 to 63 percent more frequently than a control group, black families from 15 to 73 percent more, and Hispanics had a 37 percent greater incidence of family breakups.[9]

The conclusion, therefore, is that the guaranteed income is not a suitable alternative for the present system.

Probably the most innovative solution to the present welfare mess has been proposed by Cong. Dave Stockman of Michigan. He proposes that means-tested welfare be abolished altogether. It would be replaced by a universal system of child payments, on the theory that child support is the fundamental basis for the welfare system. This would be combined with a modified negative income tax and abolishment of the minimum wage. This would encourage employers to hire workers at low wages while still ensuring an adequate income for the worker. Presumably, as the worker's skills increase his income would improve and the income support could be safely phased out without penalizing the worker.[10]

A still more radical solution would be to abolish cash welfare payments altogether and give only in-kind benefits. In other words, give the poor the actual food, clothing and shelter they need, but no money. Interestingly, this was proposed recently by former New York State Social Services Commissioner Philip Toia. He proposed elimination of the present New York State welfare system in lieu of a "soup-line." All other welfare programs would be turned over to voluntary agencies whose functions have been usurped over the years by government. "State and local governments simply can no longer afford to pay for the range of services we've been providing for the past decade," Toia said. "It's time we gave a majority of the provisions of those services back to the nonprofit agencies created to serve the clientele on our welfare rolls." In other words, try and voluntarize the welfare system as much as possible by giving back to private welfare agencies the functions they served in the past and provide only what is needed for actual survival.[11] (Of course, Toia is talking only about state-administered welfare programs, not federal.)

In light of all the money spent on welfare, perhaps the truly amazing thing is that so many American families continue to be classified as living below the poverty line. According to the latest Census

Bureau report, in 1978 there were 24.5 million people in the United States living in officially defined poverty—$6,662 per year income for a family of four—or 11.4 percent of the population.[12] Yet, in 1978 income transfers in the U.S. amounted to $224.1 billion, or $9,150 for every person in the country defined as living in poverty, or $36,600 per year for a family of four. How can this be? One answer is that administrative costs eat up an enormous amount of money. In 1978 the U.S. Department of Health, Education and Welfare had 153,000 employees and a budget of $163 billion, while state and local governments had 364,000 people employed as welfare workers earning $4.2 billion in salaries.

Another explanation is that poverty is defined in such a way that virtually no amount of welfare spending will ever eradicate it. The Census Bureau, for example, measures poverty only on the basis of money income and excludes from measurement all in-kind benefits, such as food stamps, medicare, and housing subsidies. Yet the income which is excluded is very real. Thus the Congressional Budget Office recently studied the Census Bureau figures and found that by including the value of in-kind benefits the estimated number of people living in poverty was reduced by 50 percent.[13]

In response to these facts, defenders of the unemployment insurance and welfare systems argue that they are important in order to maintain aggregate demand. The idea behind this is that unemployment and economic slowdowns occur because individuals save too much, rather than spending their money on goods and services. Thus governments should run budget deficits and increase both taxes and government spending. Unemployment compensation and welfare, because they go up automatically when unemployment occurs, are therefore considered fiscal stabilizers which help to maintain aggregate demand during slowdowns.

Now we know that increasing budget deficits only deprive the private sector of needed capital and cause "crowding out" in financial markets, or cause inflation when the debt is covered by increasing the quantity of money. If taxes and spending are raised equally the reduction in incentive will continue to depress the economy. Those whose taxes are raised and those who receive government handouts will both find that the tradeoff between work and leisure has been reduced. In other words, not working costs both groups less in terms of lost income.

We need to reorient our thinking to the view that national wealth is only created when people work and save, thereby increasing the nation's capital stock. For too many years the government has been solely concerned with maintaining the level of personal income so that people could spend, whether or not they worked or saved.

Unemployment compensation, like social security and other income transfer programs, unfortunately continues to embody outmoded Keynesian ideas in public policy long after we have learned the fallacies of the underlying concepts. If unemployment compensation or social security has any value at all it is not in maintaining aggregate demand but in providing an absolute income floor so that people do not starve from adversity. It is a gross perversion of the system when people can live as well or better on unemployment compensation than they could by working.

Notes

1. U.S. Congress, Joint Economic Committee, *Income Security for Americans: Recommendations of the Public Welfare Study,* Joint Committee Print, 93rd Cong., 2d sess. (Washington: U.S. Government Printing Office, 1974), p. vi.

2. Comptroller General of the United States, *Unemployment Insurance— Inequities and Work Disincentives In the Current System* (Washington: General Accounting Office, 1979).

3. Martin Feldstein, "Unemployment Compensation: Adverse Incentives and Distributional Anomalies," *National Tax Journal* (June 1974), p. 232.

4. Ibid., p. 233; see also Martin Feldstein, "The Economics of the New Unemployment," *The Public Interest* (Fall 1973), pp. 3–41; idem, "The Effect of Unemployment Insurance on Temporary Layoff Unemployment," *American Economic Review* (December 1978), pp. 834–46; idem, "Unemployment Compensation: Its Effect on Unemployment," *Monthly Labor Review* (March 1976), pp. 39–41; Ronald G. Ehrenberg and Ronald L. Oaxaca, "Do Benefits Cause Unemployed to Hold Out for Better Jobs?" *Monthly Labor Review* (March 1976), pp. 37–39.

5. For further elaboration, see Arthur B. Laffer, *Prohibitive Tax Rates and the Inner-City: A Rational Explanation of the Poverty Trap* (Boston: H.C. Wainwright & Co., June 27, 1978); idem, "Disincentives Drag Non-Whites," *Los Angeles Times* (August 28, 1978); Martin Anderson, *Welfare: The Political Economy of Welfare Reform in the United States* (Stanford, CA: Hoover Institution Press, 1978), pp. 43–58.

6. Joseph G. Gordon and Robert N. Schoeplein, "Tax Impact From Elimination of the Retirement Test," *Social Security Bulletin* (September 1979), pp. 22–32; Michael J. Boskin, "Social Security and Retirement Decisions," *Economic Inquiry* (February 1977), pp. 1–25; Anthony J. Pellechio, *The Social Security Earnings Test, Labor Supply Distortions, and Foregone Payroll Tax Revenue* (Cambridge, MA: National Bureau of Economic Research, Working Paper No. 272, August 1978).

7. David A. Stockman, "Welfare Is the Problem," *Journal of the Institute for Socioeconomic Studies* (Fall 1978), pp. 45–46.

8. Quoted in Gordon L. Weil, *The Welfare Debate of 1978* (White Plains, NY: Institute for Socioeconomic Studies, 1978), pp. 46–47.

9. Congress of the United States, *Welfare Research and Experimentation: Hearings Before the Subcommittee on Public Assistance of the Committee on Finance, United States Senate*, 95th Cong., 2nd sess. (Washington: U.S. Government Printing Office, 1978), pp. 74–92; for similar results related to other welfare experiments, see also Congress of the United States, Committee on Finance, U.S. Senate, *Materials Related to Welfare Research and Experimentation*, Committee Print, 95th Cong., 2nd sess. (Washington: U.S. Government Printing Office, 1978); John F. Cogan, *Negative Income Taxation and Labor Supply: New Evidence From the New Jersey-Pennsylvania Experiment* (Santa Monica, CA: The Rand Corporation, 1978).

10. Stockman, "Welfare Is the Problem," pp. 47–50.

11. "Welfare Chief Backs 'Soup-Line Concept,' " *New York Times* (January 21, 1977).

12. U.S. Bureau of the Census, *Money Income and Poverty Status of Families and Persons in the United States: 1978 (Advance Report)*, Series P–60, No. 120 (Washington: U.S. Government Printing Office, 1979).

13. Congress of the United States, Congressional Budget Office, *Poverty Status of Families Under Alternative Definitions of Income* (Background Paper No. 17, January 13, 1977); Morton Paglin, "Poverty in the United States: A Reevaluation," *Policy Review* (Spring 1979), pp. 7–24.

5

Taxation and Regional Growth and Decline

ALTHOUGH ECONOMISTS ARGUE ABOUT WHETHER THE UNITED States is approaching a limit to its taxable capacity (a point beyond which an increase in tax rates will reduce tax revenue), there is no question that state and local governments can and do exceed their limits. If taxes in the U.S. as a whole were excessive it would be very hard to escape the tax burden by moving to another country—although the number of tax-exiles from Sweden, Great Britain, and elsewhere shows that it can happen. But if taxes at the state level are excessive it is much easier to move to another state. And it is easier still to escape excessive local taxation, where it may only be a matter of moving a few miles or even a few blocks to find tax relief. Thus the constraints upon state and local governments to avoid counter-productive tax policies are much more stringent than those upon the federal government. Many state and local governments have vi-olated these constraints. The result is that they have lower rates of economic and employment growth and, in the long run, take in less revenue than they would if they had adopted a more moderate approach to taxation.

An early, well-documented example of counterproductive state tax policies can be found in Wisconsin, which had the first comprehensive and effectively administered income tax. The Wisconsin income tax, in fact, was considered a model for both the federal government and numerous state governments during the progressive era. However, Wisconsin paid a heavy price for its "progressivism." A definitive study of Wisconsin economic growth in the early twentieth century by W. Elliot Brownlee, Jr., concludes that the income tax severely retarded Wisconsin's economic growth. As Brownlee writes:

> The Wisconsin income tax likely prevented the state from making the most of her growth opportunities. If we accept certain assumptions about business behavior, especially the eminently plausible premise that firms sought to maximize profits, then we are led to the conclusion that the income tax retarded capital formation in the manufacturing sector. Indications of the extent of the impact of this retardation on economic growth are plain, even without measurement of the precise influence. The state's pace of manufacturing development fell behind that for its region as a whole during the critical period between 1909 and 1929. In the light of the centrality of manufacturing expansion to the process of economic growth during the period, the importance of manufacturing to the Great Lakes during the period, and Wisconsin's locational situation, the pattern implies that the income tax had an acute inhibiting influence on Wisconsin's growth.[1]

More recently, there has been much written about the rise of the sunbelt states of the South and West and the decline of the older industrial states of the Northeast and upper Midwest. There is a substantial body of thought which argues that the snowbelt's decline and the sunbelt's prosperity are the result of federal government policies. Relatively little, however, has been written about policies within the states which either create prosperity or promote decline. There is no doubt that federal policies do have regional consequences, but insofar as they exist they are working to aid the Northeast at the expense of the sunbelt. It is the governmental policies of the northeastern states themselves which are responsible for their own condition, and it will not be reversed by federal action.

The current debate got started in 1976 when the *National Journal* published estimates showing that the federal government was taking substantially more out of the northeastern states in tax revenue than they received in federal spending.[2] The reaction of politicians in the Northeast was inevitable. Soon they organized the Coalition of Northeast Governors and, in Congress, the Northeast-Midwest Economic Advancement Coalition to lobby for more federal aid to the Northeast and Midwest (and less to the sunbelt).[3]

A powerful voice was added to the debate with the election of Sen.

Daniel Patrick Moynihan in 1976. He has since made the issue of federal responsibility for the decline of the Northeast his principal concern in Congress. In mid-1977 he first presented his thesis in a long report which said, "The overall pattern of federal taxation and expenditure has the effect of systematically deflating the economy of New York. In effect, national prosperity is traded for New York's decline."[4] He has since used his position on the powerful Senate Finance Committee and virtually every opportunity to obtain further federal aid to New York and the rest of the Northeast. Because he is so articulate, he has managed to keep the debate going long after his central points have been refuted.[5]

It soon became clear that the data used by Moynihan and others to bolster their case was seriously flawed. It was noted, for example, that the *National Journal* had allocated the total value of federal contracts to the state in which the company's headquarters were located. But little of the money might actually have been spent in that state, since plants, factories, and subcontractors which actually fulfill the contract may be located elsewhere. Similarly, taxes allocated to a particular corporation were deemed to have come entirely from the state where its headquarters are located. Obviously, one could hardly say that the people of Michigan carry the entire burden of General Motors' corporation taxes, yet this is precisely what the data showed.[6]

Additionally, it was pointed out that federal policies inevitably redistribute income between wealthier regions of the country and poorer regions. The fact that the U.S. has a steeply graduated income tax system inevitably hurts areas where per capita incomes are higher, and federal welfare money is inevitably going to go where per capita incomes are lower. Historically, this means that the Northeast paid more taxes and the South got more welfare. It is precisely the success of these policies in reducing the disparities in per capita incomes between regions which we are observing. Nevertheless, despite the growth of incomes in the sunbelt, average per capita incomes are still higher than the national average in most snowbelt states and lower than average in most sunbelt states.[7]

In any case, it is now clear that the Northeast, far from being unfairly treated by federal aid programs, is clearly receiving more in expenditures than it sends to Washington. This is due to a major increase in welfare spending in the Northeast. According to recent data, the Northeast, with 20.7 percent of the population in poverty, as defined by the Census Bureau, received 24.7 percent of federal welfare spending (AFDC, SSI, Food Stamps, and CETA funds), while the South, with 39.7 percent of the poverty population, received only 33.6 percent of the welfare money.[8]

Furthermore, it is by no means clear that a positive federal spending/taxation balance necessarily translates into regional prosperity. A recent study by the Congressional Budget Office found the link between federal spending and local economic conditions to be quite weak:

> While there are large differences in federal spending among counties, these discrepancies are only marginally related to differences in local economic circumstances. . . . The factors influencing the location choices of businesses or individuals are so numerous, and the interrelationship among factors so complex, that researchers have been unable to specify with any degree of precision the effects of federal actions on geographic patterns of economic development.[9]

Although the relationship between federal policies and local economic conditions is weak, there is a high degree of correlation between state and local policies and economic conditions. This stands to reason considering that the differences in government spending per capita and individual tax burdens between states dwarf any differences in federal spending and taxation. In the most recent Census Bureau report, for example, state and local tax revenues per capita ranged between $1,871 and 17.5 percent of personal income in the highest taxed state (Alaska) and $553 and 10.2 percent of personal income in the lowest taxed state (Arkansas), with the national average being $888 in taxes per capital, constituting 12.7 percent of personal income.[10]

Another way of comparing tax burdens between states is to measure state tax revenues as a percentage of taxable capacity; meaning the relative ability of state and local governments to obtain revenues out of their own sources through taxes as compared to the extent to which they actually use their taxable capacity. According to such an index those states with the greatest tax effort are invariably in the Northeast (New York is the highest of all), and those with the lowest are in the South and West (Texas being the lowest).[11]

The differences become even more dramatic when one looks at actual tax burdens for particular income levels. Someone with a gross income of $50,000 might pay as little as $2,777 in state and local taxes in Texas or as much as $8,555 per year in New York. Such differences have been shown to have a significant impact on the recruitment of skilled individuals for high technology industries.[12]

This may lead one to believe that the low-tax states of the sunbelt are methodically stealing industry away from the Northeast. The evidence, however, suggests that 50 percent of the North's employment losses occurred as a direct result of the "death" of firms, while

64.3 percent of southern employment gains were due to existing firms' expansion. Inmigration of businesses to the South accounted for a mere 1.2 percent increase in employment, while outmigration in the North resulted in a 1.5 percent loss of employment opportunities.[13]

As one might expect, jobs and population have been steadily moving from the high-tax states of the Northeast and upper Midwest to the lower-tax states of the South and West. Between 1968 and 1978, for example, the four major regions of the country experienced the following net migration: Northeast, minus 2,384,000; North Central, minus 2,034,000; South, plus 2,655,000; and West, plus 1,763,000. Studies indicate that tax burdens are a major factor in individuals' decisions to move into or out of a particular area.[14]

Of course, other factors such as climate and quality of life, also play a role in the decision to move, but the evidence suggests that taxes may be a dominant factor. Consider the case of New Hampshire compared to Vermont and Massachusetts. The three states are contiguous and share the same climate and geography, yet Vermont and Massachusetts have suffered population loss and slow economic growth, while New Hampshire has prospered. An examination of the three states shows that the major difference which would explain such a situation is that the burden of government is much greater in Vermont and Massachusetts than in New Hampshire. A very detailed study comparing Vermont and New Hampshire by Colin and Rosemary Campbell, for example, produced the following findings:

1. The burden of state and local taxes is much heavier in Vermont than in New Hampshire.

2. All the major types of expenditures—education, highways, and welfare—are much higher as a percentage of personal income in Vermont than in New Hampshire.

3. The adoption of broad-based taxes in Vermont has contributed to the rise in the ratio of taxes to personal income and to the rapid expansion of the major types of state and local government expenditures.

4. There is little evidence that public services are better in Vermont than in New Hampshire despite the high tax burden.

5. The adoption of broad-based taxes in Vermont has not been followed by a reduction in the burden of property taxes.

6. The burden of state and local government debt has become much greater in Vermont than in New Hampshire.

7. Vermont receives a larger percentage of its revenues from Federal grants than does New Hampshire.

8. In the 1970s, state aid to local governments as a percentage of state expenditures has become larger in New Hampshire than in Vermont.

9. In New Hampshire, the total revenues and expenditures of local

governments are much larger than those of state government. It is the opposite in Vermont.[15]

These conclusions refute almost every liberal cliché about state government fiscal policy. Yet the bottom line is that New Hampshire not only has greater economic growth than Vermont, but a sounder, more equitable fiscal system as well.[16] The same could be said of New Hampshire compared to Massachusetts, which years of liberal policies had turned into "Taxachusetts." Interestingly, recent spending and tax cuts enacted by conservative Gov. Ed King have already begun to reverse the trend.[17]

The Massachusetts example confirms a newer view of the relationship between taxes and economic growth which says that *changes* in tax burden are more important than the absolute burden of taxation. Thus, a heavily taxed state with a declining tax burden may be better able to attract industry than a lower taxed state with a rising tax burden. According to a recent report by the Harris Bank of Chicago:

1) Between 1969 and 1976 the economic growth achieved by a particular state relative to the average U.S. performance was not directly related to its average state and local tax burden; 2) over this same period, a state's relative economic growth was loosely related to the *change* in a state's relative tax burden, with those states displaying above average increases in their tax burden tending to show below average economic growth and vice versa; and 3) once allowance is made for a three-year adjustment to tax changes, there is a strong relationship suggesting that above average increases in a state's tax burden can lead to below average economic growth, while below average increases in tax burdens lead to above average growth.[18]

While Massachusetts may finally be starting to reverse the trend toward higher taxes and bigger government, New York City, that other bastion of old-fashioned liberalism, still has a long way to go. In many respects, New York City is the epitome of big government gone wild. As Ken Auletta put it, New York City is liberalism's Vietnam. It was the showcase for all the big-spending, big-government programs of the Great Society type. Unfortunately, paying for all the social welfare programs required huge amounts of money. A lot of it came from the federal government and a lot was borrowed, but most came from increased taxes on New York's citizens and businesses. These taxes are responsible for driving out of New York, perhaps forever, the people who are so desperately needed to reinvigorate the city. Unless taxes are permanently reduced it will be impossible for New York to attract a new generation of people and businesses who will ultimately restore the economic and tax base of the city and provide the money and vitality for it to continue as one of America's greatest cities.

New York is almost certainly taking in less tax revenue today than it would with lower tax rates. A number of studies done since 1975 confirm the counterproductive nature of the city's tax structure. The most important of these was done by the Temporary Commission on City Finances, appointed by Mayor Abraham Beame in 1975. Among its most interesting findings was that the city could eliminate virtually *all* taxes on manufacturing companies and yet increase total city tax revenues, owing to increased returns from auxiliary taxes.

The commission estimated that approximately 44,500 manufacturing jobs were lost for each one point increase in the business income tax. Therefore, reducing business income taxes will increase employment in the same ratio. New York City lost 500,000 manufacturing jobs between 1950 and 1975. And since each manufacturing job produces approximately $1,395 per year in revenue to the city from individual income, property, sales, and other taxes, this implies that the loss of those jobs cost the city a minimum of $700 million per year. Although reducing business income taxes may initially reduce city revenues, increasing employment ultimately will increase them. The commission estimated that if its recommended program of tax reduction for manufacturing firms were followed, by 1981 the city would show a net tax gain of $145 million per year, largely because higher manufacturing employment would increase individual income taxes an estimated $175 million per year.[19]

Another study confirms these conclusions by showing that for every 10 percent increase in business income taxes on manufacturing firms, employment and output go down 3.5 percent. For nonmanufacturing firms the negative response was found to be insignificant.[20] This would suggest that more revenue could be raised at less economic cost by shifting local business taxes from manufacturing to nonmanufacturing firms.

New York's high taxes on personal income have also been counterproductive, driving people out of the city and state, where combined state and city tax rates go as high as 16 percent. The strong incentive that high taxes create for people to leave New York (or almost any major city in the East) may be seen in table 1. As one can see, the tax burden in New York and most other eastern cities is far above the national average and cities in the South and West.

Adjusting incomes for both taxes and the cost of living would show the true magnitude of the incentive which exists for people to move out of high tax, high cost-of-living states like New York, to low tax, low cost-of living-states like Texas. It is very hard to measure this magnitude, but according to the U.S. Bureau of Labor Statistics, a family of four would need $29,677 to live comfortably in New York City, but would need only $20,628 to have the same standard of living in Austin, Texas. One important reason for the difference is that the New York family pays $7,596 per year in personal income taxes and the Austin family pays only $2,780 per year. Moreover, these data exclude many other taxes that are also higher in New York, such as sales and property taxes.[21]

Another effort to show the magnitude of differences in tax burden between different parts of the country was made by the First National Bank of Chicago. In its study per capita personal income in each state was adjusted for both per capita state and local taxes and per capita federal taxes and the cost of living, to get figures for real, after tax differences in personal income between states. Although New York starts out with one of the highest per capita personal incomes in the U.S., it ends up with a real, after tax per capita personal income which is lower than in 47 other states, after adjustment for the cost of living, federal, state, and local taxes (see table 2).

Perhaps the most dramatic example of difference between tax rates in New York and the incentive they create to leave the state is this: According to the Temporary Commission on City Finances, a New York City resident would have had to earn 9.9 percent more in 1976 than someone who lived in Connecticut or New Jersey to keep $25,000 of after tax income. At still higher income levels the tax differential becomes enormous. For a New Yorker to keep $150,000 after taxes, his or her income would have to be $43,000 higher than in New Jersey or Connecticut.[22]

New York City lost 413,000 in population between 1970 and 1975, and since 1972 New York State has lost more than 510,000 people. While there is no way to precisely correlate this population loss with the heavy tax burden, it is nevertheless clear that any loss of population reduces the tax base, or taxable capacity. Thus the loss of 510,000 people in New York State represents the loss of at least $640 million in state and local government revenue (based on the per capita state and local tax burden for New York in fiscal 1977). Without a corresponding reduction in government spending, the result must be an increased per capita tax burden. Thus the vicious cycle of higher taxes leading to loss of population leading to higher taxes takes place.

Not only does decreased population mean a permanent reduction in the tax base, but a permanent reduction in the economic base as well, for the population loss also results in fewer jobs and businesses. This fact was confirmed in a study by the Special Task Force on Taxation appointed by New York Gov. Hugh Carey in 1976.

The task force found that those most sensitive to the high level of

TABLE 1

Tax Burden in Thirty Major U.S. Cities

Income

City	$7,500		$15,000		$22,500		$30,000		$40,000		$50,000	
	Tax*	%	Tax*	%	Tax*	%	Tax*	%	Tax*	%	Tax*	%
Atlanta	$571	7.6	$1,291	8.6	$2,032	9.0	$2,865	9.6	$3,805	9.5	$4,690	9.4
Baltimore	937	12.5	1,922	12.8	2,855	12.7	3,847	12.8	4,956	12.4	5,815	11.6
Boston	1,783	23.8	3,535	23.6	5,012	22.3	6,804	22.7	8,575	21.4	10,306	20.6
Chicago	603	8.0	1,098	7.3	1,542	6.9	1,995	6.7	2,591	6.5	2,987	6.0
Cleveland	551	7.4	1,048	7.0	1,563	7.0	2,132	7.1	2,782	7.0	3,321	6.6
Columbus	465	6.2	895	6.0	1,370	6.1	1,882	6.3	2,492	6.2	3,010	6.0
Dallas	505	6.7	1,116	7.4	1,518	6.8	2,270	7.6	3,222	8.1	4,132	8.3
Denver	546	7.3	1,208	8.1	1,742	7.7	2,374	7.9	3,174	7.9	3,744	7.5
Detroit	748	10.0	1,685	11.2	2,488	11.1	3,366	11.2	4,384	11.0	5,196	10.4
Honolulu	331	4.4	1,106	7.4	1,912	8.5	2,713	9.0	3,748	9.4	4,644	9.3
Houston	493	6.6	1,072	7.2	1,457	6.5	2,162	7.2	3,049	7.6	3,889	7.8
Indianapolis	742	9.9	1,409	9.4	1,984	8.8	2,644	8.8	3,378	8.5	4,145	8.3
Jacksonville	348	4.6	652	4.4	915	4.1	1,183	3.9	1,485	3.7	1,639	3.3
Kansas City	518	6.9	1,063	7.1	1,628	7.2	2,214	7.4	2,907	7.3	3,554	7.1
Los Angeles	569	7.6	1,382	9.2	2,436	10.8	3,306	11.0	4,555	11.4	5,905	11.8
Memphis	604	8.1	993	6.6	1,307	5.8	1,642	5.5	2,014	5.0	2,257	4.5
Milwaukee	769	10.3	1,869	12.5	2,975	13.2	4,132	13.8	5,516	13.8	6,737	13.5

TABLE 1 (Continued)

TAX BURDEN IN THIRTY MAJOR U.S. CITIES

INCOME

CITY	$7,500 Tax*	%	$15,000 Tax*	%	$22,500 Tax*	%	$30,000 Tax*	%	$40,000 Tax*	%	$50,000 Tax*	%
Nashville	462	6.2	733	4.9	953	4.2	1,168	3.9	1,446	3.6	1,619	3.2
New Orleans	331	4.4	736	4.9	972	4.3	1,281	4.3	1,726	4.3	2,036	4.1
New York	932	12.4	1,983	13.2	3,131	13.9	4,575	15.3	6,620	16.6	8,412	16.8
Philadelphia	1,140	15.2	2,098	14.0	2,982	13.3	3,871	12.9	4,866	12.2	5,684	11.4
Phoenix	653	8.7	1,221	8.1	1,857	8.3	2,569	8.6	3,355	8.4	4,086	8.2
Pittsburgh	794	10.6	1,447	9.7	2,049	9.1	2,650	8.8	3,346	8.4	3,854	7.7
San Antonio	510	6.8	1,107	7.4	1,504	6.7	2,229	7.4	3,137	7.8	3,995	8.0
San Diego	587	7.8	1,369	9.1	2,397	10.7	3,235	10.8	4,458	11.2	5,791	11.6
San Francisco	657	8.8	1,534	10.2	2,638	11.7	3,566	11.9	4,864	12.2	6,249	12.5
San Jose	474	6.3	1,178	7.9	2,144	9.5	2,899	9.7	4,059	10.2	5,352	10.7
Seattle	566	7.6	926	6.2	1,229	5.5	1,557	5.2	1,920	4.8	2,260	4.5
St. Louis	670	8.9	1,337	8.9	1,996	8.9	2,696	9.0	3,479	8.7	4,163	8.3
Washington	647	8.6	1,425	9.5	2,296	10.2	3,266	10.9	4,584	11.5	5,609	11.2
30-city average	650	8.7	1,348	9.0	2,029	9.0	2,770	9.2	3,683	9.2	4,503	9.0

*Includes income, sales, auto, and property taxes for a family of four.

SOURCE: Government of the District of Columbia, Department of Finance and Revenue, *Tax Burdens in Washington, D.C., Compared With Those in the Nation's Thirty Largest Cities, 1977.*

TABLE 2

Estimated Real After-Tax Income Per Capita (1977)
(Adjusted for Taxes and Relative Living Costs)

State	Per Capita Personal Income	Per Capita Federal Taxes*	Per Capita State and Local Taxes*	After-Tax Per Capita Income	Adjusted Per Capita Income†
Alabama	5,622	1,163	507	3,952	4,357
Alaska	10,586	2,516	2,296	5,774	4,246
Arkansas	5,540	1,382	494	3,664	4,103
Arizona	6,509	1,143	827	4,539	4,728
California	7,911	1,756	1,089	5,066	5,102
Colorado	7,160	1,557	824	4,779	4,957
Connecticut	8,061	2,040	885	5,136	4,796
Delaware	7,697	1,964	829	4,904	5,004
Florida	6,684	1,530	628	4,526	4,957
Georgia	6,014	1,298	609	4,107	4,543
Hawaii	7,677	1,749	974	4,954	4,271
Idaho	5,980	1,255	639	4,085	4,475
Illinois	7,768	1,903	860	5,005	4,960
Indiana	6,921	1,541	652	4,728	4,889
Iowa	6,878	1,643	749	4,486	4,798
Kansas	7,134	1,627	728	4,779	5,068
Kentucky	5,945	1,258	601	4,086	4,315
Louisiana	5,913	1,260	636	4,017	4,424
Maine	5,734	1,246	658	3,830	3,785
Maryland	7,572	1,858	892	4,822	5,049
Massachusetts	7,258	1,709	1,002	4,547	4,552
Michigan	7,619	1,666	878	5,075	5,111
Minnesota	7,129	1,549	906	4,674	4,869
Mississippi	5,030	987	527	3,516	3,968
Missouri	6,654	1,472	609	4,573	4,804
Montana	6,125	1,402	766	3,957	4,301
Nebraska	6,720	1,670	774	4,276	4,539
Nevada	7,988	1,903	892	5,193	5,376
New Hampshire	6,536	1,467	618	4,451	4,372
New Jersey	7,994	1,992	931	5,071	4,528

taxation in New York City and New York State were those in middle and upper management positions. They, in turn, put pressure on their companies to move out of New York to lower taxed areas in New Jersey, Connecticut, or even sunbelt states like Texas. The executives, managers, and highly skilled employees tend to follow their companies to new locations, but unskilled and clerical workers are usually left behind. The task force report said:

There is evidence that the present tax structure is, in many respects, counterproductive, fostering as it has an exodus of business, industry and individuals, eroding the tax base, and shifting the burden of taxation relentlessly down the income scale. Either New York reduces tax levels now, or New York, by inaction, will suffer an even greater revenue loss

TABLE 2 (Continued)

ESTIMATED REAL AFTER-TAX INCOME PER CAPITA (1977)
(ADJUSTED FOR TAXES AND RELATIVE LIVING COSTS)

State	Per Capita Personal Income	Per Capita Federal Taxes*	Per Capita State and Local Taxes*	After-Tax Per Capita Income	Adjusted Per Capita Income†
New Mexico	5,857	1,217	625	4,015	4,491
New York	7,537	1,848	1,252	4,437	3,979
North Carolina	5,935	1,275	593	4,067	4,509
North Dakota	6,190	1,395	682	4,113	4,404
Ohio	7,084	1,599	641	4,844	5,004
Oklahoma	6,346	1,389	598	4,359	4,790
Oregon	7,007	1,554	793	4,660	4,736
Pennsylvania	7,011	1,653	770	4,588	4,740
Rhode Island	6,775	1,626	793	4,356	4,056
South Carolina	5,628	1,167	549	3,912	4,327
South Dakota	5,957	1,308	629	4,020	4,341
Tennessee	5,785	1,339	564	3,882	4,243
Texas	6,803	1,485	637	4,681	5,061
Utah	5,923	1,227	652	4,044	4,199
Vermont	5,823	1,293	810	3,720	3,720
Virginia	6,865	1,536	675	4,654	4,773
Washington	7,528	1,722	821	4,985	4,980
West Virginia	5,986	1,271	622	4,093	4,568
Wisconsin	6,890	1,521	870	4,499	4,591
Wyoming	7,562	1,707	988	4,867	5,407
District of Columbia	8,999	2,073	1,071	5,855	5,684
U.S. Average	7,019	1,600	813	4,606	4,606

* Tax Foundation, Inc.

† After-tax per capita income adjusted by the Bureau of Labor Statistics index of comparative costs. Four person family, intermediate budget less personal income taxes (weighted by percentage of state's population in metropolitan areas).

SOURCE: *First Chicago World Report* (May–June, 1979).

through further erosion of its tax base. It is very likely that such inaction will lead to increased tax burdens on lower and middle income families as wealthier and more mobile individuals leave New York and, in many cases, take their businesses with them.[23]

"Thus," the report concluded, "ultimately, the loss of business is borne by those least able to pay."

The General Accounting Office reached the same conclusion, in a comprehensive report on New York City's long-term financial outlook. Its report strongly argued that any effort to balance the city's budget by raising taxes still further would probably lead to a reduction in revenue in the long run from further erosion of the tax base. As the report said:

Budgetary decisions have both direct and indirect effects on the economy. A City action to raise taxes to balance its budget in a given year may or may not accomplish its stated goal for that year; but it may also affect the tax base in later years. This indirect effect may actually lead to smaller future revenues—a result counter to the purpose of the short-run action.[24]

In 1977 two studies were made of the "Fortune 500" companies that had left New York or planned to do so. Interestingly, both confirmed the view that individual income taxes are most critical in the business decision to leave, in addition to business taxes. This is because it increases salaries which must be paid to workers in New York to give them an after-tax income equivalent to that of workers elsewhere. Thus, it is more difficult in New York than elsewhere to hire and retain high-salaried employees. Typical is the view expressed by Frank B. Millikan, president of Kennecott Copper Corporation, responding to an inquiry by the New York State Senate Labor Committee:

The individual income tax burden (City, State and Federal) is such that New York salaries for competent employees have to be considerably higher than salaries for similar jobs outside the state. . . . It is not only the taxes on business but also to an increasing extent the taxes on the individuals who manage the businesses that are governing factors in the decisions of corporations to leave New York City.[25]

The tax burden also appears to be discouraging new college graduates from starting their business careers in New York City. This point was emphasized by Raymond C. Hagel, chairman of the Macmillan Company, who told the Labor Committee:

The cumulative effect of Federal, State and City taxes on individuals is counterproductive and is a significant factor in depriving businesses located in New York City of the services of outstanding graduates specializing in business administration and finance. . . . New graduates, seeing little advantage in assuming the heavy New York State/New York City tax burden, prefer to take other jobs offered to them for employment with large firms having headquarters out of New York.[26]

Thus it is not surprising that 38 Fortune 500 firms took their headquarters out of New York City between 1965 and 1975. A study of these 38 firms by the Conservation of Human Resources Project at Columbia University found that high taxes were the leading factor in management's decision to move.[27]

The conclusion is therefore inescapable that there is indeed a limit to taxation in terms of revenue. If taxes are raised too high—especially at the state and local level—they may lead to such an exodus of population and industry from the area that revenues will be lower than if taxes had not been raised.

Does this mean that New York City could reduce its taxes and *raise* revenues? Undoubtedly, the answer is yes, *if* the tax reductions are concentrated on those taxes which are most counterproductive, in that they affect those people and businesses most that are most sensitive to high taxes. This will mean cutting taxes for manufacturing firms and high income individuals initially, but the benefits will soon accrue most at the lowest income level. The expansion of business will create jobs and ultimately expand the tax base enough that more revenue will be available to initiate programs which otherwise could not have been attempted for lack of money. The reality of this fact is now so obvious that we hear many politicians, who were never before thought of as probusiness calling for tax cuts to aid business. During the race for mayor of New York in 1977, Cong. Herman Badillo, a Puerto Rican who represented the poorest section of New York City (the South Bronx), called for total abolition of four major taxes in New York City. As the *New York Times* reported Badillo's proposal:

> Elimination of the New York City income tax and three business taxes was proposed yesterday by Representative Herman Badillo, who is seeking the Democratic nomination for Mayor. . . . He proposed a 10-year phase-out of the city income tax, the occupancy tax, the unincorporated business tax and the corporation tax, a total of $1.5 billion.
>
> A gusty breeze riffled the eight-page press release in which he cited studies by the Temporary Commission on City Finances as support for his contention that—after the first two years—*the economy would be spurred so by the tax cuts that it would generate enough new revenue to compensate for them.* [28] (Emphasis added.)

Notes

1. W. Elliot Brownlee, Jr., *Progressivism and Economic Growth: The Wisconsin Income Tax, 1911–1929* (Port Washington, NY: Kennikat Press, 1974), p. 88.

2. "Federal Spending: The North's Loss Is the Sunbelt's Gain," *National Journal* (June 26, 1976).

3. Neal Peirce, "Northeast Governors Map Battle Plan for Fight Over Federal Funds," *National Journal* (November 27, 1976), pp. 1695–1703; Martin Tolchin, "Congressmen From Northeast and Midwest Establish Economic Coalition," *New York Times* (September 2, 1976).

4. *Congressional Record* (June 27, 1977), pp. S 10829–34 (daily ed.); see also Daniel Patrick Moynihan, "The Senator Explains His Point," *New York Times* (August 4, 1977); idem, "What Will They Do For New York?" *New York Times Magazine* (January 27, 1980), pp. 30–40.

5. For attacks on Moynihan's position, see James L. Buckley, "Moynihan's Message," *New York Times* (July 29, 1977); William F. Buckley, "Moynihan Fires One," *National Review* (July 22, 1977); Editorial, "Too Honest," *Wall Street Journal* (August 4, 1977); Remarks of Senator Henry Bellmon, *Congressional Record* (April 6, 1978), pp. S 4901–6 (daily ed.).

6. See Maureen McBreen, "Analyzing Statistical Data: Federal Revenues and Outlays in the States," in Congressional Research Service, *Selected Essays on Patterns of Regional Change: The Changes, the Federal Role, and the Federal Response* (Washington: Government Printing Office, 1977), pp. 613–21; see also Gurney Breckenfeld, "Business Loves the Sunbelt (and Vice Versa)," *Fortune* (June 1977), pp. 140–42.

7. Janet Rothenberg Pack, "Frostbelt and Sunbelt: Convergence Over Time," *Intergovernmental Perspective* (Fall 1978), pp. 8–15; Howard L. Friedenberg, "Regional Differences in Personal Income Growth, 1929–77," *Survey of Current Business* (October 1978), pp. 27–41; "State Personal Income, 1958–78," *Survey of Current Business* (August 1979), Part II, pp. 28–31.

8. "Regional Flow of Federal Welfare Dollars," *Congressional Quarterly* (December 10, 1977), p. 2552; Charles Vehorn, *The Regional Distribution of Federal Grants-in-Aid* (Columbus, Ohio: Academy for Contemporary Problems, November 1977); Comptroller General of the United States, *Changing Patterns of Federal Aid to State and Local Governments, 1969–75* (Washington: U.S. General Accounting Office, December 20, 1977).

9. Congressional Budget Office, *Troubled Local Economies and the Distribution of Federal Dollars* (August 1977), p. 49.

10. U.S. Bureau of the Census, *Governmental Finances in 1977–78,* Series GF78, No. 5 (Washington: U.S. Government Printing Office, 1980), pp. 90, 94.

11. D. Kent Halstead, *Tax Wealth in Fifty States* (Washington: Department of Health, Education and Welfare, National Institute of Education, 1978); D. Kent Halstead and H. Kent Weldon, *Tax Wealth in Fifty States, 1977 Supplement* (Washington: Department of Health, Education and Welfare, National Institute of Education, 1979); see also Advisory Commission on Intergovernmental Relations, *Measuring the Fiscal "Blood Pressure" of the States—1964–1975* (Washington: Advisory Commission on Intergovernmental Relations, 1977).

12. Deborah S. Ecker and Richard F. Syron, "Personal Taxes and the Interstate Competition for High Technology Industries," *New England Economic Review* (Sept./Oct. 1978), pp. 25–32; "More Elbowroom for the Electronics Industry," *Business Week* (March 10, 1980), pp. 94–100.

13. C. L. Jusenius and L.C. Ledebur, *A Myth in the Making: The Southern Economic Challenge and Northern Economic Decline* (Washington: Department of Commerce, Economic Development Administration, Office of Economic Research, 1976), reprinted in the *Congressional Record* (January 25, 1977), pp. S 1421–31 (daily ed.); idem, "The Northern Tier and the Sunbelt: Conflict or Cooperation," *Challenge* (March-April 1977), pp. 44–49.

14. Lynn E. Browne, "The Shifting Pattern of Interregional Migration," *New England Economic Review* (Nov./Dec. 1979), pp. 17–31; Philip L. Rones, "Moving to the Sun: Regional Job Growth, 1968 to 1978," *Monthly Labor Review* (March 1980), pp. 12–19.

15. Colin D. Campbell and Rosemary G. Campbell, *A Comparative Study of the Fiscal Systems of New Hampshire and Vermont, 1940–1974* (Hampton, NH: Wheelabrator Foundation, 1976), p. 7.

16. "New Hampshire: Mecca for Industry," *Dun's Review* (June 1977), pp. 81–111; Michael Knight, "2 Neighboring States Far Apart on Controlling Growth," *New York Times* (June 22, 1979); Editorial, "New Hampshire's Story," *Wall Street Journal* (January 4, 1978).

17. Michael Knight, "Taxes Hurt Massachusetts Jobs," *New York Times* (March 26, 1979); James Ring Adams, " 'Taxachusetts Turns Around," *Wall Street Journal* (February 5, 1980).

18. Robert J. Genetski and Young D. Chin, *The Impact of State and Local Taxes on Economic Growth* (Chicago: Harris Economic Research Office Service, 1978).

19. Temporary Commission on City Finances, *The Effects of Taxation on Manufacturing in New York City* (New York: Temporary Commission on City Finances, 9th Interim Report, December 1976), p. 45.

20. Ronald Grieson, William Hamovitch, Albert M. Levenson, and Richard D. Morgenstern, "The Effect of Business Taxation on Location of Industry," *Journal of Urban Economics* 4(1977), pp. 170–185.

21. U.S. Department of Labor, Bureau of Labor Statistics, *Handbook of Labor Statistics 1978* (Washington: U.S. Government Printing Office, 1979), p. 488.

22. Temporary Commission on City Finances, *The City in Transition: Prospects and Policies for New York* (New York: Temporary Commission on City Finances, Final Report, June 1977), p. 142.

23. Adrian DeWind, et al., *Report of the Special Task Force on Taxation* (New York: Municipal Assistance Corporation, 1976), pp. 3–4.

24. Comptroller General of the United States, *The Long-Term Fiscal Outlook for New York City* (Washington: General Accounting Office, 1977), p. 58; see also Comptroller General of the United States, *New York City's Fiscal Problems: A Long Road Still Lies Ahead* (Washington: General Accounting Office, 1979), pp. 26–28.

25. New York State Senate Labor Committee Press Release, April 3, 1977.

26. Ibid.

27. The Conservation of Human Resources Project, Columbia University, *The Corporate Headquarters Complex in New York City* (Montclair, NJ: Allenheld Osmun Co., 1977).

28. Maurice Carroll, "Dropping of 4 Taxes Proposed by Badillo," *New York Times* (August 11, 1977).

6

Inflation and Taxation

ONE OF THE MOST PERNICIOUS EFFECTS OF INFLATION IS THE way it distorts the tax code, leading to an increase in both the average and marginal rates of taxation. This distortion results because both tax law and accounting theory assume that the American dollar is a fixed value, like a yard, an ounce, or a quart. For most of U.S. history this was largely true.

In 1800, the consumer price index (CPI) stood at 51 (1967=100). It went up a bit during the War of 1812, reaching 63 in 1814. There followed a steady and continuous decline in the CPI until the Civil War. Yet even at the height of the war in 1864 the index was only up to 47—lower than it had been in 1814. Once again there followed a long, steady decline on prices until the eve of World War I.

The CPI doubled between 1915 and 1920, from 30 to 60. But, as in previous cases, once the war was over prices began to decline and did so steadily until the mid-1930s. Since 1939 the price level has increased every single year, with the only variation being in the rate of increase. The CPI is now above 200 and rising at a rapid rate.

The truly alarming thing is that the rate of increase in prices has gone up so significantly in recent years. The price index in 1943 was approximately the same as it was in 1800. By 1967 the index had roughly doubled. Since 1967 it has doubled again. At this rate prices will double yet again by the mid-1980s.

In short, through most of our nation's existence there has been a regular pattern to price level behavior: Prices have tended to remain stable, with some ups and downs, except during wartime when they increased rapidly. After each war the price level tended to decline gradually to about its prewar level. Through the vast bulk of American history—roughly 150 years—the price level was relatively stable, remaining between about 40 and 50 on the price index.

The reason for this fundamental stability is relatively simple: Throughout most of our history the quantity of money was tied to a relatively fixed standard—gold. The rate of increase in the quantity of money was held to the rate at which gold was mined. But during wartime, when government's need for revenue greatly exceeded its ability to borrow real savings and to tax, the restraints on the money supply were cast aside. When peace was reestablished, a high level of economic growth restored, and the gold standard put back in place, the supply of goods and services tended to "catch up" with the larger quantity of money, price level reduction ensued, and real incomes increased.[1]

The question, therefore, is, What has happened since World War II that has broken the pattern which held throughout all previous American history? The answer is twofold: (1) The check on the government's ability to increase the quantity of money—the gold standard—is gone. (2) Government officials now have a powerful vested interest in maintaining a steady rate of inflation, an interest which never existed before. The most important aspect of this is that inflation increases taxes without the necessity of legislative action.

The increase in individual income taxes due to inflation is the result of graduated tax rates, fixed exemptions, and a fixed standard deduction. The more money one earns, the higher the percentage of his income he pays in taxes. The problem is that the tax rate schedule applies equally whether real income or just nominal (money) income has increased.[2] Table 1 illustrates this phenomenon.

Inflation affects every income class, with the magnitude of the inflation tax increase rising as one gets into higher tax brackets. Thus, a 10 percent inflation rate, with gross family income rising by the same amount—leaving real, pretax income unchanged—will lead to a first year tax increase of $123 for a family of four earning $10,000, a $249 tax increase for a family earning $30,000, and a $1,342 tax increase for a family earning $100,000. Within three years the annual tax increase will rise to $448, $1,061 and $5,177, respectively.

TABLE 1

INCREASE IN FEDERAL INCOME TAX BURDEN DUE TO INFLATION*

1979 Income	1979 Taxes	INFLATION TAX INCREASE			1981 Taxes	1981 Income
		1980	1981	1982		
$10,000	$370	$123	$268	$448	$941	$13,310
15,000	1,238	77	207	350	2,007	19,965
20,000	2,013	125	309	511	3,200	26,620
25,000	2,901	188	462	780	4,640	33,275
30,000	3,917	249	630	1,061	6,292	39,930
40,000	6,312	500	1,146	1,984	10,396	53,240
50,000	9,323	748	1,558	2,715	15,093	66,550
100,000	28,534	1,342	3,129	5,177	43,111	133,100

*Figures assume a family of four with one wage earner, 10 percent inflation per year with gross family income rising at the same rate, 1979 tax law, and deductions equal to 23 percent of gross income.

As a result, the percentage of federal income taxes paid by a family of four earning $10,000 in 1979 would increase from 3.7 percent of gross income to 7.1 percent in 1982, unless taxes were cut by Congress. For a family earning $30,000 in 1979 the percentage of taxes paid would increase from 13.1 to 15.8 percent, and for a family earning $100,000 it would increase from 28.5 percent to 32.4 percent (see table 2).

All of this translates into enormous increases in tax revenue for the federal government (and state governments with graduated income tax rates) and a reduction in real, after-tax, income for most Americans. It is estimated by Congress' Joint Committee on Taxation that individual income tax revenues increase 1.67 percent for every one percent inflation. Table 3 shows the estimated aggregate amount of

TABLE 2

INCREASE IN EFFECTIVE FEDERAL INCOME TAX RATES DUE TO INFLATION

1979 INCOME	PERCENT FEDERAL TAXES			
	1979	1980	1981	1982
$10,000	3.7	4.8	5.9	7.1
15,000	8.3	8.8	9.4	10.1
20,000	10.1	10.7	11.4	12.0
25,000	11.6	12.3	13.1	13.9
30,000	13.1	13.9	14.8	15.8
40,000	15.8	16.9	18.2	19.5
50,000	18.6	20.0	21.2	22.7
100,000	28.5	29.7	31.1	32.4

increase in individual income taxes resulting from inflation over the next five years. By 1985 the cumulative increase in taxation will amount to a staggering $138 billion.

It has been argued that the damage to the economy is really minimal because Congress has periodically reduced taxes. As Prof. Edward Gramlich of the Brookings Institution recently put it, "Congress has periodically adjusted income tax rates so as to prevent average effective tax rates from rising in response either to inflation or economic growth. Thus although the personal income tax rate structure is not formally indexed, it has changed much as it would have if indexed."[3] As table 4 shows, this statement is technically correct. But it requires the Congress to be very alert to changing tax

TABLE 3

INFLATION TAX "WINDFALL" TO FEDERAL GOVERNMENT,* INCREMENTAL AND CUMULATIVE ($ IN BILLIONS)

Year	Assumed Inflation Factor	1981	1982	1983	1984	1985
1981	13.3%	$23.4	$26.2	$29.3	$32.9	$36.8
1982	10.0	—	19.7	22.1	24.7	27.7
1983	9.7	—	—	21.4	24.0	26.8
1984	8.7	—	—	—	21.5	24.1
1985	8.3	—	—	—	—	23.0
Cumulative Totals		$23.4	$45.9	$72.8	$103.1	$138.4

*Estimated by indexing the rate brackets, the zero bracket amount, personal exemptions and the earned income credit for the increase in the Consumer Price Index of the years ending in the third quarter of the preceding year. The inflation rates are those assumed in the First Concurrent Budget Resolution for fiscal year 1981 and out to 1985. Also assumed are real growth rates in GNP of 0.4% for FY81, 3.1 percent for FY82, 3.4 percent for FY83, 3.8 percent for FY84 and 3.8 percent for FY85.

SOURCE: Joint Committee on Taxation.

burdens and their effect on the economy. It has been argued that the great virtue of indexing is that it prevents inflationary recessions from snowballing downward. The 1974 recession, for example, was unquestionably aggravated by the rising tax burden caused by inflation.[4]

More important, Congress' tax reductions have not treated all taxpayers equally. The vast bulk of tax reductions passed since 1964 have been concentrated in the lowest income tax brackets. As a result, those in upper income tax brackets have been most affected by inflation.[5] It is not surprising, therefore, that the percentage of total income taxes paid by those in the upper 50 percent of gross income classes has increased over the years, while those in the lower brackets are paying less. As table 5 shows, those in the upper 50 percent of gross income classes, with incomes above $10,960 per year, pay more than 93 percent of all individual income taxes.[6]

TABLE 4

FEDERAL INCOME TAXES AND PERSONAL INCOME (1962–1974) ($ IN BILLIONS)

YEAR	PERSONAL INCOME	Federal Income Taxes			LEGISLATED INCOME TAX CUTS*
		$	% of Personal Income		
1962	$ 438.4	$ 45.6	10.4		
1963	462.3	47.6	10.3		
1964	490.4	48.7	9.9		$11.5
1965	527.3	48.8	9.3		
1966	576.8	55.4	9.6		
1967	625.6	61.5	9.8		
1968	674.9	68.7	10.2		
1969	740.4	87.2	11.8		
1970	803.0	90.4	11.3		
1971	858.2	86.2	10.0		8.0
1972	928.8	94.7	10.2		
1973	1,033.2	103.2	10.0		
1974	1,147.6	119.0	10.4		
1975	1,251.9	122.4	9.8		22.8
1976	1,372.8	131.5	9.6		
1977	1,547.9	157.6	10.2		18.4
1978	1,726.4	181.0	10.5		18.7
1979	1,924.2	217.8	11.3		
1980†	2,137.6	234.2	11.0		
1981†	2,372.6	277.2	11.7		
1982†	2,626.1	322.8	12.3		
1983†	2,884.3	370.0	12.8		
1984†	3,153.6	421.9	13.4		

*First full year effect.
†Estimates based on current law.
SOURCE: Office of Management and Budget.

TABLE 5

Federal Income Taxes Paid by High and Low Income Taxpayers, 1971, 1977, and 1978

Adjusted Gross Income Class	Income Level			% of Tax Paid			Average Tax		
	1971	1977	1978	1971	1977	1978	1971	1977	1978
Highest 10%	$18,034 or more	$27,105 or more	$29,415 or more	46.5%	50.2%	49.7%	$5,324	$9,239	$10,429
Highest 25%	12,125 or more	18,520 or more	19,860 or more	70.0	73.6	73.8	3,208	5,421	6,208
Highest 50%	7,292 or more	10,207 or more	10,960 or more	91.1	93.9	93.5	2,086	3,460	3,924
Lowest 50%	7,291 or less	10,206 or less	10,959 or less	8.9	6.1	6.5	205	234	272
Lowest 25%	3,291 or less	4,245 or less	5,039 or less	0.7	0.3	0.4	34	25	32

SOURCE: Tax Foundation computations based on Internal Revenue Service, *Statistics of Income.*

It has frequently been argued that individual income taxes should be "indexed" to inflation. This means increasing the personal exemption, the standard deduction (or "zero-bracket amount"), and widening tax brackets by some index for inflation, such as the consumer price index or the GNP deflator. This would keep the tax burden constant as a percentage of one's real income and deny government the extra revenue it gets because of the progressivity of the tax code.[7] The experience of several states and foreign countries suggests that such a system works quite well, making any legislated tax reductions meaningful, making the income tax system more equitable, and helping to hold down growth of the public sector.[8]

The main argument against indexing is that it signifies "giving up" on the fight against inflation. It is said that the pain inflicted by a rising tax burden creates an incentive to stop inflation. If this were so, then the fair thing to do would be to eliminate the present indexing of federal spending programs, so that everyone would suffer, rather than just taxpayers.[9] In any case, government is still the major beneficiary of "taxflation," and indexing at least removes the government's incentive to inflate. As Dr. Rudolph Penner recently testified before the Joint Economic Committee:

> Indexing might make inflation less painful for the voter, but it also makes it less profitable for political decision makers. They no longer have the "inflation tax" with which to provide pseudo tax cuts or expanded programs. That may act as a more important curb on inflation than imposing slightly more pain on voters.[10]

Of course, to completely adjust the tax system for inflation one also needs to index corporate and capital gains taxes. Consider the case of someone who buys a stock and holds it for the average holding period—7.2 years—and then sells it for twice what he paid for it, at a nominal profit of 100 percent. If inflation rises at 10 percent per year, the real, after-tax, rate of return on this investment would be a *loss* of 2 percent. If inflation were to rise by the 18 percent rate experienced in early 1980, this 2 percent loss would become an 8.6 percent yearly loss.

The magnitude of losses suffered by investors in recent years by having to pay taxes on nonexistent capital gains is enormous. A recent paper by Martin Feldstein and Joel Slemrod shows that in 1973 individuals paid nearly $500 million in extra taxes on corporate stock capital gains because of the distorting effect of inflation. This resulted because after adjustment for inflation the $4.5 billion of nominal capital gains reported was actually a $1 billion loss. Moreover, in many cases, individuals with similar real capital gains were subject to very different tax liabilities.[11]

Inflation's distortion of corporate income taxes has to do with the fact that depreciation expenses are based on historical costs rather than replacement costs, and because inventory profits become artificially inflated.

In order to calculate real economic profits, one must first compute the amount by which profits have been overstated because firms calculate inventories on a first-in-first-out (FIFO) basis. Inflation gives the firm "paper" profits on the sale of inventory stock which was accumulated when prices were lower. But since a firm must maintain a given level of inventories, such "profits" are immediately eaten up by inventory replacement. Hence, such profits are not "real." The inflation distortion could be minimized by using a last-in-first-out (LIFO) accounting basis, since inventories would be valued at the higher prices of the most recently purchased stocks, rather than the older, lower priced ones.

The second adjustment has to do with the understatement of costs the firm is allowed to charge against earnings. The most important of these is depreciation, which is the pro rata cost of plant and equipment. Depreciation allowances allow the firm to recapture its capital investment over the life of its plant and equipment so that the firm can replace them when their useful life is finished. Unfortunately, depreciation under the United States Tax Code is based upon the original purchase price, or historical cost, of plant and equipment, rather than what it would really cost to replace such plant and equipment during a period of inflation. Thus, on a historical cost basis, depreciation is greatly understated compared to what it would be under replacement cost principles. The result is that business profits are *over*stated, business costs *under*stated, and, therefore, taxes *over*stated.

Although great harm is done to firms because their taxes are overstated by inventory and depreciation rules, management has not been moved to change existing accounting rules or tax laws (LIFO accounting is already permitted under law). Managers evidently prefer high nominal profits to the lower real ones. As the *Wall Street Journal* recently put it:

> Many corporate executives are not anxious to move to accurate profit reporting. The understatement of depreciation and inventory costs translates into a better profit performance figure. In some cases, replacement cost accounting would push the income statement into the red. Managements would rather over-pay taxes than report poorer profit. They would rather be publicly pilloried for gouging than explain losses and low profits to shareholders.[12]

The Commerce Department each year calculates the amount by which inventories have been overvalued and the amount by which depreciation costs have been understated. The first figure is the "inventory valuation adjustment" and the second is the "capital consumption adjustment." If we apply these adjustments against reported profits, we can derive a figure for real economic profits (see table 6).

As one can see, the magnitude of these adjustments has been growing steadily as inflation exacts a higher and higher toll on corporate finances. This fact is of critical importance, for corporations are paying taxes on inflationary profits as well as on real profits. The higher taxes deny corporations funds needed for capital investment. These higher taxes also shortchange shareholders (the owners of the corporation) and depress stock prices, making it difficult for firms to issue stock.

The tax drain is growing yearly. In 1978, the overstatement of corporate profits by roughly $42 billion caused U.S. corporations to overpay their taxes by roughly $20 billion. Table 7 shows the variance between taxes as a percentage of real profits and taxes as a percentage of reported profits.

TABLE 6

REAL ECONOMIC PROFITS ($ IN BILLIONS)

Year	Reported Profits	Inventory Valuation Adjustment	Capital Consumption Adjustment	Real Economic Profits
1960	39.5	0.3	−2.3	37.5
1961	39.2	0.1	−1.8	37.5
1962	43.7	0.1	1.2	44.8
1963	48.3	−0.2	1.9	50.0
1964	54.6	−0.5	2.6	56.7
1965	64.4	−1.9	3.6	66.1
1966	69.5	−2.1	3.8	71.2
1967	65.4	−1.7	3.6	67.3
1968	71.9	−3.4	3.6	72.1
1969	68.4	−5.5	3.5	66.4
1970	55.1	−5.1	1.5	51.5
1971	63.3	−5.0	0.5	58.6
1972	75.9	−6.6	2.7	71.8
1973	92.7	−18.6	1.8	76.0
1974	102.9	−40.4	−3.0	59.6
1975	101.3	−12.4	−11.9	77.0
1976	130.2	−14.5	−14.3	101.4
1977	143.5	−14.8	−14.7	114.0
1978	166.1	−25.2	−12.6	128.3
1979	190.2	−41.8	−15.6	132.9

SOURCE: Department of Commerce, Bureau of Economic Analysis.

TABLE 7

TAXATION OF CORPORATE PROFITS

Year	Income Tax ($ in billions)	Tax as a % of Reported Profits	Tax as a % of Real Economic Profits
1960	$19.2	48.6	51.2
1961	19.5	49.7	52.0
1962	20.6	47.1	46.0
1963	22.8	47.2	45.6
1964	24.0	43.9	42.3
1965	27.2	42.2	41.1
1966	29.5	42.4	41.4
1967	27.7	42.3	41.1
1968	33.6	46.7	46.6
1969	33.3	49.1	50.1
1970	27.3	49.5	53.0
1971	29.9	47.2	51.0
1972	33.5	44.1	46.6
1973	39.6	42.7	52.1
1974	42.7	41.5	71.6
1975	40.6	40.1	52.7
1976	53.0	40.7	52.3
1977	59.0	41.1	51.7
1978	68.8	41.4	53.6
1979	75.1	39.5	56.5

SOURCE: Department of Commerce, Bureau of Economic Analysis.

From 1951 to 1964, the maximum corporate tax rate was 52 percent. In 1964, it was reduced to 50 percent and further reduced to 48 percent in 1965. In 1979 the corporate tax rate was reduced again to a maximum of 46 percent. Thus, effective corporate tax rates were dropping, both as a percentage of nominal profits and real profits, beginning in 1964. The low rate of inflation during the mid-1960s also reduced the disparity between the two tax rates. Starting around 1968, however, there was an increasingly wide differential between corporate taxes as a percentage of nominal profits and taxes as a percentage of real profits because inflation began to accelerate. When prices rose by more than 12 percent in 1974, the disparity between real and nominal profits was enormous. The effective corporate tax rate on real economic profits reached 71.6 percent that year. Though inflation subsided, the effective corporate tax rate on real profits continued to exceed the maximum statutory rate.

Some prominent policymakers are now beginning to realize that the inflated level of nominal profits and the excessively heavy tax burden which results from it have important policy implications. Harold M. Williams, chairman of the Securities and Exchange Commission, for example, recently said:

The public perception seems increasingly to be that American business profits—particularly those of the largest firms, those most able and most responsible for aiding in accomplishing our national objectives—are huge, growing larger, and accruing exclusively to the benefit of a small and select group of wealthy individuals. This mis-impression leads inevitably to demands that the government take steps—often through tax policy—to moderate those profits and to divert them to the common weal.

In my judgement, American corporations, as a whole, are—rather than generating shockingly high profits—earning at dangerously low levels, if they are to discharge the responsibilities we expect them to shoulder.[13]

Among the responsibilities which Williams says we have imposed on American corporations without adequately understanding their cost is that of environmental protection. According to the Department of Commerce, total business expenditures for pollution abatement and control in recent years amounted to $125 billion between 1972 and 1978.[14]

Since pollution abatement expenditures do nothing to economize on costs or to enhance production as ordinarily measured (however socially desirable they may be in other ways), they ought not to be considered capital investments in the normal sense of the term. Indeed, government-mandated expenditures by business are economically no different than taxes.[15] In such a case, a firm's resources are being directed away from market-directed purposes to politically directed purposes. Yet, for tax purposes, expenditures for pollution control are considered additions to a company's capital stock and must be depreciated over many years, rather than charged as a current outlay. Furthermore, pollution abatement expenditures distort the corporate earnings picture, since such expenditures ought to be subtracted from reported profits in order to get a truer picture of real profits.

A big step forward in making corporate profit statements more truly reflect reality came when the Securities and Exchange Commission began requiring large firms to begin reporting alternative profit figures based on the replacement cost of inventories, plant, and equipment. Subsequently, the Financial Accounting Standards Board adopted rules requiring all corporations to provide inflation-adjusted profit figures. The results are startling. According to a survey by Price Waterhouse of 215 of the Fortune 500 companies: sales growth, which averaged 76 percent as historically reported, was reduced to 33 percent—less than 8 percent compounded annually—when adjusted for inflation; income from continuing operations declined 40 percent; return on net assets computed to reflect changing rrices declined from 17 percent—when based on historical measures —to 8 percent; and effective tax rates increased from 39 percent to 53 percent—well above the statutory 46 percent limit.[16]

In 1978 Congress almost voted to index capital gains, so that taxes would only be paid on profits exceeding the rate of inflation over the time an asset was held. An amendment offered by Cong. Bill Archer of Texas passed the House, but did not get through the Senate. In the 96th Congress, most interest focused on radically reducing the period of time over which a firm may depreciate its capital investments. The Capital Cost Recovery Act would allow firms to depreciate structures in 10 years, equipment in 5 years, and trucks and autos in 3 years.[17] A study by Martin Feldstein concluded that at moderate rates of inflation, such a procedure would closely approximate full indexation of depreciation.[18]

Although it is not clear at this writing whether any indexing proposals will be approved by the 96th Congress, it is certain that, unless inflation is halted or there are massive across the board tax cuts, taxflation is going to continue to exert an ever more harmful effect until the economy either collapses or indexing is instituted.

Notes

1. See E. J. Hamilton, "The Role of War in Modern Inflation," *Journal of Economic History* 37 (March 1977), pp. 13–19.

2. For a technical discussion, see Randall K. C. Kau and Michael L. Schler, "Inflation and the Federal Income Tax," *Yale Law Journal* 82 (March 1973), pp. 716–44.

3. Edward M. Gramlich, "The Economic and Budgetary Effects of Indexing the Tax System," in Henry Aaron, ed., *Inflation and the Income Tax* (Washington: Brookings Institution, 1976), p. 277.

4. U.S. Congress, Joint Economic Committee, *Indexing the Individual Income Tax For Inflation: Will This Help to Stabilize the Economy?*, by Thomas F. Dernberg, Joint Committee Print, Studies in Fiscal Policy Paper No. 2 (Washington, D.C.: U.S. Government Printing Office, 1976).

5. Dan Throop Smith, "Progressive Income Taxation Discriminates Against Larger Incomes During Inflation," *Tax Review* (June 1975).

6. See Paul Craig Roberts, "Disguising the Tax Burden," *Harper's* (March 1978), pp. 32–38; idem, "Some Tax Myths: Who Pays What?" *National Review* (April 28, 1978), pp. 524–26, 547; Paul Craig Roberts and Richard E. Wagner, "The Tax Reform Fraud," *Policy Review* (Summer 1979), pp. 121–39. For an attack on this view, see the *Congressional Record* (August 4, 1978), pp. H 7924–30 (daily ed.). For a rejoinder, see the *Congressional Record* (August 23, 1978), pp. S 14234–35 (daily ed.).

7. See Congress of the United States, *Indexation of Certain Provisions of the Tax Laws: Hearings Before the Subcommittee on Taxation and Debt*

Management Generally of the Committee on Finance, United States Senate, 95th Cong., 2nd sess. (Washington: U.S. Government Printing Office, 1978); William Fellner, Kenneth Clarkson, and John H. Moore, *Correcting Taxes for Inflation* (Washington: American Enterprise Institute, 1975); Donald J. Senese, *Indexing the Inflationary Impact of Taxes: The Necessary Economic Reform* (Washington: The Heritage Foundation, 1978); Editorial, "Inflation and Fair Taxation," *New York Times* (February 12, 1979); idem, "Tax Cuts for Inflationary Times," *New York Times* (September 14, 1979); Robert J. Samuelson, "The Future Is Now," *National Journal* (January 28, 1978), p. 157; Nancy Jianakoplos, "Paying More Taxes and Affording It Less," *Federal Reserve Bank of St. Louis Review* 57 (July 1975), pp. 9–13.

8. On state indexing, see Laurence Ingrassia and Laurel Leff, "Several States Adjust Income Tax Brackets to Discount Inflation," *Wall Street Journal* (March 4, 1980); Advisory Commission on Intergovernmental Relations, *The Inflation Tax: The Case for Indexing Federal and State Income Taxes* (Washington: U.S. Government Printing Office, 1980), pp. 17–26. On foreign indexing, see American Institute of Certified Public Accountants, *Indexation of the Tax Laws for Inflation* (New York: American Institute of Certified Public Accountants, 1980), pp. 13–18; C.F. Steiss, "Indexation of Canada's Individual Income Tax System," *Tax Review* (May 1978).

9. On indexation of federal spending programs, see Congress of the United States, Congressional Budget Office, *The Effect of Inflation on Federal Expenditures* (Washington: U.S. Government Printing Office, 1976); Comptroller General of the United States, *An Analysis of the Effects of Indexing for Inflation on Federal Expenditures* (Washington: U.S. General Accounting Office, 1979); Robert S. Kaplan, *Indexing Social Security* (Washington: American Enterprise Institute, 1977).

10. Hearings before the Joint Economic Committee, July 27, 1979.

11. Martin Feldstein and Joel Slemrod, *Inflation and the Excess Taxation of Capital Gains on Corporate Stock* (Cambridge, Mass.: National Bureau of Economic Research, Working Paper No. 234, February 1978); Martin Feldstein, "Adjusting Tax Rules for Inflation—Capital Gains and Capital Income," *Tax Review* (January 1979).

12. Editorial, "The Profit Famine," *Wall Street Journal* (March 26, 1979).

13. From a speech given on October 18, 1977.

14. Gary L. Rutledge and Susan L. Trevathan, "Pollution Abatement and Control Expenditures, 1972–78," *Survey of Current Business* 60 (February 1980), pp. 27–33.

15. Richard A. Posner, "Taxation By Regulation," *Bell Journal of Economics and Management Science* (Spring 1971), pp. 22–50.

16. *Disclosure of the Effects of Inflation: An Analysis* (New York: Price Waterhouse & Co., 1980); see also Phillip H. Wiggins, "Inflation's Impact on Companies," *New York Times* (April 16, 1980); "The Closest Look Yet At Inflation's Corporate Toll," *Business Week* (June 16, 1980), pp. 148–49; Editorial, "Timely Reckoning," *Wall Street Journal* (April 3, 1980).

17. See *The Capital Cost Recovery Act Proposal* (Washington: American Enterprise Institute, 1980).

18. Martin Feldstein, *Adjusting Depreciation in an Inflationary Economy: Indexing versus Acceleration* (Cambridge, MA: National Bureau of Economic Research, Working Paper No. 395, October 1979).

7

Econometrics and Politics

ECONOMIC FORECASTING IN RECENT YEARS HAS BECOME AN IN-creasingly important factor in government policy. Decisions about the budget, the deficit, tax rates and the quantity of money are made on the basis of how forecasters, using complex computer models, predict the course of the economy and the results of proposed policy changes. Unfortunately, they are often wrong. As Charles Schultz, chairman of the Council of Economic Advisors, recently put it, "As someone paid to be a forecaster, I have to admit that I am often paid for wrong forecasts."[1] The consistent failure of the forecasters has now led many economists and policymakers to examine the fundamental theoretical basis upon which the forecasters' econometric models are grounded, the suspicion being that there are certain biases and errors built into the models which consistently lead to incorrect forecasts.

The first important macroeconometric model—a series of mathematical equations used to simulate the U.S. economy and predict the consequences of various policies—was built by Lawrence Klein after World War II. His model, the Wharton model, contains 669 equations and is one of the three most widely used econometric models in the United States today. The other two are the Data Resources, Inc.

(DRI) model and the Chase Econometrics model. The DRI model contains some 800 equations and was developed by Otto Eckstein of Harvard. The Chase model was built by Michael Evans and has about 455 equations. Before 1969 such models were rarely used by either businesses or government. Today, virtually every major corporation, government department and agency, and congressional committee has access to one or more of these models. Another measure of their influence is the fact that Eckstein recently sold DRI to McGraw-Hill for $100 million. Evans also recently sold his interest in the Chase model for a multimillion dollar amount and is now working on a new model.[2]

Unfortunately, for all their sophistication, the forecasting record of the major econometric models is dismal at best. The National Bureau of Economic Research keeps track of their performance. A major study of economic forecasts by Victor Zarnowitz for the NBER, for example, concluded that the models' "record of the numerical forecasts of GNP does not indicate an ability to forecast the turn several months ahead. Not only were actual turns missed but also turns were predicated that did not occur."[3]

Fortunately for the forecasters, no one pays much attention to their track record. In fact, even dramatic mistakes by forecasters rarely come back to haunt them. Consider the case of economist Pierre Rinfret, who said just before the 1969 recession, "We ain't going to have no recession." When asked about this statement some years later he said, "That was a stupid statement, but not a very big mistake. My clients don't really care about the GNP."[4]

In 1974, however, the general record of all forecasters in predicting the length and depth of the recession was so bad that *Business Week* said economists will remember 1974 "as the year the forecasters blew it."[5] Although their failure obviously did no lasting harm to the influence or profitability of econometric models or economic forecasting, the almost universal lack of ability by the economists to explain what went wrong did have some long-term consequences.

Many economists now argue that today's econometric models are ill-equipped to simulate the actual reactions of people to policy changes. This is because, as Paul Anderson of the Federal Reserve Bank of Minneapolis recently put it,

> most models are built on the assumption that people form their expectations by extrapolating past experience in a mechanical way. Expectations formed in this way are not very sensitive to changes in policy; they change very slowly regardless of policy changes. So simulations using such models implicitly assume that people change their expectations about economic conditions—and thus their behavior—very slowly even

when important government policies have obviously changed substantially. In a sense, then, these models assume that people can be fooled for long periods of time into acting against their own best interests.[6]

As an example of this fact, it is pointed out that virtually all macro-econometric models assume a tradeoff between inflation and unemployment: the higher the inflation the lower the unemployment and vice versa.[7] The basis for this tradeoff is found in John Maynard Keynes' *General Theory of Employment Interest and Money,* in which he argued that since unemployment is caused by the unwillingness of workers to accept a reduction in their wage rates they must be fooled into doing so through a "money illusion." By causing inflation the government can effect a general reduction in real wages while money wage rates remain unchanged. As Keynes put it:

> Whilst workers will usually resist a reduction of money-wages, it is not their practice to withdraw their labor whenever there is a rise in the price of wage-goods. It is sometimes said that it would be illogical for labor to resist a reduction of money-wages but not to resist a reduction of real wages.... But, whether logical or illogical, experience shows that this is how labor in fact behaves.[8]

Econometric models in the late 1960s predicted a sustained unemployment rate of 4 percent as consistent with a 4 percent annual rate of inflation. The budget deficits and money supply growth of the 1970s, therefore, should have produced the lowest average unemployment rates for any decade since the 1940s. In fact, as we know, they produced the highest unemployment rates since the 1930s. "This was econometric failure on a grand scale," say Robert Lucas of the University of Chicago and Thomas Sargent of the University of Minnesota.[9] Of course, the problem is that politicians believed the models when they said that budget deficits were necessary to lower unemployment and that inflation would not result unless unemployment got down to 4 percent or less.

Consequently, many economists now argue in favor of steady, consistent economic policies, with no attempts to straighten out short-run kinks in the business cycle. They say, for example, that the way to stop inflation with minimal disruption to the economy is for the government to announce that the budget deficit will be gradually reduced, that the rate of growth of the money supply will be gradually slowed, and then stick with it no matter what. As soon as people realize that the government will not alter its policies, they will reorient their behavior to accept the new state of affairs. According to Mark Willes, former president of the Federal Reserve Bank of Minneapolis:

Once the program of gradually slowing growth in aggregate demand has begun and the government has unambiguously demonstrated its determination to carry it out, the costs of the program will decline. When the new approach is well known and understood, then even large steps will not lead to higher unemployment. As surprises gradually disappear, so will the high costs of fighting inflation with macroeconomic policies.[10]

Another criticism often made of the major econometric models is that they are entirely demand-oriented and do not take into sufficient consideration supply factors.[11] Thus, in a letter to the *Wall Street Journal,* Otto Eckstein recently went to great pains to explain how the DRI model really is a supply-side model. Michael Evans replied that

the comments offered in Mr. Eckstein's letter indicate a fundamental lack of understanding of the current state of the art of supply-side economics. . . . The true meaning of supply-side economics is far different, and refers to the fact that a combination of high tax rates and a maze of government regulations have combined to reduce the growth in output per unit of factor input. High taxes lead to disincentives both for personal and corporate saving and for the supply of labor. Attempts to "soak the rich" result in less savings and investment and less revenue for the federal government. When the after-tax rate of return on savings is minus 5% per year, the personal savings rate declines to an all-time low. Perhaps all these facts are elementary, but they have not yet been incorporated in any of the popular large-scale econometric models.

Evans added that the DRI model "does not contain any true supply-side effects."[12]

Evans' criticism of the DRI model might be dismissed as mere professional jealousy except for the fact that they have been repeated by others with no axe to grind. In the Joint Economic Committee's mid-year report for 1979 it noted that the DRI model "is based on the results of past experience and is unable to incorporate or accommodate significant changes in the interrelationships of economic forces that may result from new patterns of behavior. For this reason, the analysis [in the report] was not based solely on the model but includes calculations, assessments, and judgments that go beyond econometric modeling."[13]

The 1978 debate over the shape of Congress' periodic tax reduction bill brought out into the open some of the questions being raised within the economics profession about the biases and accuracy of macroeconometric models. The debate over whether to cut capital

gains tax rates was particularly significant because of the wide agreement that it would raise tax revenues, since more people would be
inclined to sell assets with capital gains at a lower tax rate than at the
higher one. Russell Long, chairman of the Senate Finance Committee, was especially interested in the possibilities of cutting taxes without reducing revenue. It had been a long-held pet peeve of his that
the Treasury Department's revenue estimates of the losses from
various tax reductions were almost always way off the mark, because
the department calculated its figures on an arithmetic basis without
considering dynamic or feedback effects. On paper, a tax cut obviously involves a revenue loss, but if it stimulates the economy
enough, more total revenue may actually be collected because the
lower tax rate will apply to a large tax base. Long's experience with
the investment tax credit is a case in point. As he said during hearings
in June 1977:

These revenue estimates have a way of being very, very far off base
because of their failure to anticipate everything that happens. We are
now estimating, I would think, that the investment tax credit would be
costing us $9 billion in revenue. . . . Now, when we put the investment
tax credit on, we estimated that we were going to lose about $5 billion.
. . . Instead of losing money, the revenue went up in corporate income
tax collections alone. Then we thought it was overheating the economy.
We repealed it. We would have thought that the government would
have taken in more money, but instead of making $5 billion, we lost $5
billion. Then, after a while we thought we made a mistake, so we put
it back on again. Instead of losing us money, it made us money. Then,
after a while, we repealed this thing again and it did just exactly the
opposite from what it was estimated to do again by about the same
amount.
    It seems to me, if we take all factors into account, it winds up with
the conclusion that taking the investment tax credit alone and looking
at it by itself, it is not costing us any money because the impression I
gain from it is that it stimulates the economy to the extent, and brings
about additional investment to the extent, that it makes us money
rather than loses us money. It just convinced me that something has to
be done to try to find somebody who knows more how to put the answer
in the computer so that it comes out the right way. Otherwise, I gained
the impression that we are moving on bad advice, that this thing that
stimulates the economy is costing us money, when the sum total effect
is to make us money.[14]

Actually, the notion that a tax increase may reduce revenue rather
than raise it is not novel. In 1919, for example, President Woodrow
Wilson said:

The Congress might well consider whether the higher rates of income and profits taxes can in peace times be effectively productive of revenue, and whether they may not, on the contrary, be destructive of business activity and productive of waste and inefficiency. There is a point at which in peace times high rates of income and profits taxes discourage energy, remove the incentive to new enterprise, encourage extravagant expenditures and produce industrial stagnation with consequent unemployment and other attendant evils.[15]

Conversely, the view that a tax reduction may raise revenue rather than reduce it is also not new. The tax rate reductions of the 1920s, under Presidents Harding and Coolidge, and those of the 1960s, under Presidents Kennedy and Johnson, both increased revenue within a short time.

The political importance of whether or not a tax cut will increase revenue or reduce it, or whether an econometric model can accurately predict what will happen, relates directly to passage of the Congressional Budget and Impoundment Control Act of 1974. This legislation was Congress' response to the feeling that it needed new procedures in order to get control of the federal budget, which seemed totally out of control. The Budget Act established the Congressional Budget Office (CBO) to provide Congress with an equivalent to the President's Office of Management and Budget, House and Senate Budget Committees, and a new congressional budget process for dealing with tax and spending issues on a comprehensive basis. The idea was to balance total spending and total revenues, rather than dealing with each individual spending and tax bill on an ad hoc basis. In theory this should have led to balanced budgets, instead of chronic deficits.

Unfortunately, the congressional budget process has failed to control spending. The first fiscal year in which the process was in effect (1976), the federal government ran the largest deficit in history: $66.4 billion. Since then we have had deficits of $45 billion and $49 billion in 1977 and 1978, and deficits of $28 billion in 1979 and almost $40 billion in 1980.

Since the budget committees have been unable to eliminate deficits by controlling spending they have turned increasingly to the tax system for increased revenue to balance the budget. Fortunately for them it is not necessary for Congress to explicitly raise taxes by passing new legislation (although it does this too, such as with the so-called windfall profits tax). Because of our steeply graduated tax structure inflation increases tax revenue faster than the rate of inflation, as people get pushed up into higher tax brackets even though there may be no real increase in their income. According to the Joint

Committee on Taxation, the individual income tax increases revenue approximately two-thirds faster than the rate of inflation. Thus, Congress can easily raise the total tax burden just by not cutting taxes as much as revenues go up.

The budget committees' desire to increase taxes to balance the budget, however, pits then squarely against the tax-writing committees of Congress, whose power lies in being able to cut taxes. Russell Long, in particular, has no intention whatsoever of having his power to cut taxes blocked by Ernest F. Hollings' Senate Budget Committee. This is why he has become such a devotee of supply-side econometric models. If he can prove that his tax reduction bills will not cost the Treasury significant revenue, or even that they will increase revenue, then Long is free to do what he wants without interference from the Budget Committee.

Under the congressional budget process, Congress sets overall spending and revenue targets in a budget resolution. Any legislation which would throw these targets off by reducing revenue or increasing spending may be prohibited from consideration. Thus if Senator Long were to bring to the Senate floor a major tax cut bill without getting a budget waiver or having it previously incorporated into the budget resolution, Senator Hollings would probably raise a point of order against it and have it taken out of consideration.

Despite the evidence that certain kinds of tax cuts can lead to an increase in revenue through expanded economic activity, the budget committees have steadfastly refused to consider this possibility when considering tax cuts. All tax cuts are assumed to involve a dollar-for-dollar revenue loss, and thus to create larger budget deficits. With the clamor for a balanced budget so great these days, legislators have been forced to decide which is more important, a balanced budget or a tax cut. Other options, such as simultaneously cutting taxes and spending, are not seriously considered because the CBO always warns that this will do serious harm to the economy and create unemployment. This is because the CBO assumes that there is a stronger multiplier effect to government spending than to tax cuts, because if taxes are reduced some of the money will be saved, thereby reducing aggregate demand. Conversely, if taxes and spending are simultaneously increased aggregate demand will be stimulated, because the tax increase will reduce private saving.[16]

Thus far, the CBO has been totally immune to supply-oriented thinking and has continued to argue in favor of demand-management policies, to be for spending and against tax cuts. And because the CBO has more than 200 professional economists on its staff, it has been able to back up its recommendations with impressive studies and reports which intimidate congressmen and senators into going along in the belief that the CBO speaks for the economics profession.[17] Economics is far from monolithic, however, and there are any number of serious disagreements on the issues. In short, CBO's views are opinions and little more. And like all those who offer opinions, CBO has its biases. A recent paper by David Meiselman and Paul Craig Roberts spells out some of the institutional problems with CBO's outlook:

> In the CBO analysis there is demand without supply, inflation without money, interest rates without capital, output without inputs, employment without wage rates or a capital market, and investment without saving or any change in the capital stock, Expectations are assumed to be static, and consumption is assumed to depend only on current disposable income. . . . The study concludes that the new budget process has institutionalized Keynesian fiscal policy rather than budget balance as the concept of budget control. Now, deficits are rationalized in terms of scientific economic policy prior to the appropriations process. This tends to loosen rather than tighten constraints on government expenditures.[18]

The CBO and its model have also come in for attack before Congress. Michael Evans testified before the Senate Budget Committee in 1978 as follows:

> To give one example, without being too technical, most people believe that the function that explains consumer behavior depends on a long period of past income as well as the present level of income. This was established practice 20 years ago and is now part of the literature. The CBO model made no distinctions between the short term and the long term. They say you get the income and spend it and that is it. That is why savings is down because there are no feedbacks to the spending for consumers.
> This is bad economics. This is a step backward because this is not right. If you lower corporate tax rates or do other things it has some positive effect on investment. The problem is that economists do not agree on the magnitude. Some say that cutting corporate rates or expanding the investment tax credit is best. . . . The third fact is that the CBO model is only four or five equations so there was not room to include any supply side at all. If you asked anyone, if you increase productivity will you lower inflation, I think the answer would have to be yes. Yet there is no mention of that in the CBO model.[19]

Evans' testimony was endorsed by Herbert Stein, former chairman of the Council of Economic Advisors, who added that the CBO gives very little consideration to the money supply and also has a unique way of deciding what is the optimum size of the federal deficit necessary to maintain the economy, rather than saying we have a choice of a large number of different combinations of fiscal and monetary policies which would give the same overall results.[20]

The CBO reacts to such criticism by proclaiming its nonpartisanship and lack of any intention to steer the Congress toward adopting specific policies. However, a recent paper by Preston Miller and Arthur Rolnick of the Federal Reserve Bank of Minneapolis points out that there are inevitably policy implications in the way the CBO carries out its studies. They point out, for example, that the CBO generally produces only short-range forecasts—two years or less. This fact inevitably biases the results because almost all econometric models will show that an expansionary fiscal policy will stimulate output and have little effect on inflation for two years. Subsequently, the real output effect will die out while the inflationary effect will grow. By limiting its forecasts to two years and less, therefore, the CBO gives the misleading impression that changes in policy will have positive effects on real output and negligible effects on inflation.[21]

Other examples of bias may be found in the CBO's own publications. A paper entitled "Temporary Measures to Stimulate Employment" lists only five alternative ways for Congress to deal with unemployment: public service jobs, aid to state and local governments, accelerated public works, increased government purchases, and a tax cut (type unspecified). The figures clearly imply that public service jobs are the superior method, costing only about $8,000 each, compared to a tax cut which would cost as much as $122,000 per job. The reason why it comes up with such figures is that the CBO assumes that all tax cuts are the same, in that they impact on the economy only in the form of stimulus to aggregate demand and because the CBO is only looking at the effect of a tax cut on employment in the short run. The incentive effects of various kinds of tax cuts are irrelevant. To the CBO it is all the same whether the corporate tax rate is cut or if the government hands out one-shot tax rebates to everyone. At least in the short run, the effects will be exactly the same if their aggregate dollar size is the same. In other words, the only thing that matters is whether or not people have more dollars to spend, whether it is because of a tax cut or a government check sent to every American.[22]

Russell Long has had to fight against this view, not particularly because he disagrees with it, but because it inevitably puts him in competition with the Senate's budget and appropriations committees. If a tax cut is all the same to the economy as an increase in spending, and an increase in spending for, say, public service jobs gives us more "bang for the buck" than tax cuts, then his power is severely undermined unless he can prove that there is something special about tax cuts. This leads him inevitably to the matter of incentive effects of various different fiscal policies. If Long can find a respectable econometric model which can measure incentive effects and thereby produce feedback from tax reduction legislation then he does not have to fight the Budget Committee when he wants to cut taxes. This is what led the Senate Finance Committee to give Michael Evans $250,000 to build a new econometric model sensitive to supply-side considerations, which will show how revenue can increase from tax cuts.[23]

Evans has completed his model, but in the meantime many other economists have developed what they claim to be supply-side models. Dr. Norman Ture has had such a model for years. In 1979 Dr. Arthur Laffer unveiled another such model, developed in conjunction with the American Council for Capital Formation and the H. C. Wainwright Company. Among the findings of Laffer's model is the forecast that passage of the Kemp-Roth Tax Reduction Act, which would reduce marginal tax rates on individuals by about a third, would increase aggregate tax revenue by the fifth year after passage above what it would have been in the absence of any tax cut, due to its dynamic effects on the economy.[24] Another such model has been developed by D. Evans Vanderford.[25]

Interestingly, Otto Eckstein and DRI now claim to have produced a supply-side model, developed in conjunction with the Joint Economic Committee. The principle finding of Eckstein's model thus far is to show that a properly designed tax cut may reduce inflation rather than increase it, by increasing productivity, which in turn has a multiplier effect in terms of reducing inflation.[26] This is important because heretofore it has been a fundamental principle of Keynesian economics that tax cuts stimulate inflation by increasing aggregate demand, whereas tax increases slow inflation by reducing demand.

Nevertheless, despite the work of Evans, Ture, Laffer, and Eckstein, the House and Senate Budget Committees refuse to use such models or even to acknowledge their value. Recently, Senator Orrin Hatch, a member of the Senate Budget Committee, requested that the committee hold hearings on problems with the models. In a memo which later became public, the committee's staff director, John McEvoy, told then committee chairman Sen. Edmund Muskie that Alice Rivlin, head of the CBO, did not want such hearings. McEvoy said that Rivlin considered critics of the models to be "an extreme right-wing claque who should not be given an audience, lest it legitimize their views."[27] In light of the fact that some of the most eminent men in the economics profession now agree that there are serious problems with the major macroeconometric models (Eckstein was a member of the Council of Economic Advisors under

President Johnson), it would appear that the CBO's attitude relates more to its liberal biases than to objective economic opinion.

The fact is that economics is far more political than anyone realizes. Economists try to pass themselves off as scientists by mimicking the methods and using the tools of science (computers, mathematics, statistics), when in fact there is no comparison between economics and hard science because in economics there are no constants. All economic relationships vary with time, and the same individual cannot even be depended upon to react the same way to the same circumstances twice. Ultimately, one's economic outlook is determined philosophically, not empirically. If one believes that an expansion of government power can improve life then one will incline toward one school of economic thought. If one believes that an expansion of state power is contrary to individual welfare then one is going to incline toward another school. Moreover, one is going to get a different forecast from an econometric model depending on one's worldview. As a recent report from the Joint Economic Committee observes, whether a model is used for forecasting or policy analysis "its results are always subject to modification by the analyst if they appear 'unreasonable.' This means that different analysts may derive different results from the same model if they alter the model's output to conform to their own judgement."[28]

Econometric models cannot really tell policymakers what to do. All they can do is give reinforcement to decisions that have already been made on other grounds, whether they be political or philosophical. Unfortunately, they can give the appearance of providing exact proof for a particular view which can be influential on those who do not hold strong political or philosophical views on a particular matter.[29]

The great economist Joseph Schumpeter understood the interaction between politics and economics as well as anyone and knew that the development of econometrics would increase the influence of economists on policy, precisely because it quantifies everything and gives the illusion of exactness. Thus Schumpeter was surely correct when he wrote in the first issue of *Econometrica* (January 1933):

> The only way to a position in which our science might give positive advice on a larger scale to politicians and businessmen, leads through quantitative work. For as long as we are unable to put our arguments into figures, the voice of our science, although occasionally it may help to dispel errors, will never be heard by practical men. They are, by instinct, econometricians all of them, in their distrust of anything not amenable to exact proof.[30]

Notes

1. Quoted in the *New York Times* (January 28, 1980).

2. "New Vogue in Forecasting," *Dun's Review* (October 1979), pp. 94–100; "Right or Wrong, Forecasts Pay," *Business Week* (May 28, 1979), pp. 134–143; Comptroller General of the United States, *Uses of National Economic Models by Federal Agencies* (Washington: General Accounting Office, 1979); "The Economist as Prophet," *Morgan Guaranty Survey* (August 1978), pp. 9–14; James Henry, "The Future Hustle," *New Republic* (February 4, 1978), pp. 16–20; "A Big Business in Credibility," *Business Week* (March 7, 1977), pp. 84–86.

3. Victor Zarnowitz, *An Appraisal of Short-Term Economic Forecasts* (New York: Columbia University Press, 1967), p. 7; see also W. Allen Spivey and William Wrobleski, *Econometric Model Performance in Forecasting and Policy Assessment* (Washington: American Enterprise Institute, 1979); idem, *Surveying Recent Econometric Forecasting Performance* (Washington: American Enterprise Institute, Reprint No. 106, 1980); Lindley H. Clark, Jr., "Econometrics Gains Many New Followers, But the Accuracy of Forecasts Is Unproven," *Wall Street Journal* (August 2, 1977); Stephen K. McNees, "The Forecasting Record for the 1970s," *New England Economic Review* (Sept./Oct. 1979), pp. 33–53.

4. Quoted in Roger Leroy Miller, *Economics Today: The Macro View* (San Francisco: Canfield Press, 1974), p. 62.

5. "Theory Deserts the Forecasters," *Business Week* (June 29, 1974), p. 50.

6. Paul A. Anderson, "Rational Expectations: How Important for Econometric Policy Analysis?" *Federal Reserve Bank of Minneapolis Quarterly Review* (Fall 1978), p. 5.

7. Robert E. Lucas, Jr., "Econometric Policy Evaluation: A Critique," in Karl Brunner and Allan Meltzer, eds., *The Phillips Curve and Labor Markets* (New York: North-Holland Publishing Co., 1976), pp. 19–46.

8. John Maynard Keynes, *The General Theory of Employment Interest and Money* (New York: Harcourt, Brace and Co., 1936), p. 9.

9. Robert E. Lucas, Jr. and Thomas J. Sargent, "After Keynesian Macroeconomics," *Federal Reserve Bank of Minneapolis Quarterly Review* (Spring 1979), p. 6.

10. *Federal Reserve Bank of Minneapolis 1978 Annual Report*, p. 7; see also Mark Willes, "The Rational Expectations Model," *Wall Street Journal* (April 2, 1979).

11. Paul Craig Roberts, "The Breakdown of the Keynesian Model," *The Public Interest* (Summer 1978), pp. 20–33; Irving Kristol, "The Foxes vs. the Hedgehog," *Wall Street Journal* (June 14, 1977); Arthur B. Laffer and R. David Ranson, *The "Prototype Wedge Model": A Tool for Supply-Side Economics* (Boston: H. C. Wainwright & Co., 1979); Michael K. Evans, "The Bankruptcy of Keynesian Econometric Models," *Challenge* (January-February 1980), pp. 13–19; idem, "Confessions of an Economic Forecaster," *New York Times* (February 17, 1980).

12. Otto Eckstein, "Value of Econometric Models," *Wall Street Journal* (August 27, 1979); Michael Evans, "The Supply Side of Econometric Models," *Wall Street Journal* (August 30, 1979).

13. Congress of the United States, Joint Economic Committee, *Midyear Review of the Economy: The Outlook for 1979* (Washington: U.S. Government Printing Office, 1979), pp. 53–54.

14. Congress of the United States, *Incentives for Economic Growth: Hearings before the Subcommittee on Taxation and Debt Management Generally of the Committee on Finance, United States Senate,* June 14, 1977 (Washington: U.S. Government Printing Office, 1977), p. 242.

15. From his annual message to Congress, *Congressional Record* (December 2, 1919), p. 53.

16. Congress of the United States, Congressional Budget Office, *Understanding Fiscal Policy* (April 1978); idem, *Closing the Fiscal Policy Loop: A Long-Run Analysis* (December 1977); idem, *The CBO Multipliers Project: A Methodology for Analyzing the Effects of Alternative Economic Policies* (August 1977).

17. See Tom Bethell, "Fooling With the Budget," *Harper's* (October 1979), pp. 41–52, 116–17; Senator Orrin Hatch, "Congressional Irresolution," *Barron's* (July 9, 1979), pp. 11–25.

18. David Meiselman and Paul Craig Roberts, "The Political Economy of the Congressional Budget Office," in Karl Brunner and Allan Meltzer, eds., *Three Aspects of Policy-making: Knowledge, Data and Institutions* (New York: North-Holland Publishing Co., 1979), p. 283.

19. Congress of the United States, *Second Concurrent Resolution on the Budget—Fiscal Year 1979: Hearings Before the Committee on the Budget, United States Senate,* July 27, 1978 (Washington: U.S. Government Printing Office, 1978), pp. 178–79; see also idem, *Special Study on Economic Change: Hearings Before the Joint Economic Committee,* June 13, 1978 (Washington: U.S. Government Printing Office, 1978), Pt. 2, pp. 678–79.

20. *Budget Hearings,* p. 179.

21. Preston J. Miller and Arthur J. Rolnick, *The CBO's Policy Analysis: An Unquestionable Misuse of a Questionable Theory* (Federal Reserve Bank of Minneapolis, Staff Report No. 49, August 1979).

22. Congress of the United States, Congressional Budget Office, *Temporary Measures to Stimulate Employment: An Evaluation of Some Alternatives* (September 1975), pp. 68–72.

23. Juan Cameron, "The Economic Modelers Vie for Washington's Ear," *Fortune* (November 20, 1978), pp. 102–5; Edward Cowan, "Model Is Due in Senate On Benefits of Tax Cuts," *New York Times* (February 18, 1980).

24. Laffer and Ranson, *Wedge Model,* p. 33.

25. D. Evans Vanderford, "Building A Supply Side Model: The Permanent Money Balances Hypothesis," *Taxing & Spending* (Winter 1980), pp. 21–42.

26. Congress of the United States, Joint Economic Committee, *Joint Economic Report 1980: Plugging in the Supply Side* (Washington: U.S. Government Printing Office, 1980), pp. 35–37; Otto Eckstein, *Tax Policy and Core Inflation: A Study Prepared for the Use of the Joint Economic Committee* (Washington: U.S. Government Printing Office, 1980).

27. Rowland Evans and Robert Novak, "Backstage at the Budget Committee," *Washington Post* (April 11, 1980); "Mrs. Rivlin Rejects Supply-Side

View," *New York Times* (April 14, 1980); Editorial, "The 'Right-Wing Claque,'" *Wall Street Journal* (April 9, 1980).

28. L. Douglas Lee, *A Comparison of Econometric Models: A Study Prepared for the Joint Economic Committee* (Washington: U.S. Government Printing Office, 1978), p. 2.

29. In general, see F.A. Hayek, *The Counterrevolution of Science* (New York: The Free Press, 1955); Murray N. Rothbard, "The Mantle of Science," in Helmut Schoeck and James Wiggins, eds., *Scientism and Values* (Princeton: Van Nostrand, 1960), pp. 159–80; Ludwig von Mises, *Human Action* (New Haven: Yale University Press, 1949), pp. 347–54; Leland Yeager, "Measurement as Scientific Method in Economics," *American Journal of Economics and Sociology* 16 (July 1957), pp. 337–46.

30. Joseph Schumpeter, "The Commonsense of Econometrics," *Econometrica* 1 (January 1933), p. 12.

8

The Mellon Tax Cuts

A S WAS NOTED IN CHAPTER 3, IT HAS LONG BEEN KNOWN THAT most tax systems get their start during war and that they rarely change thereafter.[1] The experience in the United States confirms this view. The individual income tax got started just in time for World War I, but originally it only affected taxpayers earning more than $3,000 per year (a very good income in those days) and only taxed them at 1 percent up to $20,000. The top rate was only 7 percent and applied to incomes above $500,000. Less than 0.5 percent of the American population paid any income tax at all and the average tax per return was a mere $114.80. This changed quickly with the outbreak of war. The war not only led to a vast increase in tax rates but made the income tax an institution. As Gerald Carson put it: "World War I built an acceptance for the income tax that would probably never have occurred otherwise, since paying soon became an act of patriotism."[2]

Tax rates were roughly doubled across the board in 1916, raising the lowest rate from 1 to 2 percent and the highest rate from 7 to 15 percent. In 1917 they were increased even more significantly, with the top rate going all the way to 67 percent. By 1918 the bottom rate was up to 6 percent, beginning at $2,000 of income, with the top rate increased to 77 percent. As a result of imposing the progressive income tax and its subsequent increases, federal budget receipts had gone from a mere $624 million in 1910 ($6.75 per capita), to $5,728 million in 1920 ($53.80 per capita).[3]

With the end of war it was clear that tax rates needed to be cut, but the Democrats refused to acquiesce in any kind of tax rate reduction which included a reduction in tax rates on upper incomes. So although taxes were cut somewhat in 1919, the wartime rate structure remained largely in effect, with the bottom rate at 4 percent and the top rate at 73 percent. But it was already clear that such high rates were counterproductive. As Treasury Secretary Carter Glass said in his annual report for 1919:

> The uppermost brackets of the surtax have already passed the point of productivity and the only consequence of any further increase would be to drive possessors of these great incomes more and more to place their wealth in the billions of dollars of wholly exempt securities, as well as those heretofore issued by the United States. This process not only destroys a source of revenue to the Federal Government, but tends to withdraw the capital of very rich men from the development of new enterprises and place it at the disposal of State and municipal governments upon terms so easy to them (the cost of exemptions from taxation falling more heavily upon the Federal Government) as to stimulate wasteful and nonproductive expenditure by State and municipal governments.[4]

Again in 1920, Treasury Secretary David Houston called attention to the adverse effects of high income tax rates in his annual report:

> Since the adoption of the heavy war surtaxes in the revenue act of 1917, the Treasury has repeatedly called attention to the fact that these surtaxes are excessive; that they have passed the point of maximum productivity and are rapidly driving the wealthier taxpayers to transfer their investments into the thousands of millions of tax-free securities which compete so disastrously with the industrial and railroad securities upon the ready purchase of which the development of industry and the expansion of foreign trade intimately depend.
>
> It seems idle to speculate in the abstract as to whether or not a progressive income-tax schedule rising to rates in excess of 70 per cent is justifiable. We are confronted with a condition, not a theory. The fact is that such rates cannot be successfully collected. Tax returns and statistics are demonstrating what it should require no statistical evidence to prove. For the year 1916 net income amounting to $992,-972,985 was included in the returns of taxpayers having net income over $300,000 a year.
>
> This aggregate fell to $731,372,153 for the year 1917 and to $392,-

247,329 for the year 1918. There is little reason to believe that the actual income of the richer taxpayers of the country had fallen in that interval. It is the taxable income which has been reduced and almost certainly through investment by the richer taxpayers in tax-exempt properties. Whatever one may believe, therefore, about the abstract propriety of projecting income-tax rates to a point above 70 per cent, when the taxpayers affected are subject also to State and local taxation, the fact remains that to retain such rates in the tax law is to cling to a shadow while relinquishing the substance. The effective way to tax the rich is to adopt rates that do not force investment in tax-exempt securities.[5]

In 1920 Republican Warren G. Harding was elected president while Republicans increased their narrow majorities in the House and Senate to substantial majorities. Harding appointed Andrew Mellon Secretary of the Treasury. Both he and Mellon shared the goal of getting tax rates reduced as soon as possible. In his inaugural address Harding spoke of the need to "strike at war taxation," and shortly after taking office he spoke to a joint session of Congress, saying, "I know of no more pressing problem at home than to . . . lift the burdens of war taxation from the shoulders of the American people."[6]

Shortly thereafter the Congress began work on the Revenue Act of 1921. The Republican plan to eliminate the excess profits tax and limit surtaxes on individual incomes drew heavy criticism from liberal Democrats on the House Ways and Means Committee. In minority views to the committee report on the Revenue Act of 1921 the Democrats said their position was that

not a dollar of taxes should be reduced on these profiteering corporations and on the millionaires and multimillionaires that reaped harvests of wealth during the war, as long as a single disabled or wounded soldier or a single widow or orphan of a dead soldier or a single veteran is in need.[7]

Nonetheless, the Revenue Act was enacted on November 23, 1921, increasing the personal exemption for married couples, increasing the surtax exemption, reducing all income tax rates, and reducing the top rate from 73 to 58 percent. In addition, the excess profits tax on corporations was repealed and preferential treatment for capital gains was instituted. Previously, capital gains had been treated as ordinary income, but under the new provision gains from capital assets held for more than two years could be taxed at an alternate rate of 12.5 percent.[8]

On August 2, 1923, President Harding died of pneumonia, elevating Vice President Calvin Coolidge to the presidency. With Coolidge's blessing, Mellon immediately launched a new campaign for further tax reductions. On November 10, 1923, he put forward his plan in a letter to the chairman of the House Ways and Means Committee, Congressman William R. Green. Mellon asked for a 25 percent reduction in the tax on earned income, a one to two percentage point reduction in normal tax rates, a further increase in the surtax exemption and revision of the surtax rates, the repeal of various excise taxes, and numerous technical changes in the tax law.[9]

Mellon's plan once again came under attack from liberal Democrats. Coming to his defense, however, was the *New York Times,* which ran almost daily editorials in favor of the Mellon plan. Typical of the *Times'* view is the following editorial, entitled "Relieving the Rich," from December 23, 1923:

Parts of Secretary Mellon's plan to cut taxes are accepted by everybody. No one can directly oppose easing the lot of people of moderate means. But there is much pother about lowering the rate of surtaxes. Senator Simmons of North Carolina declares that his party will yield to none in its desire to reduce the taxes of the middle classes, but that it will withstand to the last gasp the Mellon scheme which is intended to "relieve the rich."

The great point of Secretary Mellon's main argument is that the rich have found ways to relieve themselves. They are progressively escaping the heavy taxes levied specially upon them. It was certain from the first that they would do so. The Treasury figures cited by Mr. Mellon prove that they have done it. He wants in reality to get more money out of them than they are now paying. But he proposes to do it by making their rate of taxation lower. This is in line with economic theory and with experience running over many years, though of course it seems a ridiculous proposition to those whose thoughts are all of aiming sharp arrows of taxation at wealth.

Suppose the surtaxes on large incomes are not reduced—suppose that they are increased; what will happen? The rich may or may not be relieved, but it is certain that the poor will be hit harder than ever. For a large proportion of the heavy taxation of rich corporations is inevitably passed on to the consumer. The tax is necessarily entered as an item in the total cost of production. The result is to make prices rise, to increase rents, to cause the poor man to feel that the necessities of life are less within his reach than ever. This sure course of economic events has been followed in all countries, and it has plainly been followed during the last few years in the United States. The lawmakers gleefully start out to lay oppressive taxes on the rich, but really are all the while striking at the poor. The true way to help the latter is to make it possible for the former to put more money into enterprise and industry and less into tax-exempt securities.[10]

On another occasion the *Times* asked:

Why should our rulers and lawmakers show themselves so indifferent
to the reasoned convictions of the leaders of industry and finance in the
United States? What the latter desire has repeatedly been made public.
They feel in a thousand ways the drag of heavy taxation which checks
enterprise and keeps production down. They would be almost ready to
underwrite a period of general prosperity if the taxing hand of the
Government could be lightened and if Congressional appropriations
could be held down. Existing taxes come perilously near to being a levy
upon capital. That inevitably means a check to expansion and a discour-
agement of initiative. Every dollar needlessly voted by Congress is a
dollar taken away from the country's productive capacity and turned
into wasteful, because unproductive, channels. These are elementary
truths, admitted by all. They are admitted in private even by the great
majority of the Members of Congress. Why do they ignore or defy them
in their public and collective action? It is because some of them think
they have discovered a philosopher's stone, by which money enough
can be created to cover all public deficits and to pay for every form of
governmental extravagance.

What they think is that they can indefinitely increase the taxes laid
upon wealth. They have their eye upon the very rich men of the country, and believe that they can take from the large incomes and great
accumulations of property all that is needed to finance a lavish Government. But all men of sense know that this is a vain thing. The evidence
of the past three years has conclusively shown that unjustly high surtaxes defeat their own end. When the Government threatens to take 65
per cent of big incomes, those incomes have a way of shrinking ere the
taxgatherer can lay a finger upon them. They take flight into tax-exempt
securities, or in other ways manage, within the law, to frustrate the
short-sighted intent of those who framed the law. Even if it were otherwise, and the immense collections from great wealth could be made as
planned, an obvious misfortune for the country would be involved.
Capital would be denied to industries clamoring for it. The sources of
large-scale production would be dried up. Money that ought to be
continually feeding private enterprise would be squandered in unproductive public outlay.[11]

Secretary Mellon helped his own case by writing a book on tax
policy published in 1924 and called *Taxation: The People's Business*.
In this book he made a powerful case for a reduction in high marginal
tax rates, on the grounds that they were counterproductive and not
yielding enough revenue (see also President Coolidge's remarks in
Appendix A). As Mellon wrote:

The history of taxation shows that taxes which are inherently excessive are not paid. The high rates inevitably put pressure upon the

taxpayer to withdraw his capital from productive business and invest it in tax-exempt securities or to find other lawful methods of avoiding the realization of taxable income. The result is that the sources of taxation are drying up; wealth is failing to carry its share of the tax burden; and capital is being diverted into channels which yield neither revenue to the Government nor profit to the people. . . . Experience has shown that the present high rates of surtax are bringing in each year progressively less revenue to the Government. This means that the price is too high to the large taxpayer and he is avoiding a taxable income by the many ways which are available to him. What rates will bring in the largest revenue to the Government experience has not yet developed, but it is estimated that by cutting the surtaxes in half, the Government, when the full effect of the reduction is felt, will receive more revenue from the owners of large incomes at the lower rates of tax than it would have received at the higher rates . . . just as Mr. Ford makes more money out of pricing his cars at $380 than at $3,000.[12]

The Revenue Act of 1924 was enacted on June 2, 1924. It gave taxpayers a 25 percent tax reduction retroactive to 1923 income. It increased personal and surtax exemptions, instituted an earned income credit, and reduced normal and surtax rates across the board, bringing the top rate down to 46 percent from 58 percent.[13]

However, Mellon and Coolidge were not finished. Further tax reductions were voted in 1926 and 1928 (enacted February 26, 1926, and May 29, 1928, respectively). Personal and surtax exemptions were again increased, the earned income credit broadened, and normal and surtax rates sharply reduced. The highest tax rate came down to 25 percent on incomes over $100,000.[14]

The economic effects of these tax rate reductions were dramatic. During the 1920s the stock market more than quadrupled, and nominal GNP went from $69.6 billion to $103.1 billion, but because prices were falling real GNP rose much more, by 54 percent over the period. Output per man hour increased by 66.5 percent while the index of industrial production doubled. Thus Jude Wanniski argues that the Mellon-Coolidge tax reductions were the fundamental basis for the economic boom of the 1920s.[15]

Proving Mellon's point about lower tax rates raising more revenue from larger incomes, the statistics show that in 1916 there were 6,633 tax returns reporting $100,000 or more of income. In total, these taxpayers reported $1,856 million of income and paid $17 million in income tax. But as the rates went up, the income went down. In 1918 there were only 4,499 returns with $100,000 or more of income, reporting a total of $990 million in income and paying $470 million in tax. By 1920 the number of returns had fallen to 3,649, the amount

TABLE 1

SUMMARY OF INDIVIDUAL INCOME TAX RATE CHANGES, 1913–29

INCOME YEAR	FIRST BRACKET		TOP BRACKET	
	Rate (percent)	Income Up to	Rate (percent)	Income in Excess of
1913–15	1	$20,000	7	$ 500,000
1916	2	20,000	15	2,000,000
1917	2	2,000	67	2,000,000
1918	6	4,000	77	1,000,000
1919–21	4	4,000	73	1,000,000
1922	4	4,000	58	200,000
1923	3	4,000	58	200,000
1924	1 ½*	4,000	46	500,000
1925–28	1 ⅛*	4,000	25	100,000
1929	⅜*	4,000	24	100,000

*After earned income credit equal to 25 percent of tax on earned income.
SOURCE: Congressional Research Service.

of income to $727 million, and the amount of tax to $321 million. But the reduction in rates reversed the trend. By 1924 there were 5,715 returns reporting income of $100,000 or more, generating $1,238 million in total income and $304 million in taxes. A mere four years later, in 1928, the number of returns virtually tripled, to 15,977; total income leaped to $4,451 million and tax revenue from incomes over $100,000 jumped to $714 million.[16]

Similarly, one finds that the preferential treatment of capital gains, which tax "reformers" have long abhorred, substantially increased the amount of capital gains generated. In 1922 $249 million in long-term capital gains were reported. This increased to $305 million in 1923, $389 million in 1924, $940 million in 1925, $1,081 million in 1927, $1,880 million in 1928, and $2,347 million in 1929.[17]

And because a tight rein was kept on spending—a task made much easier by the fact that with so much economic output and so many jobs there was little need for government expenditures for relief or welfare—Mellon was able to pay off a substantial portion of the war debt. The national debt stood at $25.5 billion in 1919. It was reduced every single year during the 1920s, to $16.2 billion in 1930.

As early as 1927 the Treasury Department was crediting the reduction in tax rates for the nation's economic prosperity and the increased tax revenue. In his annual report for the fiscal year ending in 1927, Secretary of the Treasury Mellon said:

The Revenue Act of 1926 made sweeping changes affecting the taxation of individual incomes by increasing the personal credit exemption for single persons 50 percent and that for married persons and heads of families 40 percent, by increasing the earned income credit and by decreasing the normal and surtax rates. More than 44 percent of the individual taxpayers were relieved from income-tax payments. . . . It was very naturally anticipated that these changes would result in considerable loss of revenue. In fact, the report of the Ways and Means Committee submitted to the House estimated a reduction of $46,000,-000 in normal tax paid and a reduction of $98,575,000 in returns from the surtax. As a matter of fact, however, the individual returns for the calendar year 1925 showed a larger tax than did those for 1924. . . . The results are attributable to several causes: First and most important was the increased prosperity of the country as exemplified by the increased income from certain sources, despite the reduction in number of returns. . . . In the second place, the entire decrease in taxable incomes occurred in the classes not in excess of $5,000, while for those in excess of $5,000 it materially increased. The number of taxable returns with income of less than $5,000 decreased 55 percent, while the number in excess of $5,000 increased 18 percent; in excess of $25,000, 32 percent; in excess of $100,000, 67 percent; in excess of $300,000, 104 percent; and in excess of $1,000,000, 176 percent.

The Treasury Department has always contended that in the long run the taxation of income at moderate rates would be more productive than at very high rates. The soundness of this contention appears to have been amply borne out by the tax returns under the law of 1926, for both the calendar years 1925 and 1926.[18]

Unfortunately, the stock market crash and the onset of the Great Depression and later World War II led to severe increases in tax rates.[19] The top rate went from 25 percent in 1931 to 63 percent between 1932 and 1935, increasing again to 79 percent in 1936, to 81 percent in 1941, 88 percent in 1942, and 94.4 percent in 1944. But when the war ended, we no longer had great men like Andrew Mellon in the Treasury Department. The World War II tax rates stayed essentially in effect until John F. Kennedy became president.

Notes

1. Edward Ames and Richard Rapp, "The Birth and Death of Taxes: A Hypothesis," *Journal of Economic History* 37 (March 1977), pp. 161–76; C. Northcote Parkinson, *The Law and the Profits* (Boston: Houghton Mifflin, 1960), pp. 38–50.

2. Gerald Carson, "The Income Tax and How It Grew," *American Heritage* (December 1973), p. 84.

3. *Facts and Figures on Government Finance,* 20th ed. (Washington: Tax Foundation, 1979), pp. 98, 102.

4. *Annual Report of the Secretary of the Treasury, 1919* (Washington: U.S. Government Printing Office, 1920).

5. *Annual Report of the Secretary of the Treasury, 1920* (Washington: U.S. Government Printing Office, 1921), pp. 36–37.

6. *Inaugural Addresses of the Presidents of the United States* (Washington: U.S. Government Printing Office, 1974), p. 211; *Congressional Record* (April 12, 1921), p. 169.

7. House of Representatives Report No. 350, part 2, 67th Cong., 1st sess., p. 4.

8. For details, see a report by the Treasury Department on tax cuts in the 1920s in Hearings before the House Ways and Means Committee on Individual Income Tax Reduction, 80th Cong., 1st sess. pp. 38–43.

9. Reprinted in Andrew Mellon, *Taxation: The People's Business* (New York: Macmillan, 1924), pp. 175–93.

10. Editorial, "Relieving the Rich," *New York Times* (December 23, 1923).

11. Editorial, "Taxes and Extravagance," *New York Times* (October 21, 1923).

12. Mellon, *Taxation,* pp. 13, 17.

13. See note 8.

14. Ibid.

15. Jude Wanniski, *The Way the World Works* (New York: Basic Books, 1978), pp. 121–22.

16. *Facts and Figures on Government Finance,* p. 107.

17. Cited in the *Congressional Record* (January 9, 1947), p. A59.

18. *Annual Report of the Secretary of the Treasury, 1927* (Washington: U.S. Government Printing Office, 1928), pp. 10–11.

19. See Benjamin M. Anderson, *Economics and the Public Welfare* (Princeton, NJ: D. Van Nostrand, 1949), pp. 370–89, 530–40.

9

The Rediscovery of Incentive, 1946–1954

F OLLOWING THE DEFEAT OF HERBERT HOOVER AND THE ELEC-
tion of Franklin D. Roosevelt, in 1932, a significant change
occurred in United States tax policy. The tax reductions of the 1920s
were replaced by almost annual tax increases under the Roosevelt
administration. By 1936 the bottom tax rate was up to 4 percent,
from ⅜ percent in 1929, and the top rate was up to 79 percent, from
25 percent in 1929. Such tax rate increases during peacetime are
unprecedented in American history.

By 1938 these tax increases began to produce a reaction. Early that
year, Cong. Thomas W. Phillips, Jr. of Pennsylvania proposed a constitutional amendment to repeal the Sixteenth Amendment to the
Constitution, the income tax amendment, and limit federal taxes on
incomes, gifts, and inheritances to 25 percent. Shortly thereafter, on
June 15, 1938, Cong. Emanuel Celler of New York, later to become
chairman of the House Judiciary Committee, introduced such an
amendment. The text of the proposed amendment read as follows:

> Section 1. The sixteenth amendment to the Constitution of the
> United States is hereby repealed.
> Section 2. The Congress shall have power to lay and collect taxes on

incomes, from whatever source derived, without apportionment among the several States and without regard to any census or enumeration: *Provided,* That in no case shall the maximum rate of tax exceed 25 per centum.

Section 3. The maximum rate of any tax, duty, or excise which Congress may lay and collect with respect to the devolution or transfer of property, or any interest therein, upon or in contemplation of death, or by way of gift, shall in no case exceed 25 per centum.[1]

Congressman Celler reintroduced his proposed amendment on the first day of the next Congress, January 3, 1939.[2] As with his previous proposal, this resolution was referred to the Judiciary Committee, but no further action taken.

Shortly thereafter, Wyoming became the first state to petition for the calling of a constitutional convention, pursuant to Article V of the Constitution, to propose such an amendment. In 1940 Mississippi and Rhode Island joined Wyoming in calling for a constitutional convention to limit federal taxes to 25 percent. In 1941 Iowa, Maine, Massachusetts and Michigan followed suit. In 1943, following the passage of high wartime tax rates, several more states joined the vanguard, including Alabama, Arkansas, Delaware, Illinois, Indiana, New Hampshire, Pennsylvania, and Wisconsin. Kentucky and New Jersey adopted resolutions in 1944, Louisiana in 1950; Florida, Kansas, Montana, Nevada, and Utah in 1951; and Georgia in 1952. In total, at least 24 states asked for a constitutional convention to limit federal tax rates. Subsequently, 7 states rescinded their applications, while two governors attempted to veto their state legislatures' actions. But these actions apparently had no constitutional validity and the original petitions remained valid.[3]

As the number of state petitions grew, opponents of the 25 percent tax limit mounted their attack. Congressman Wright Patman of Texas was particularly outspoken, saying that passage of the amendment would wreck small business and make it impossible to make payments on the national debt, veterans' benefits, social security benefits, and unemployment benefits. The Treasury Department warned that its power to adapt to changing economic conditions would be constrained. Prof. Harold M. Groves called the proposed amendment "exceedingly undesirable." The *Nation* called the state petitions the work of a "millionaire's lobby." And the *Washington Post, The New Republic,* and *The Philadelphia Record* also editorialized against the amendment.[4]

Supporters of the amendment argued that it would not wreck federal finances for two reasons: first, it would ensure economy in government expenditures, causing only waste to be cut, and second, the increase in economic incentive would cause the tax base to grow and government revenue to increase. The experience of the Mellon tax cuts of the 1920s was frequently pointed to as an example of what would happen.[5]

The tax reduction movement shifted gears in 1946, with the election of the first Republican Congress in 15 years. During the 1946 campaign Republicans had promised that the first bill introduced in a Republican-controlled Congress would be a 20 percent reduction in all income tax rates. When the Republicans gained 55 seats in the House and 13 in the Senate, giving them control in both houses, they kept their promise. On January 3, 1947, Congressman Harold Knutson, new chairman of the House Ways and Means Committee, introduced H.R. 1 to provide a flat 20 percent reduction in all income tax rates. Such a tax reduction was frequently justified on the grounds that it would increase revenues as the Mellon cuts did.[6]

The House Ways and Means Committee completed its work quickly, reporting the tax reduction bill on March 24, 1947. It was brought up in the House three days later and passed by a vote of 273 to 137. The Senate Finance Committee made few changes in the bill and reported it on May 14. It passed the Senate on May 28 by a vote of 52 to 34. The Congress completed final action on H.R. 1 on June 3, sending it to the president for his signature.

President Truman opposed passage of H.R. 1 from the beginning, on the grounds that it was inflationary and gave too much to those with upper incomes. On June 16, 1947, he vetoed the tax reduction bill, saying "this bill represents the wrong kind of tax reduction, at the wrong time. It offers dubious, ill-apportioned, and risky benefits at the expense of a sound tax policy and is, from the standpoint of Government finances, unsafe."[7] An effort to override the president's veto failed the next day when Republicans in the House were unable to get a two-thirds majority.

Representative Knutson promptly reintroduced the vetoed measure as H.R. 3950, changing only the effective date. The Ways and Means Committee reported the bill on July 3, 1947, and it passed the House on July 8. The Senate took up the House-passed bill on July 14, passing it by a vote of 60 to 32. On July 18 President Truman returned the measure as being "at complete variance with the fundamental requirements of a good tax bill."[8] This time the House voted the same day to override, with 27 more votes than necessary. But the Senate, voting the same day, was 5 votes short of an override, killing the chances of an across-the-board tax reduction for the first session of the 80th Congress.

In November 1947 the Special Tax Study Committee, appointed by the House Ways and Means Committee to make a general study of the tax code, issued its report. The committee, headed by prominent Connecticut attorney Roswell Magill, found high marginal tax rates on income to be highly counterproductive:

Income-tax rates have been raised to heights well beyond those imposed in World War I. Moreover, far more citizens are paying far more Federal taxes today than would have been thought possible 10 or 20 years ago. Total taxes, local, State, and Federal, are estimated to amount to the staggering annual total of $50,000,000,000. This means that, if taxes were evenly spread (which, of course, they are not), every workingman would owe the Government $800 per year. At $10 per day, he would have to work for the Government more than 3 months out of the year.

For many members of the income-tax-paying groups, now about 48.5 millions of people, the picture is worse than that. A young man starting out in life with no dependents and an income of $2,000 per year must pay the Federal Government $247 of it. He works for the Government one-eighth of his time. He makes his way up the ladder to $5,000 and marries; his Federal income tax is $694. He is now working for the Government about one-seventh of his time. After he has two children the tax is still $484.

Suppose he is industrious and successful. His salary goes up to $10,-000. The Government takes $1,577 of it. If he can increase his earnings to $25,000 the Government share is $7,163. In other words, although he increased his gross income $15,000 he can keep only $9,414 of it. He works for the Government not one-eighth or one-seventh but nearly one-third of his time.

The man with $50,000 net income pays about half of what he makes to the Government, and the man with $100,000 net income about two-thirds. Moreover, the man with $50,000 net income has only $9,410 more to spend than the man with $25,000 net income. By increasing his income to $100,000 he gets only $11,810 more free money than if he were receiving $50,000.

Our businesses are managed by men with incomes of these amounts. Our country has grown great by the chances we have offered to every country boy and workingman to build himself up by his industry and thrift to as good a position as his capabilities justify. Our great productivity results from the work of men who have made their own ways to the top.

With the present scale of tax rates we have put the brake on men's incentives to a dangerous degree by piling heavier and heavier burdens on them as they try to climb the ladder. Not only is this stultifying to the kind of dynamic long-term growth that has characterized this country in the past, but—to the extent that it impedes production—it is an element in our inflationary pressures today. The builder who doesn't build the extra house, the farmer who doesn't market the extra carload of cattle or grain, the wage earner who doesn't put in the extra day, because doing so would put him in a higher tax bracket and multiply his tax, afford examples of how a tax program adopted to control inflation may, when carried to extremes, tend to defeat its purpose.[9]

On December 18, 1947, Congressman Knutson made his third effort to get an across-the-board tax reduction during the 80th Congress. H.R. 4790 was a compromise tax bill designed to win Democrat votes by limiting the tax rate reduction to 10 percent in the upper brackets and giving more of a reduction to those in lower brackets by increasing the personal exemption.

The bill was reported from the House Ways and Means Committee on January 27, 1948, and passed the House on February 2 by an overwhelming 297 to 120 vote. The Senate Finance Committee reported the House bill on March 16 and it passed the Senate on March 22 by well over a two-thirds majority, 78 to 11. President Truman vetoed this tax cut too, saying that it "would exhibit a reckless disregard for the soundness of our economy and the finances of our Government."[10] The same day Truman vetoed the bill, however, both the House and Senate voted to override the veto by wide margins.

Although Keynesian economists of the time had opposed the tax cut on the grounds that it would be inflationary, this proved not to be the case. In fact, as it turned out, the country was on the brink of a recession. Thus the current judgment of the 1948 tax cut is that it was enacted just in time, making the subsequent recession much milder than it would otherwise have been.[11]

Nevertheless, the Republicans lost control of Congress in the 1948 elections. With the onset of the Korean War in 1950, the post–World War II cuts in individual income tax rates were rescinded, restoring the 1945 rates. The corporation tax rate was increased to 47 percent, and an excess profits tax was reimposed. Again in 1951 taxes were raised again. Individual income tax rates were increased by about 11 percent, the maximum corporate tax rate raised to 52 percent, and the excess profits tax broadened. In addition, excise taxes on liquor, beer, cigarettes, gasoline, autos and other items were raised.

In 1952 voters returned the Republicans to power in Congress and elected Republican Dwight Eisenhower president. The first bill introduced in the new Republican Congress—H.R. 1, introduced by House Ways and Means Committee chairman Daniel Reed—was a bill to cut income tax rates across the board. Republicans in Congress naturally assumed that this time they need have no fear of a presidential veto. But they were wrong to think they would receive support for their efforts from President Eisenhower. On February 17, 1953, the Ways and Means Committee reported H.R. 1, which would have advanced scheduled tax reductions from December 31 to July 1, 1953. That same day, President Eisenhower told a press conference:

> In spite of some things that I have seen in the papers over the last 8 or 9 months, I personally have never promised a reduction in taxes. Never.
>
> What I have said is, reduction of taxes is a very necessary objective of government—that if our form of economy is to endure, we must not forget private incentives and initiative and the production that comes from it. Therefore, the objective of tax reduction is an absolutely essential one, and must be attained in its proper order.
>
> But I believe, and I think this can be demonstrated as fact by economists, both on the basis of history and on their theoretical and abstract reasoning, that until the deficit is eliminated from our budget, there is no hope of keeping our money stable. It is bound to continue to be cheapened, and if it is cheapened, then the necessary expenses of government each year cost more because the money is worth less. Therefore, there is no end to the inflation; there is finally no end to taxation; and the eventual result would, of course, be catastrophe.
>
> So, whether we are ready to face the job this minute or any other time, the fact is there must be balanced budgets before we are again on a safe and sound system in our economy. That means, to my mind, that we cannot afford to reduce taxes, reduce income, until we have in sight a program of expenditures that shows that the factors of income and of outgo will be balanced. Now that is just to my mind sheer necessity.[12]

Eisenhower then put heavy pressure on the Congress not only to stop H.R. 1 from coming up for a vote, but to delay still further scheduled tax reductions. On May 20, 1953, he asked for a six-month extension of the excess profits tax (worth $800 million), repeal of the 5 percent reduction in the normal corporate tax rate due to take place on April 1, 1954 (worth $2 billion per year), and postponement of excise tax reductions scheduled for the same date.

Congressman Reed and other proponents of tax reduction opposed Eisenhower's request and continued to push for H.R. 1, but were frustrated by the House leadership. Although H.R. 1 had been reported by the Ways and Means Committee on February 17, it remained bottled up in the Rules Committee, which refused to send it to the floor for a vote. On April 13, 1953, Reed filed a discharge petition, but was only able to get 115 signatures—far less than the necessary number.

Meanwhile, Reed steadfastly opposed an extension of the excess profits tax. Until June he was able to use his position as chairman of the Ways and Means Committee to block action on the extension request. But the House leadership outmaneuvered him. On June 25 the House Rules Committee approved a resolution which would have allowed a vote on the extension bill, H.R. 5899, without the approval of the Ways and Means Committee. But on June 29 Majority Leader Halleck called off floor action on the resolution. Finally, on July 8, the Ways and Means Committee overrode Reed and voted to report an extension bill. Rushed to the floor under a closed rule— barring any amendments—the excess profits tax extension passed the House on July 10, 1953, with only 38 Republicans opposing. During debate, Republican Cong. Noah Mason of Illinois predicted that extension of the excess profits tax, which was much hated by businessmen, would cost the Republicans 40 borderline seats in the 1954 elections. As it turned out, they only lost 18 seats, but it was enough to give the Democrats control once again.

When the Republicans lost control of Congress in 1954 it ended all chance of reducing the high wartime tax rates. Eisenhower remained committed to a balanced budget and refused to endorse any significant tax cut as long as the budget stayed in deficit. Presumably, it would have been necessary to accumulate a large budget surplus before Eisenhower would have approved a tax cut. But with the world crisis and increasing demands for domestic spending, no such surplus ever occurred, foreclosing the tax-cut option. It took a liberal Democrat, John F. Kennedy, a Democratic Congress, and a group of Keynesian economists to finally get the rates down to a tolerable level.

Notes

1. H. J. Res. 722, 75th Cong., 2nd sess.

2. H. J. Res. 1, 76th Cong., 1st sess.

3. U.S. Congress, Joint Economic Committee, *Constitutional Limitation on Federal Income, Estate, and Gift Tax Rates,* Joint Committee Print, 82nd Cong., 2nd sess. (Washington: U.S. Government Printing Office, 1952). See also *Amendment of the Constitution by the Convention Method Under Article V* (Washington: American Bar Association, 1974).

4. See "Should the Federal Taxing Power Be Limited?" *Congressional Digest* (November 1944), pp. 259–88; "Should a Constitutional Limit Be Placed on Federal Income Tax Rates?" *Modern Industry* (March 15, 1944), pp. 109–19.

5. Ibid.; see also *17 States Say—Repeal the Income Tax Amendment; Limit U.S. Taxes to 25%* (Washington: National Research Institute, 1944); Robert B. Dresser, "The Case for a Constitutional Limitation on Federal Taxes," *Bulletin of the National Tax Association* 29 (March 1944), pp. 170–77.

6. *Congressional Record* (January 9, 1947), pp. A58–61; *Congressional Record* (January 21, 1947), pp. A241–42; Henry Hazlitt, "High Taxes Versus Incentive and Revenue," *Newsweek* (April 7, 1947).

7. *Congressional Record* (June 16, 1947), pp. 7073–74.

8. *Congressional Record* (July 18, 1947), pp. 9303–4.

9. U.S. Congress, House, *Revenue Revision, 1947–48: Reports of the Special Tax Study Committee to the Committee on Ways and Means*, H. Doc. 523, 80th Cong., 2nd sess., 1947, pp. 8–9.

10. *Congressional Record* (April 2, 1948), pp. 4051–53.

11. Herbert Stein, *The Fiscal Revolution in America* (Chicago: University of Chicago Press, 1969), pp. 217–20; Wilfred Lewis, Jr., *Federal Fiscal Policy in the Postwar Recessions* (Washington: The Brookings Institution, 1962), pp. 91–96. On the history of the 1948 tax cut in general, see Susan M. Hartmann, *Truman and the 80th Congress* (Columbia, MO: University of Missouri Press, 1971), pp. 74–78, 95–96, 132–36; Frank Gregorsky, "1948 Tax Cut: Some Lessons for 1979," *Human Events* (April 28, 1979), pp. 13–15.

12. *Public Papers of the Presidents: Dwight Eisenhower, 1953* (Washington: U.S. Government Printing Office, 1960), pp. 47–48.

10

The Kennedy Tax Cuts

W HEN PRESIDENT JOHN F. KENNEDY TOOK OFFICE IN JAN-
uary 1961 the economy was still recovering from a recession.
During the last three quarters of 1960 real gross national product
"grew" at a negative rate and unemployment rose. Although GNP
rebounded in 1961 the unemployment rate remained high, averag-
ing 6.7 percent for the year. By mid-1962, Kennedy and his economic advisors had decided on the need for an across-the-board tax
cut. He first mentioned this possibility at a press conference on June
7, but he did not fully elaborate his plans until later in the year. In
a speech before the Economic Club of New York on December 14,
1962, Kennedy outlined his thinking:

> The most direct and significant kind of Federal action aiding eco-
> nomic growth is to make possible an increase in private consumption
> and investment demand—to cut the fetters which hold back private
> spending. In the past, this could be done in part by the increased use
> of credit and monetary tools—but our balance of payments situation
> today places limits on our use of those tools for expansion. It could also
> be done by increasing Federal expenditures more rapidly than neces-
> sary—but such a course would soon demoralize both the government

and the economy. If government is to retain the confidence of the people, it must not spend a penny more than can be justified on grounds of national need and spent with maximum efficiency.

The final and best means of strengthening demand among consumers and business is to reduce the burden on private income and the deterrents to private initiative which are imposed by our present tax system —and this Administration pledged itself last summer to an across-the-board, top-to-bottom cut in personal and corporate income taxes to be enacted and become effective in 1963.[1]

Kennedy seemed to be saying that although Keynesian economics held that aggregate demand could be just as easily stimulated by increasing government spending or by increasing the quantity of money, because of the U.S. balance of trade deficit and resistence to increased expenditures solely for macroeconomic reasons, a tax cut was the only viable option. A tax cut also had special political appeal. As Walter Heller, chairman of the Council of Economic Advisors, put it, "The use of tax reduction made it possible to induce a coalition of conservative and liberal forces to endorse and work for an expansionary fiscal policy even in the face of an existing deficit, an expanding economy, and rising government expenditures."[2]

Nevertheless, although conservatives generally favored tax reduction, they were even more concerned about deficit spending. Thus Kennedy made clear from the very beginning his belief that high tax rates were reducing revenues and that lower tax rates would increase revenue. Again from his Economic Club of New York speech:

Our true choice is not between tax reduction, on the one hand, and the avoidance of large Federal deficits on the other. It is increasingly clear that no matter what party is in power, so long as our national security needs keep rising, an economy hampered by restrictive tax rates will never produce enough revenue to balance the budget—just as it will never produce enough jobs or enough profits. Surely the lesson of the last decade is that budget deficits are not caused by wild-eyed spenders but by slow economic growth and periodic recessions—and any new recession would break all deficit records. In short, it is a paradoxical truth that tax rates are too high today and tax revenues are too low—and the soundest way to raise revenues in the long run is to cut rates now. . . . I repeat: our practical choice is not between a tax-cut deficit and a budgetary surplus. It is between two kinds of deficits—a chronic deficit of inertia, as the unwanted result of inadequate revenues and a restricted economy—or a temporary deficit of transition, resulting from a tax cut designed to boost the economy, increase tax revenue and achieve a future budget surplus. The first type of deficit is a sign of waste and weakness—the second reflects an investment in the future.[3]

In his Economic Report, issued on January 21, 1963, Kennedy continued his tax cut theme. As he put it, "The main block to full employment is an unrealistically heavy burden of taxation. The time has come to remove it."[4] Three days later, on January 24, Kennedy sent his tax cut message to Congress, outlining the specifics of his proposal:

(1) A reduction in all individual income tax rates. Rates would be lowered from a range of 20 percent at the bottom and 91 percent at the top—rates essentially the same as those during World War II— to 14 percent at the bottom and 65 percent at the top. The reductions would average 20 percent in every bracket and be phased in over three years.

(2) The corporate tax rate would be reduced from 52 percent to 47 percent, with special reductions for small businesses.

In addition, Kennedy proposed numerous tax "reforms" designed to raise $3.4 billion and offset some of the revenue loss from rate reductions.[5]

The House Ways and Means Committee deliberated on the tax bill, H.R. 8363, most of the summer, not completing action until September 13, 1963. Interestingly, Section One of the bill declared that it was the sense of Congress that the tax reduction provided by the bill, through stimulation of the economy, would, after a brief transitional period, raise (rather than lower) revenues. The committee report elaborated this point:

> It is recognized that to many it may seem inconsistent to think of cutting taxes as a way of increasing revenues. Nevertheless, past experience demonstrates that this can happen; in fact, given today's conditions it can be expected to happen. The events of the period 1954–56 demonstrate how this can occur. In 1954 Congress allowed the individual income tax increases imposed during the Korean War to expire, made certain excise tax reductions, allowed the excess profits tax to expire and made certain other tax reductions as well. The total of these reductions amounted to about $7.4 billion. Yet, only 2 years later, in 1956, receipts were $3.2 billion above the level existing before the reductions were made.[6]

The Republicans on the Ways and Means Committee, however, opposed the Kennedy tax reduction as fiscally irresponsible, because taxes were being reduced while expenditures were not. In other words, they believed that it was more important to balance the budget by raising taxes than to suffer a temporary deficit.[7] They seem not to have understood (as many today do not) that tax rates are not fixed; as inflation or real income growth occurs people are pushed up into higher tax brackets. Kennedy and his advisors referred to this as "fiscal drag" which must be offset by "fiscal dividends," such as tax cuts or expanded federal programs.[8]

On the floor of the House, Wilbur Mills, chairman of the Ways and Means Committee, attempted to refute the view that the proposed tax reductions would lead to larger deficits, as charged by the Republicans:

> The idea . . . that tax reductions will provide the rate of growth we need in this country to solve the problems I have listed for you, and that the tax reductions, after a brief transition period, will actually increase revenues above the levels that would have been achieved in the absence of tax reductions are not new or novel ideas as some would suggest. . . . It is on the basis of this type of reasoning, Mr. Chairman, that I have reached the conclusion that this bill will provide a sufficient increase in the gross national product so that the larger revenues derived from this additional income will result in the Federal budget being balanced sooner than would be the case in the absence of this tax cut.
>
> Mr. Chairman, there is no doubt in my mind that this tax reduction bill, in and of itself, can bring about an increase in the gross national product of approximately $50 billion in the next few years. If it does, these lower rates of taxation will bring in at least $12 billion in additional revenue.[9]

Similar statements were made during Senate debate by Senate Majority Leader Mike Mansfield and Senator Russell Long, later to become chairman of the Senate Finance Committee.[10]

What did the tax cut actually do for the economy? Virtually all of the econometric studies of the Kennedy tax cut agree that it was highly stimulative to the economy. Arthur Okun, chairman of the Council of Economic Advisers under President Johnson, has stated that "the tax cuts of 1964 are credited with a $25 billion contribution to our GNP by mid-1965, a $30 billion effect by the end of 1965, and an ultimate $36 billion increment."[11] Similar estimates have been made by Lawrence Klein; Data Resources, Inc.; Wharton Econometric Forecasting Associates, Inc.; and the Congressional Budget Office.[12]

The effects of the tax cut can probably be seen most dramatically, however, in the unemployment rate. As shown in table 1, the unemployment rate for all workers dropped almost by half between 1961 and 1969. In terms of adult black males the drop was phenomenal, going from 11.7 percent unemployment in 1961 to a mere 3.7 per-

TABLE 1

UNEMPLOYMENT RATES (1961–69)

(PERCENT)

YEAR	WHITES				FEMALES OVER 20
	Total	Males	Males Over 20	Females	
1961	6.0	5.7	5.1	6.5	5.7
1962	4.9	4.6	4.0	5.5	4.7
1963	5.0	4.7	3.9	5.8	4.8
1964	4.6	4.1	3.4	5.5	4.6
1965	4.1	3.6	2.9	5.0	4.0
1966	3.3	2.8	2.2	4.3	3.3
1967	3.4	2.7	2.1	4.6	3.8
1968	3.2	2.6	2.0	4.3	3.4
1969	3.1	2.5	1.9	4.2	3.4
BLACKS AND OTHER					
1961	12.4	12.8	11.7	11.9	10.6
1962	10.9	10.9	10.0	11.0	9.6
1963	10.8	10.5	9.2	11.2	9.4
1964	9.6	8.9	7.7	10.7	9.0
1965	8.1	7.4	6.0	9.2	7.5
1966	7.3	6.3	4.9	8.7	6.6
1967	7.4	6.1	4.3	9.1	7.1
1968	6.7	5.6	3.9	8.3	6.3
1969	6.4	5.3	3.7	7.8	5.8

SOURCE: Department of Labor, Bureau of Labor Statistics.

cent in 1969. In no other time in recent history have minorities fared so well.

While there may be little debate about the overall economic effects of the tax cut there is still considerable debate about the revenue impact. Congressman Jack Kemp has argued, based on a study by the Congressional Research Service, that the tax cut increased revenues substantially.[13] The Treasury Department strongly disagrees with this view, citing the closeness of revenue estimates contained in the president's budgets during the early 1960s with actual receipts.[14] This obviously proves nothing, for the estimates themselves took into consideration the feedback effects. Interestingly, Ohio's Democrat Cong. Charles Vanik, who serves on the House Ways and Means Committee recently charged that the revenue was never recovered; that the government is still losing revenue because of the Kennedy tax cut. As he told the House:

> Yes, Government spending and Government waste have contributed to our debt and deficit. However, the major impact on our debt and our deficit has resulted 10 times more from tax cuts which have taken place

TABLE 2

COMPARISON OF ESTIMATED REVENUE LOSS AND ACTUAL REVENUE GAIN, 1965

ADJUSTED GROSS INCOME CLASS ($ IN THOUSANDS)	MILLIONS OF DOLLARS				DIFFERENCE AS % OF ESTIMATE
	Estimated Revenue Loss	Estimated 1965 Tax	Actual 1965 Tax	Difference	
0–5	$1,656	$4,374	$4,337	−$37	−0.8
5–10	3,411	13,213	15,434	+2,221	+16.8
10–15	1,412	6,845	10,711	+3,866	+56.5
15–20	467	2,474	4,188	+1,714	+69.3
20–50	914	5,104	7,440	+2,336	+45.8
50–100	342	2,311	3,654	+1,343	+58.1
100+	204	2,086	3,764	+1,678	+80.4
Total	8,406	36,407	49,530	+13,123	+36.0

SOURCE: Internal Revenue Service, *Statistics of Income—1965, Individual Income Tax Returns*; Joseph A. Pechman, "Evaluation of Recent Tax Legislation: Individual Income Tax Provisions of the Revenue Act of 1964," *The Journal of Finance* (May 1965), p. 268.

over the last 15 years. . . . The 1962 tax cut has had a cumulative cost to the Treasury of $10 billion; the 1964 tax cut, $228 billion; the 1971 tax cut, $73.6 billion; and the 1975 tax cut, $56 billion.[15]

This is clearly absurd. It is just the old trick of holding everything else constant while breaking all the rules. In other words, Vanik is assuming that even without all those tax cuts we still would have gotten the same amount of economic growth. Such an assumption is obviously invalid.

Nevertheless, data does exist to suggest that revenues increased fairly quickly to above where they otherwise would have been. For example, a 1965 study of the tax cut done by Joseph Pechman forecast a revenue loss of $8.4 billion in 1965. But a study of actual receipts showed revenues to be $13.1 billion above the forecast (see table 2).

Another study, by Dr. Michael K. Evans, showed that there was substantial revenue growth in upper tax brackets (see table 3). The percent of total income tax revenues paid by those with incomes over $100,000 increased from 5.1 percent in 1963 to 6.3 percent in 1964, 7.6 percent in 1965, 8.5 percent in 1967, and 9.2 percent in 1968. As Evans notes, these data strongly rebut the view that tax cuts for the wealthy are a "raid on the Treasury."[16]

It is for this reason that many people argue today, as Andrew Mellon did in the 1920s, that the best way to get more tax revenue from the rich is to lower their tax rates. As the *Wall Street Journal* recently put it:

> It stands to reason, and we thoroughly believe, that the U.S. economy would benefit enormously if the rich paid more taxes. We have been arguing this, at least implicitly, for years. What we have not been able to get the politicians to understand, though, is that you can't get rich people to pay more in tax *revenues* by raising their tax *rates*. If you raise the rates, it becomes even more profitable for them to hire lawyers and accountants to find them loopholes, and the cost of this misdirected effort is a dead loss to the economy. Or they stop working entirely and dissipate their capital drinking champagne and sailing yachts, which is also a dead loss to the economy. Either way, they contribute less in tax revenues, and the burden of supporting government expenditures falls on the middle class and the poor.[17]

Lastly, on the question of whether the Kennedy tax cut increased revenues, one should note that in 1977 Walter Heller testified before the Joint Economic Committee that it did. In response to a question

TABLE 3

THE KENNEDY TAX CUT AND THE RICH

YEAR	MAXIMUM TAX RATE	TAXES ($ IN MILLIONS) COLLECTED FROM ADJUSTED GROSS INCOME CLASSES OF:		
		Over $1,000,000	$500,000 to $1,000,000	$100,000 to $500,000
1961	91%	342	297	1,970
1962	91	311	243	1,740
1963	91	326	243	1,890
1964	77	427	306	2,220
1965	70	603	408	2,752
1966	70	590	457	3,176

from Senator Jacob Javits, who cited the same figures used by Congressman Kemp, Heller replied:

> What happened to the tax cut in 1965 is difficult to pin down, but insofar as we are able to isolate it, it did seem to have a tremendously stimulative effect, a multiplied effect on the economy. It was the major factor that led to our running a $3 billion surplus by the middle of 1965 before escalation in Vietnam struck us. It was a $12 billion tax cut which would be about $33 or $34 billion in today's terms, and within one year the revenues into the Federal Treasury were already above what they had been before the tax cut. . . . Did it pay for itself in increased revenues? I think the evidence is very strong that it did.[18]

The reason why the stimulative effects of the Kennedy tax cut did not continue is because the excessive government spending and increases in the quantity of money which took place from 1965 on created inflation that pushed everyone up into higher tax brackets. Considering the magnitude of the tax increase that has taken place over the last 15 years it would seem quite in order to have a reduction in tax rates which would put everyone back into the same relative tax position they were in following the Kennedy tax cut.

As table 4 shows, despite numerous tax cuts since 1964–65, which have tended to keep the aggregate tax burden as a percentage of personal income from rising, the progressivity of the tax code has greatly increased due to inflation.

As one can see, there has been a significant upward movement in the percentage of taxpayers who are affected by high marginal tax rates—the tax on each additional dollar earned. This translates into a massive erosion of incentive, as year after year people keep less and less out of each additional dollar they earn.

It is ironic that the most important reduction in tax rates since the 1920s was accomplished by a liberal Democrat for decidedly liberal reasons—to pump up demand. Yet today liberal Democrats are the

TABLE 4

DISTRIBUTION OF TAXABLE INCOME BY MARGINAL TAX RATE,
FEDERAL INCOME TAX, 1968, 1972, AND 1977

| | SUMMARY TABLE | | |
| | Percent of Taxable Income | | |
MARGINAL RATE	1968	1972	1977
14–19%	72.78	65.45	49.13
22–32	19.90	26.97	39.06
36–48	3.52	4.00	6.65
50–70	4.11	3.60	5.12

DISTRIBUTION BY INDIVIDUAL RATE

| | Percent of Taxable Income at Each Marginal Rate | | |
MARGINAL TAX RATE	1968	1972	1977
14%	13.80	11.20	7.52
15	12.06	9.81	6.61
16	11.35	9.67	6.82
17	9.85	8.34	5.97
19	25.72	26.40	22.21
22	11.12	13.72	15.90
25	4.70	7.79	12.45
28	2.48	3.33	6.39
32	1.60	2.13	4.32
36	1.12	1.35	2.50
39	0.82	0.90	1.49
42	0.65	0.75	1.18
45	0.51	0.60	0.91
48	0.42	0.40	0.57
50	2.25	1.54	2.65
53	0.53	0.38	0.47
55	0.32	0.27	0.34
58	0.21	0.17	0.20
60	0.14	0.14	0.18
62	0.16	0.17	0.22
64	0.10	0.12	0.15
66	0.07	0.09	0.11
68	0.05	0.07	0.09
69	0.03	0.06	0.06
70	0.25	0.59	0.65

SOURCE: Internal Revenue Service *Statistics of Income;* Tax Foundation computations.

major opposition to efforts to duplicate the Kennedy tax cut by Sen. William Roth and Cong. Jack Kemp. Similarly, it is ironic that the major opposition to Kennedy came from conservative Republicans concerned about the deficit. Yet today it is conservative Republicans who wish to emulate Kennedy. In any case, the economic record is clear: the period following enactment of the Kennedy program is the best this country has had in the last quarter century. If we want to restore the economic health we had in the mid-1960s a good way to start would be to put taxpayers back into the same relative tax position they were in in 1965.

Notes

1. *The Commercial and Financial Chronicle* (December 20, 1962).

2. Walter Heller, *New Dimensions of Political Economy* (Cambridge: Harvard University Press, 1967), p. 113.

3. *The Commercial and Financial Chronicle* (December 20, 1962).

4. *Public Papers of the Presidents of the United States, John F. Kennedy, 1963* (Washington: U.S. Government Printing Office, 1964), p. 60.

5. Ibid., pp. 73–92. Subsequently, the Congress only reduced the top marginal rate to 70 percent and the corporate rate to 48 percent.

6. House Report No. 749, 88th Cong., 1st sess., pp. 6–7.

7. Ibid., pp. C5–C28.

8. Heller, *New Dimensions,* p. 65; Herbert Stein, *The Fiscal Revolution in America* (Chicago: University of Chicago Press, 1969), pp. 399–400.

9. *Congressional Record* (September 24, 1963), p. 17907.

10. Idem (January 23, 1964), p. 1002; idem (February 25, 1964), p. 3397.

11. Arthur M. Okun, "Measuring the Impact of the 1964 Tax Reduction," in Walter Heller, ed., *Perspectives on Economic Growth* (New York: Random House, 1968), p. 47.

12. Lawrence R. Klein, "Econometric Analysis of the Tax Cut of 1964," in James Duesenberry, et al., eds., *The Brookings Model: Some Further Results* (Chicago: Rand McNally & Co., 1969), pp. 459–72; Committee on the Budget, U.S. House of Representatives, *Economic Stabilization Policies: The Historical Record, 1962–76* (Washington: U.S. Government Printing Office, 1978), pp. 11–147; Congressional Budget Office, *Understanding Fiscal Policy* (Washington: Congressional Budget Office, April 1978), pp. 23–25.

13. *Congressional Record* (July 14, 1977), pp. H 7156–57 (daily edition).

14. Committee on the Budget, U.S. House of Representatives, *Leading Economist's Views of Kemp-Roth* (Washington: U.S. Government Printing Office, 1978), pp. 94–96.

15. *Congressional Record* (March 15, 1979), p. H 1376 (daily ed.).

16. Michael K. Evans, "Taxes, Inflation and the Rich," *Wall Street Journal* (August 7, 1978).

17. Editorial, "Tax the Rich!" *Wall Street Journal* (March 8, 1977).

18. Statement before the Joint Economic Committee, Congress of the United States, February 7, 1977.

11

The Kemp-Roth Revolution

JACK KEMP WAS FIRST ELECTED TO CONGRESS FROM NEW YORK'S 38th Congressional district—the Buffalo suburbs—in 1970, following a distinguished career as a professional football player, most recently as quarterback for the Buffalo Bills, whom he led to the American Football League championship in 1965. He entered Congress in January 1971, and economic policy quickly became his primary interest. On May 3, 1971, Kemp made his first major House speech on the subject.[1] In 1974 he introduced his first significant piece of economic legislation—the Economic Stability Act of 1974, a companion bill to one introduced in the Senate by Sen. Bill Brock of Tennessee (later chairman of the Republican National Committee), which would limit the power of the Federal Reserve to increase the money supply.[2]

In 1974, Randall Teague joined Kemp's staff as administrative assistant. Teague put together the first of Kemp's major tax bills, the Savings and Investment Act, which would (1) increase the investment tax credit from 7 to 15 percent, (2) increase the asset depreciation range from 20 percent to 40 percent, (3) permit a 12-month write-off for pollution control equipment, (4) permit a capital gains exclusion of the first $1,000, and (5) allow a tax credit for increased saving by individuals.[3] Teague carefully constructed the bill to make it appeal to as broad a cross-section of the business community as possible. Thus, as soon as the bill was introduced, it had a firm base of support. This was important, because Kemp was not a member of the tax-writing Ways and Means Committee. The only way that he could promote a tax cut, therefore, was by getting major business organizations to get behind it.

However, although Kemp and Teague could both see the importance of their approach in terms of increasing capital formation and saving, they lacked a theoretical underpinning. This problem was solved in early 1975 when Kemp hired Dr. Paul Craig Roberts as his staff economist. Roberts, a widely respected scholar, had been interviewing in the Ford White House, but went to work for Kemp when he realized that the size of the White House staff would have precluded his having any real impact on policy. Roberts' early writing anticipated much of what later came to be called supply-side economics.[4] But in 1975 Keynesian demand-management still ruled the day, even among Republicans, and Roberts had considerable difficulty developing support for the Kemp tax cut within the economic community and among White House, Treasury, and congressional staffs.

Roberts soon made contact with Dr. Norman Ture, a Washington economic consultant who developed the first econometric model having supply-side capabilities. Through the Business Roundtable (a big-business lobby), money was obtained so that Ture could do an econometric analysis of the Kemp bill. This analysis was completed in the fall of 1975.[5]

The Ture analysis showed enormous supply response to the Kemp bill, which was renamed the Jobs Creation Act (JCA) and revised to include additional provisions cutting taxes for business. Private GNP would increase $151 billion the first year after passage of the JCA, 7.2 million jobs would be created, and federal tax revenues would show a net *increase* of $5.2 billion.[6] The Ture analysis came under heavy attack from the Treasury Department.[7] Nevertheless, Kemp and Roberts stuck with Ture's numbers, defending them as best they could.[8] Eventually, according to Roberts, the Treasury backed down from its initial position on the supply effects of the JCA and agreed that some supply effects existed—although not as great as Ture's estimates.

Meanwhile, the *Wall Street Journal* was becoming interested in Kemp and his tax-cutting strategy for creating jobs. As early as December 1974 Jude Wanniski, associate editor of the *Journal,* had published an article urging a big tax cut and tight money to fight stagflation, based on the work of Columbia University economist

Robert Mundell.[9] In 1975, the editorial page editor of the *Journal*, Robert Bartley, met Kemp in Washington. He went back to New York and told Wanniski, "You'd better get by and meet this guy Kemp; he's quite a piece of horseflesh."[10]

Wanniski got together with Kemp and there was an immediate meeting of the minds. Wanniski told Kemp about the work of Mundell and a young University of Chicago economist named Arthur Laffer, and about how Kemp's tax-cutting strategy fit in with the historical role of the Republican Party. As Wanniski wrote in an article for the *National Observer*, for the U.S. economy to be strong and growing there must be a division of labor between Democrats and Republicans; each must be a different kind of Santa Claus:

> The Democrats, the party of income redistribution, are best suited for the role of Spending Santa Claus. The Republicans, traditionally the party of income growth, should be the Santa Claus of Tax Reduction. It has been the failure of the GOP to stick to this traditional role that has caused much of the nation's economic misery. . . . It isn't that Republicans don't enjoy cutting taxes. They love it. But there is something in the Republican chemistry that causes the GOP to become hypnotized by the prospect of an imbalanced budget. Static analysis tells them taxes can't be cut or inflation will result. They either argue for a tax hike to dampen inflation when the economy is in a boom or demand spending cuts to balance the budget when the economy is in a recession. Either way, of course, they embrace the role of Scrooge, playing into the hands of the Democrats, who know the first rule of successful politics is Never Shoot Santa Claus. The political tension in the marketplace of ideas must be between tax reduction and spending increases, and as long as Republicans have insisted on balanced budgets, their influence as a party has shriveled, and budgets have been imbalanced.[11]

The *Journal* soon became Kemp's biggest supporter. On August 4, 1976, it ran the first of many editorials extolling the virtues of Kemp's tax-cutting strategy.[12] Two weeks later Wanniski wrote an article for the *Journal* about Kemp's performance at the Republican National Convention in Kansas City. He noted that under pressure from Gerald Ford and the Republican establishment, the platform committee refused to endorse the Jobs Creation Act.[13] On August 17 Kemp took his case to the convention as a whole. In a speech introducing the convention's permanent chairman, Kemp said that the Republican Party should move from defense to offense, that it should stop just opposing what the Democrats are for and offer a vision and strategy of its own. The key to this strategy was offering the people tax cuts as a political counterweight to the Democrats' promises of something-for-nothing via government spending and deficits (see Appendix E).

Shortly after the convention, Craig Roberts left Kemp to become minority staff economist for the House Budget Committee. Roberts did so because he saw that the congressional budget process offered a great opportunity to promote the fiscal ideas that he and Kemp were developing. I replaced Roberts as Kemp's staff economist after the congressman I was working for—Ron Paul of Texas—was defeated in the November election. (Dr. Paul was reelected in 1978.)

When Jimmy Carter became president on January 20, 1977, one of the first things he proposed was a one-shot $50 tax rebate for every American, as a way of pumping up demand in the economy and reducing unemployment. Roberts saw this as a great opportunity for Republicans on the Budget Committee to sharpen the difference between themselves and the Democrats by proposing a permanent tax cut in lieu of the Democrats' $50 give-away. Previously, the Budget Committee Republicans usually just opposed the Democrat proposals without offering an alternative. This time it would be different.

Working closely with Republican Representatives John Rousselot of California and Marjorie Holt of Maryland, Roberts put together a permanent tax cut as a substitute for the Carter proposal and drafted minority views to the committee report justifying a permanent tax cut for the Budget Committee Republicans. These minority views may be the first official expression of support by a Republican body of what was to become supply-side economics.[14]

When the Third Concurrent Resolution on the Budget for Fiscal Year 1977 came to the floor of the House on February 23, 1977, containing budget authority for the $50 rebate, Congressman Rousselot offered a substitute budget resolution providing for a 22 percent reduction in each tax bracket or a five percentage point reduction in each tax rate. The first cut would give more to those in the upper brackets, the second, more to those in the lower brackets. But either way, the aggregate size of the tax cut was the same—$19 billion—and could be accommodated by the Rousselot substitute, which only specified an aggregate dollar figure. (Kemp did not offer the substitute because House rules required that it be offered by a member of the Budget Committee.) Nevertheless, the Democrats attacked it as a give-away to the rich, and the Rousselot substitute was defeated, 148 to 258. But more important, the Republicans stuck together, voting 123 to 10 for the substitute.[15] Less than two weeks later, when the $50 rebate bill came to the floor, Cong. Barber Conable, ranking Republican on the Ways and Means Committee, offered another permanent tax cut substitute to the Democrats' bill.

Although it was defeated, the margin of defeat narrowed considerably, losing by a vote of only 194 to 219, with Republicans voting 140 to 1 for the Conable substitute. This was a significant vote because Conable is an important figure in the House Republican leadership who had previously been skeptical of the Kemp-Rousselot approach. Conable's action, therefore, was a kind of "seal of approval" for the tax-cutting efforts of Kemp, Rousselot and other House Republicans. Thereafter, House Republicans almost always offered substitutes for the Democrats' budget resolutions and voted against such resolutions en bloc.

TABLE 1

HOUSE REPUBLICAN BUDGET/TAX VOTES (1977)

Date	Republican Vote	Nature of Vote
2-23-77	123–10	Rousselot substitute to 3rd budget resolution for FY 1977, providing for a permanent tax cut (defeated, 148–258)
2-23-77	8–122	Final passage of the 3rd budget resolution for FY 1977 (passed, 226–173)
3-8-77	140–1	Conable amendment to H.R. 3477, $50 rebate bill, providing for a permanent tax cut (defeated, 194–219)
4-27-77	126–9	Latta amendment to 1st budget resolution for FY 1978 (defeated, 150–250)
4-27-77	2–135	Final passage of 1st budget resolution for 1978 (defeated, 84–320)
5-5-77	122–7	Conable amendment to 1st budget resolution for FY 1977, providing for budget cuts and a tax cut (defeated, 150–240)
5-5-77	7–121	Final passage of 1st budget resolution for FY 1978 (passed, 213–179)
5-17-77	29–107	Final passage of conference report on 1st budget resolution for FY 1978 (passed, 221–177)
9-8-77	115–21	Rousselot amendment to 2nd budget resolution for FY 1978 providing for a balanced budget (defeated, 169–230)
9-8-77	4–129	Final passage of 2nd budget resolution for FY 1978 (passed, 199–188)
9-15-77	4–132	Final passage of conference report on 2nd budget resolution for FY 1978 (passed, 215–187)

This cohesion among House Republicans on tax and budget matters is extremely important and continues to the present day. In contrast, Senate Republicans have not been especially united on tax cuts or opposition to the Democrats' budget. For example, on September 9, 1977, Senators Roth, Hayakawa, and Hatch offered Senate Republicans three different opportunities to vote on tax and spending cuts, in connection with the second budget resolution for fiscal 1978. First, Sen. William Roth of Delaware offered an across-the-board tax cut amendment. Senate Republicans voted 18 to 10 for the amendment, with 10 not voting. Roth's proposal was defeated, 23 to 63. To Roth's amendment, the Democrats predictably said that taxes could not be cut without corresponding spending cuts. So Sen. S. I. Hayakawa of California offered the same tax cut with specific, corresponding spending cuts. This time the Democrats said that such cuts —which largely involved cutting documented waste out of various programs—could not be tolerated. Republicans voted against the amendment 13 to 15, with 10 not voting (defeated, 16 to 69). Finally, Sen. Orrin Hatch of Utah proposed the same tax cut linked to a 2.5 percent reduction in all programs, including defense, on the theory that there is 2.5 percent waste in any program. Nevertheless, the Hatch amendment was defeated, 19 to 64, with Republicans voting against it, 12 to 15, and 11 not voting.[16] This series of votes proved once and for all that the arguments against tax cuts were phony—the Democrats had no intention of voting for a Republican-sponsored across-the-board tax cut regardless of whether it was linked to spending cuts or not.

Early in 1977, Senator Roth contacted Congressman Kemp about working together on supply-side tax cuts. At this time, Kemp was very interested in the Kennedy tax cuts of 1964–65. On numerous occasions the *Wall Street Journal* had compared Kemp's efforts to Kennedy's in 1962–63.[17] Kemp asked me to draft a bill explicitly duplicating the Kennedy tax cut. After much discussion with Norman Ture, Craig Roberts, Steve Entin of the Joint Economic Committee, and Bruce Thompson of Senator Roth's office, we decided that a reduction in the highest individual income tax rate from 70 percent to 50 percent, and the lowest tax rate from 14 percent to 8 percent, roughly duplicated Kennedy's cut of 91 percent to 70 percent at the top and 20 percent to 14 percent at the bottom. The Kemp-Roth Tax Reduction Act, embodying the Kennedy approach, was introduced on July 14, 1977, with little fanfare.[18]

Throughout the rest of 1977 we struggled mightily to drum up interest in the Kemp-Roth Bill. Kemp's colleagues in the House were receptive, their interest in tax-cutting fueled by debates on the budget resolutions. Kemp soon had virtually every Republican in the House as a cosponsor of the Kemp-Roth bill. It was endorsed by the Republican leadership in the House and later by the Republican National Committee. In short, by the end of 1977 the Kemp-Roth bill was firmly established as official Republican policy.

Meanwhile, an important behind-the-scenes debate was taking

place among congressional staffs about what the real economic effects of such a tax cut would be. Kemp insisted that it would stimulate the economy to such an extent that the government would get all the lost revenue back immediately *à la* the Laffer Curve. Although the Laffer Curve was a convenient tool for explaining the relationship between tax rates and tax revenues and was useful in the early months of the debate, when people began seriously to discuss the idea of a 30 percent tax rate reduction better analyses were needed.

Craig Roberts, who moved from the Budget Committee to Senator Hatch's staff in mid-1977, was instrumental in discrediting the Keynesian econometric models used by the Congressional Budget Office, which were showing that there would be no revenue "reflows" of any kind from passage of Kemp-Roth.[19] Roberts had made an issue of this while still with the House Budget Committee. He thought that it was particularly interesting that two of the three main commercial econometric models used by the CBO (Chase, DRI, and Wharton) all showed that GNP would decline if corporate tax rates were cut.[20] Since this conclusion is clearly nonsensical, it dealt a heavy blow to CBO's credibility. Alice Rivlin, director of the CBO, responded to Roberts' criticism, which had been forwarded to her by Congressman Rousselot, essentially by saying that taxes have no effect on work effort, saving, or investment.[21] Roberts sent copies of this letter to Dr. Michael Evans of Chase Econometrics, Dr. Otto Eckstein of DRI, and Dr. Lawrence Klein of Wharton. Evans wrote back immediately, saying Roberts' criticism of the models was exactly correct. Later, Evans proposed a new econometric model based on supply-side factors.[22] Because of his high standing among professional economists, Evans lent important credibility to the whole tax-cut/supply-side movement in Congress. Eventually, the Senate Finance Committee gave Evans $250,000 to develop a supply-side model for the committee's use. This further enhanced the credibility of the movement, because in effect it meant that the Finance Committee endorsed the supply-side approach and the criticism of existing econometric models, which were being used to beat back tax cutting.

To show how far out of line the CBO was in its denial of revenue reflows from tax cuts, even Bert Lance, President Carter's director of the Office of Management and Budget, said:

> My personal observation is that as you go through the process of permanent tax reduction, that there is an awfully good argument to be made for the fact that the revenues of the Government actually increase at a given time. I think that has been proven in previous circumstances. I have no problem in following that sort of thing.[23]

Building on the base established in 1977, Kemp and Roth moved into 1978 with considerable momentum. Not only did Republicans have the budget process as a forum, but another Carter tax bill as well. Republicans again proposed across-the-board tax cuts in lieu of Carter's so-called tax reforms.[24] Soon, Kemp began receiving national attention for his alternative to the Democrats' program. In April 1978, for example, Kemp was profiled in *Fortune.*[25] Later, came profiles in *Atlantic Monthly, Esquire,* the *Washington Post,* and elsewhere.[26]

The Kemp-Roth effort got a big boost from passage of Proposition 13 in California. Kemp-Roth was widely interpreted as being the national equivalent of Prop. 13.[27] Kemp encouraged such comparisons.[28] As a result of this momentum, the Senate Finance Committee held hearings on the Kemp-Roth bill on July 14, 1978—one year to the day after it was first introduced. Testifying in favor of the bill were Kemp (Roth was a member of the committee), Congressman Dave Stockman of Michigan, the U.S. Chamber of Commerce, Michael Evans of Chase Econometrics, former chairman of the Council of Economic Advisors Alan Greenspan, former chairman of the Council of Economic Advisors Herb Stein, and Dr. Norman Ture, among others. Testifying against were Emil Sunley, deputy assistant secretary of the treasury for tax policy, representing the administration, and Rudy Oswald of the AFL-CIO.[29]

Faced with an outpouring of support for the Kemp-Roth bill—a Roper Poll found people favoring a one-third cut in taxes by a two to one margin—the Democrat establishment counterattacked.[30] The House Ways and Means Committee and the House and Senate Budget Committees all solicited comments from prominent economists regarding the passage of Kemp-Roth. Some of those endorsing Kemp-Roth were Professors Armen Alchian, Robert Clower, and Jack Hershleifer of UCLA; Martin J. Baily of the University of Maryland; Oswald Brownlee of the University of Minnesota; William Fellner of the American Enterprise Institute; Paul McCracken of the University of Michigan; and Alan Meltzer of Carnegie-Mellon University. Those opposed included Professor Gardner Ackley of the University of Michigan, who called Kemp-Roth "the most irresponsible policy proposal . . . that I can recall"; Joseph Pechman of the Brookings Institution; John Kenneth Galbraith of Harvard; and Walter Heller of the University of Minnesota.[31]

Soon the debate was going on full steam in the press. George Will and Milton Friedman argued that an across the board tax cut would help control government spending by denying government revenue.[32] *Business Week* strongly opposed the Kemp-Roth bill, saying that without corresponding spending cuts it would ignite an inflation that would wreck the country.[33] Senator Roth responded by saying that Kemp-Roth was needed just to offset tax increases from social security tax hikes and inflation's effect on pushing people into higher tax brackets. Moreover, he said, *Business Week* ignored the importance of increased saving caused by Kemp-Roth.[34] Irving Kristol argued that Kemp-Roth was a necessary political counterweight to the prevailing trend toward greater spending, "a populist remedy for populist abuses."[35] Walter Heller called it a "free lunch."[36] And the *New Republic* and Hobart Rowan of the *Washington Post* called Kemp-Roth a give-away to the rich.[37] Paul Craig Roberts tried to make clear that the Kemp-Roth tax cut could not be evaluated in Keynesian terms, that it must be analyzed in terms of supply-side economics. Hence, the Keynesian critics of Kemp-Roth—of both liberal and conservative persuasions—were off base in their projections.[38]

Early in 1978 Kemp had brought his bill for a vote in the House as an amendment to the Humphrey-Hawkins bill. It lost by a close vote, 194 to 216. He brought it up again in August as a substitute for the Democrats' tax bill, but it was defeated by a vote of 177 to 240, Republicans voting 140 to 3 for the Kemp substitute. In the Senate, Roth was more successful. He offered Kemp-Roth as a substitute for the Democrats' bill on October 6, 1978, losing 36 to 60. However, a variation of the Kemp-Roth bill, offered by Democratic Sen. Sam Nunn of Georgia, was passed by the Senate, 65 to 20. What Nunn did was to tie the tax cut to spending cuts, making them contingent upon each other. However, although the House voted to instruct its conferees to accept the Nunn amendment to the tax bill, it was dropped in the House-Senate conference and was not enacted.[39]

Conventional wisdom later suggested that the Republicans made an error by making an issue out of tax cuts, because they did not make the big electoral gains that had been expected. However, the *Wall Street Journal* disagreed with this assessment of the alleged failure of Kemp-Roth:

We cannot help but note a stunning inconsistency in one common interpretation of last month's elections. Republicans enjoyed their greatest political success in many years—winning 57% of the Senate races, capturing 6 governorships and gaining 300 seats in state legislatures—all by running on the wrong issue! As one pundit put it, "there is now almost universal agreement" that the Kemp-Roth bill "was a political blunder of the first magnitude". . . . For us, it is a mite too far-fetched that a declining party reversed its political fortunes by making a political blunder. . . . In the days before Kemp-Roth, when politicians attempted to compete politically with spending programs by offering to cut the budget, they were always asked where they proposed to make the cuts. Did they want to cut national defense or aid to education or unemployment compensation or Social Security or agricultural subsidies? Obviously, such a political platform is treacherous, and decades of such "competition" resulted in an enormous growth in government. The Kemp-Roth bill let politicians from both parties get out of this box. The spenders, who never worried about budget deficits when they proposed spending increases, did not declare themselves against tax cuts but against the deficits they said would result if spending were not restrained. In effect, the big spenders were mousetrapped by the Kemp-Roth bill, and the Holt-Nunn version of it swept through the Congress. . . . The Kemp-Roth bill was the most successful bill in recent history in terms of what it prevented from happening.[40]

In the 96th Congress, the Democrats again took up the antideficit call in heading off Kemp-Roth II, a bill which combined tax cuts with a reduction in federal government spending as a percentage of GNP to 18 percent. Thus, the first session of the 96th Congress became dominated by calls for a balanced federal budget. Thirty states petitioned the Congress to call a constitutional convention to draft a balanced budget amendment to the Constitution, and the Senate Judiciary Committee held hearings on the issue.[41]

However, as it became clear that the budget could not be balanced and the nation began to slide into a recession, the balanced budget talk disappeared, and the Senate Judiciary Committee rejected a bipartisan balanced budget amendment.

By the second session in 1980—an election year—with massive tax increases going into effect, there were again serious efforts to enact Kemp-Roth.[42] The most important of these came in mid-June after Ronald Reagan, who strongly supported Kemp-Roth, and Senate Republicans agreed to work together on a tax cut in 1980, to take effect January 1, 1981. Throughout the spring it seemed that President Carter might be moving away from his high-tax policy toward a tax cut.[43] During the week of June 16–20, Sen. Robert Dole of Kansas, ranking Republican on the Senate Finance Committee, organized some meetings with key Republican senators and staff people to plan a tax-cut strategy. Contact was made with Reagan, and a plan was made to hold a joint press conference on June 25, 1980, announcing Reagan's support for a bill containing the first year of Kemp-Roth —a 10 percent income tax rate reduction—and the 10-5-3 depreciation reform bill, which would allow businesses to depreciate all buildings over 10 years, equipment over 5, and vehicles over 3.

The next day, the Senate took up consideration of a bill raising the temporary debt limit. Dole offered the Reagan plan as an amendment, much to the consternation of Democrats. Although the Dole amendment was tabled on virtually a straight party-line vote of 54 to 39 (only Sen. Lowell Weicker of Connecticut deserted the Republicans), the Democrats were forced to respond by offering a tax cut of their own, to be drafted by the Finance Committee no later than September 3, 1980. The effect was clearly a major political victory for Reagan and the Republicans, and showed that the tax revolt was alive and well.[44]

With Kemp being a principal advisor to Reagan (and a widely discussed vice presidential possibility prior to George Bush's selection), Reagan's firm endorsement of Kemp-Roth and supply-side economics, and the endorsement of Kemp-Roth in the Republican Party platform, one would have to say that Kemp and the Republican Party came a long way in four years. When Kemp started his effort, the Republican Party had just lost the White House; Republican members of the House and Senate had no clearly defined economic program, usually just opposing whatever the Democrats were for; and their prospects for ever becoming the majority party seemed hopeless. Kemp gave Republicans something to be *for* and helped the party shed some of its negative image. The effect of his efforts extended to the economics profession as well. Whereas in 1977 supply-side economics did not even exist, by 1980 "supply-side economics" was a buzz-phrase used by many, with the nation's most eminent economists competing with each other to develop supply-side econometric models. These are impressive achievements which surely will keep Kemp and supply-side economics in the forefront of U.S. economic policy for years to come.

Notes

1. *Congressional Record* (May 3, 1971), pp. 13086–89.

2. H. R. 14322, 93rd Cong., 2nd sess.

3. H. R. 16648, 93rd Cong., 2nd sess.

4. Indeed, Roberts may almost be called the father of what was later called the "Laffer Curve." See Paul Craig Roberts, *Alienation and the Soviet Economy* (Albuquerque, NM: University of New Mexico Press, 1971), p. 54; see also idem, "Crucifixion on a Keynesian Cross," *The Occasional Review* (February 1974), pp. 111–120.

5. Ture has a Ph.D. from the University of Chicago. From 1951 to 1955 he worked in the Treasury Department. From 1955 to 1961 he worked for Congressman Wilbur Mills on the staff of the Joint Economic Committee. From 1961 to 1968 Ture was Director of Tax Studies for the prestigious National Bureau of Economic Research. Since then he has been involved in private economic consulting. For background, see Norman B. Ture, "Growth Aspects of Federal Tax Policy," *Journal of Finance* 17 (May 1962),

pp. 269–79; idem, *Tax Policy, Capital Formation and Productivity* (Washington: National Association of Manufacturers, 1973); idem, "Federal Income Tax Rates, Incentives, and Equities," in *Essays on Taxation* (New York: The Tax Foundation, 1974), pp. 20–34; idem, "Tax Reform Should Encourage Saving," *Wall Street Journal* (June 21, 1977).

6. *Reducing Unemployment: The Humphrey-Hawkins and Kemp-McClure Bills* (Washington: American Enterprise Institute, 1976), p. 31.

7. Ibid., pp. 35–36.

8. *Congressional Record* (April 28, 1976), pp. 11638–46.

9. Jude Wanniski, "It's Time to Cut Taxes," *Wall Street Journal* (December 11, 1974).

10. Robert Bartley, "Jack Kemp's Intellectual Blitz," *Wall Street Journal* (November 29, 1979).

11. Jude Wanniski, "Taxes and a Two-Santa Theory," *National Observer* (March 6, 1976); see also idem, "The Mundell-Laffer Hypothesis—A New View of the World Economy," *The Public Interest* (Spring 1975), pp. 31–52.

12. Editorial, "The Kemp Counter," *Wall Street Journal* (August 4, 1976).

13. Jude Wanniski, "Looking for the Right Broom," *Wall Street Journal* (August 17, 1976).

14. House of Representatives Report No. 95–12, 95th Cong., 1st sess. (February 8, 1977), pp. 82–88.

15. *Congressional Record* (February 23, 1977), pp. 5040–56.

16. *Congressional Record* (September 9, 1977), pp. S14491–14510 (daily ed.).

17. Jude Wanniski, "Taxes and the Kennedy Gamble," *Wall Street Journal* (September 23, 1976); Editorial, "JFK Strikes Again," *Wall Street Journal* (February 23, 1977).

18. H.R. 8333, 95th Cong., 1st sess.; S. 1860, 95th Cong., 1st sess.

19. See Congress of the United States, Congressional Budget Office, *Understanding Fiscal Policy* (Washington: U.S. Government Printing Office, 1978); idem, *An Analysis of the Roth-Kemp Tax Cut Proposal* (Washington: U.S. Government Printing Office, 1978).

20. Roberts' memorandum criticizing the models was put into the *Congressional Record* (February 22, 1977), pp. H1308–9 (daily ed.); see also Paul Craig Roberts, "Econometrics and Politics," *National Review* (May 13, 1977), pp. 549–51; idem, "Political Econometrics," *Wall Street Journal* (July 25, 1977).

21. Alice Rivlin to Congressman John Rousselot, March 11, 1977, in possession of author.

22. *Proposal: The Effect of Changes in the Federal Tax Structure on Aggregate Supply and Economic Activity* (Bala Cynwd, PA: Chase Econometric Associates, 1977).

23. Congress of the United States, *The 1977 Economic Report of the President: Hearings Before the Joint Economic Committee,* 95th Cong., 1st sess. (Washington: U.S. Government Printing Office, 1977), pt. 3, p. 478.

24. See Kemp's testimony on the Carter bill in Congress of the United States, *The President's 1978 Tax Reduction and Reform Proposals: Hearings*

Before the Committee on Ways and Means, House of Representatives (Washington: U.S. Government Printing Office, 1978), pt. 9, pp. 5956–79.

25. Irwin Ross, "Jack Kemp Wants to Cut Your Taxes—A Lot," *Fortune* (April 10, 1978).

26. Paul Hendrickson, "Jack Kemp: From 70-Yard Spirals to Laffer Curves," *Washington Post* (June 22, 1978); Norman C. Miller, "Tax-Cut Plan Gives GOP a New Issue—And a New Face: Ex-Quarterback Jack Kemp Stars as Republicans Catch the Proposition-13 Fever," *Wall Street Journal* (September 19, 1978), p. 1; Martin Tolchin, "Jack Kemp's Bootleg Run to the Right," *Esquire* (October 24, 1978), pp. 59–69; Adam Clymer, "Washington: Quarterbacking for the GOP," *Atlantic Monthly* (December 1978), pp. 14–21.

27. Robert J. Samuelson, "Son of Proposition 13?" *National Journal* (June 17, 1978), p. 974.

28. Jack Kemp, "Prop 13 Fever," *New York Daily News* (July 23, 1978).

29. Congress of the United States, *Individual and Business Tax Reduction Proposals: Hearings Before the Subcommittee on Taxation and Debt Management Generally of the Committee on Finance, United States Senate*, 95th Cong., 2nd sess. (Washington: U.S. Government Printing Office, 1978).

30. Congress of the United States, *Roper Opinion Poll: Hearing Before the Committee on Finance, United States Senate*, 95th Cong., 2nd sess. (Washington: U.S. Government Printing Office, 1978), p. 25.

31. Congress of the United States, Committee on Ways and Means, U.S. House of Representatives, *Tax Reductions: Economists' Comments on H.R. 8333 and S. 1860, Bills to Provide for Permanent Tax Rate Reductions for Individuals and Businesses*, Committee Print, 95th Cong., 2nd sess. (Washington: U.S. Government Printing Office 1978); Congress of the United States, Committee on the Budget, House of Representatives and Senate Budget Committee, United States Senate, *Leading Economists' Views of Kemp-Roth*, Joint Committee Print, 95th Cong., 2nd sess. (Washington: U.S. Government Printing Office, 1978).

32. George Will, "Reining In The Federal Spending Urge," *Washington Post* (July 27, 1978); Milton Friedman, "The Kemp-Roth Free Lunch," *Newsweek* (August 7, 1978).

33. Editorial, "Wishing Can't Make It So," *Business Week* (August 7, 1978), p. 94; see also Seymour Zucker, "The Fallacy of Slashing Taxes Without Cutting Spending," *Business Week* (August 7, 1978), pp. 62–64.

34. William V. Roth, "How Tax Cuts Can Pay For Themselves," *Business Week* (September 11, 1978), pp. 14–16.

35. Irving Kristol, "Populist Remedy for Populist Abuses," *Wall Street Journal* (August 10, 1978).

36. Walter Heller, "The Kemp-Roth-Laffer Free Lunch," *Wall Street Journal* (July 12, 1978).

37. Michael Kinsley, "Alms for the Rich," *New Republic* (August 19, 1978), pp. 19–26; Hobart Rowan, "A Tax Bill for the Wealthy," *Washington Post* (September 7, 1978).

38. Paul Craig Roberts, "The Economic Case for Kemp-Roth," *Wall Street Journal* (August 1, 1978).

39. See *Congressional Quarterly Almanac 1978* (Washington: Congressional Quarterly Inc., 1979), pp. 233, 241, 247–48; see also Editorial, "Kemp-What?" *Wall Street Journal* (October 12, 1978).

40. Editorial, "Some Blunder," *Wall Street Journal* (December 4, 1978).

41. See Congress of the United States, *Proposed Constitutional Amendment to Balance the Federal Budget: Hearings Before the Subcommittee on the Constitution of the Committee on the Judiciary, United States Senate,* 96th Cong., 1st sess. (Washington: U.S. Government Printing Office, 1980); *Proposals for a Constitutional Convention to Require a Balanced Federal Budget* (Washington: American Enterprise Institute, 1979); "Congress Seeks Handle on Spending Restraint Issue," *Congressional Quarterly* (February 17, 1979), pp. 267–79; Maxwell Glen, "Balance-the-Budget Juggernaut Heads for Capitol Hill," *National Journal* (February 24, 1979), pp. 306–10; "A Debate Over Fiscal Discipline for Congress," *Business Week* (June 18, 1979), pp. 92–94.

42. On the rising tax burden, see John M. Berry, "Raising Taxes: The Burden Would Climb $40 Billion," *Washington Post* (January 29, 1980); Editorial, "The Planned Tax Increase," *Wall Street Journal* (January 29, 1980).

43. Rowland Evans and Robert Novak, "Tax Cut: No Becomes Yes," *Washington Post* (May 12, 1980); Edward Cowan, "Administration, in Policy Change, Is Discussing Cut in Taxes for 1981," *New York Times* (June 18, 1980).

44. Rowland Evans and Robert Novak, "Republicans Brew a Tax-Cut Elixir," *Washington Post* (June 23, 1980); idem, "The Virtue of Disorganization," *Washington Post* (July 2, 1980); *Congressional Record* (June 26, 1980), pp. S8381–419, S8514–15 (daily ed.); Art Pine, "Jittery Senate Democrats Rush Own Tax Cut," *Washington Post* (June 27, 1980); "A Stampede To Cut Taxes," *Business Week* (July 14, 1980), pp. 36–37.

12

Proposition 13
and Its Aftermath

O N JUNE 6, 1978, THE VOTERS OF CALIFORNIA APPROVED PROP-
osition 13 by a two to one margin. Initiated by tax activists
Howard Jarvis and Paul Gann, Prop. 13 set the maximum rate of
property taxation at 1 percent of cash value based on 1975 assessments. Thereafter, assessments could only increase by 2 percent per
year unless the property were sold or transferred. In addition, state
and local governments were prohibited from raising taxes or imposing new ones (property taxes excluded) without a two-thirds vote of
the people in the jurisdiction affected.

Although simple in its form and content, Prop. 13 was the culmina-
tion of 15 years of effort by California tax protesters to get a cap on
property taxes. It also initiated a wave of tax cut and tax limitation
initiatives throughout the nation, giving rise to predictions that the
long-awaited tax revolt had finally arrived. Unfortunately, the tax
revolt did not spread as its proponents had hoped, although many
states did approve more limited tax and spending limitations. But
Prop. 13 did prove to be highly stimulative to the California economy, contradicting the predictions of those who opposed it.

Jarvis became active in the property tax reform movement in
1962. He subsequently worked for the Watson Initiatives in 1968 and

1972, which were designed to require that property tax revenues be used solely for property-related services, thereby allowing for a reduction in the property tax rate to 1 percent of valuation. Unfortunately, both efforts failed badly. In 1973 Governor Reagan proposed a related tax reform measure, Proposition 1. It set limits on tax rates, required a two-thirds majority vote in the legislature for tax bills, and set a limit on the growth of state spending. In the face of massive opposition from government employees and other special interests, Prop. 1 only got 44 percent of the vote.[1]

Some time after 1973 California housing prices went into a steep upward spiral. Between 1973 and 1977 they were increasing in the Los Angeles and San Francisco metropolitan areas at a rate of 14 to 15 percent a year—far higher than for most of the rest of the country. Since, under California law, property assessments were fixed at 25 percent of market value, whenever a similar home in one's neighborhood was sold, at increasingly higher prices, it required an automatic increase in everyone else's property assessment—and a higher tax bill, despite no change in the tax rate.

A family in Los Angeles that made $18,000 in 1973 could probably have qualified to buy a $47,000 home. The annual property tax bill would have been about $1,000 per year. By 1976, however, typical reassessments would have increased the family's property tax bill by $730. By 1977, its tax bill would have risen by an additional $400 per year—an increase of over 100 percent in four years. Needless to say, the family's income could hardly have increased by an equal amount. Thus many people found themselves slowly being taxed out of their own homes.[2]

By 1977 the effective property tax rate in California had risen to 2.21 percent (tax liability as a percent of the market value of a house), compared to 1.67 percent for the United States as a whole. Similarly, property taxes as a percentage of personal income in 1977 had risen to 6.5 percent—141 percent of the national average and the third heaviest burden of any state in America. Between 1972 and 1977 per capita property tax collections in California increased an average of 6.8 percent per year, increasing the per capita property tax burden from $329 to $458. Per capita property taxes for the U.S. as a whole in 1977 were only $289.[3]

For all these reasons, the political atmosphere was much more hospitable for a property tax initiative in 1977 than it had been earlier. In May, Jarvis missed getting his property tax initiative on the ballot by 1,400 signatures. At this point, in order to broaden his base, which was primarily in Southern California, Jarvis joined with Paul Gann, whose organization, People's Advocate, was strong in Northern California. Together, they managed to collect 1.5 million signatures to get Prop. 13 on the ballot in June 1978.

Almost immediately, the political establishment in California lashed out at the Jarvis-Gann initiative. Former California Gov. Pat Brown said, "If I were a Communist and wanted to destroy this country, I would support the Jarvis amendment." Even the *Los Angeles Times,* which opposed Prop. 13, thought such remarks were "nonsense, and the senior Brown must know it. . . . To suggest that Red legions are waiting to take advantage of it is plain silly."[4]

Nevertheless, others made equally outlandish comments in opposition to Prop. 13. Southern California Edison executive director Howard Allen, president of the Los Angeles Chamber of Commerce, described the Jarvis-Gann amendment as a "fraud on the taxpayer that will cause fiscal chaos, massive unemployment and disruption of the economy." Los Angeles Mayor Tom Bradley said Prop. 13 would "hit the city like a neutron bomb, leaving some city facilities standing virtually empty and human services devastated."[5] Economist Walter Heller, former chairman of President Kennedy's Council of Economic Advisors, wrote in the *Wall Street Journal:*

> Far from being a constructive "experiment in democracy," Proposition 13 would help dig the grave of local self-government. It would rip the heart out of local finances by chopping away nearly 60 percent of the $12 billion of local property taxes. . . . Chaotic cuts in local school, hospital, police and fire services would be the order of the day. Indeed, to meet advance-notice requirements, wholesale dismissal letters have already gone out to a large number of teachers in San Diego, Los Angeles and other communities. The strangled local governments would be forced to turn to the state for fiscal handouts, not just from existing surpluses, but permanently. State sales and income taxes would have to be boosted.[6]

Other economists predicted that passage of Prop. 13 would increase the unemployment rate in California, reduce personal incomes, and reduce California's output of goods and services. UCLA's Graduate School of Management, for example, said that as many as 1.25 million more people might be unemployed by the end of 1980 if Prop. 13 passed than if it failed, virtually doubling the state's unemployment rate.[7]

The proponents of Prop. 13 responded with their own economic experts. Professor Neil Jacoby of UCLA, a former member of President Eisenhower's Council of Economic Advisors, supported Prop. 13 saying:

> Spending by California state and local governments has been booming upward nearly twice as fast as price inflation, with no end in sight.

Public officials continue to vote themselves higher salaries, put more jobholders on government payrolls, and annually boost the pay and pensions of government employees. The millions of taxpayers supporting the Jarvis-Gann Initiative are saying that a brake must be put on public spending. A start must be made in weeding out wasteful and duplicative programs. So far, neither Sacramento nor our city and county officials seem to have understood this message. . . . California's present tax system is archaic. Taxation of land and buildings according to value began when American society was predominantly rural and agricultural. A century ago, property was a fairly good measure both of a person's wealth and the benefits received from government. Today, we live in a highly industrialized and urbanized society in which wealth takes many forms and in which most government spending confers no direct benefits on property.[8]

Contradicting the pessimistic economic forecast of the UCLA econometric model, Dr. Charles Kadlec and Dr. Arthur Laffer did a study of Prop. 13 for the H. C. Wainwright Company of Boston, which showed highly positive effects from its passage. They predicted that over a 10-year period, passage of Prop. 13 would mean an increase of $110 billion in personal income in California, a $4 billion loss in property tax revenue instead of the $7 billion forecast by the state, an $8 billion increase in other state and local tax revenues, and an immigration of capital and labor into California from the rest of the nation. They predicted that the state government would soon be back in surplus and that there was little cause for concern about sharp reductions in spending for essential services.[9]

Prop. 13 also received strong support from Dr. Milton Friedman, Nobel laureate in economics, and the *Wall Street Journal.*[10] Of major California newspapers, only the *Los Angeles Herald Examiner* supported Prop. 13.

Jarvis-Gann was in considerable difficulty coming down the home stretch, under the brutal attack of government officials and even most business leaders, who supposedly are for free enterprise but more often just want government favors for themselves.[11] As Jude Wanniski reported, "Indeed, the entire Establishment is arrayed against Jarvis, including the Business Roundtable and the 'conservative' newspapers of San Diego. Those in control fear their system is threatened when people take matters into their own hands."[12] Thus, as election day neared, many informed political observers were predicting defeat for Jarvis-Gann. As Richard Reeves put it, "Nothing can stand up to the political juggernaut of the government-union-business-newspaper complex and the threat of chaos if Jarvis wins."[13]

But the day was saved when the Los Angeles County tax assessor decided to send out the fiscal year 1979 assessments in May, rather than waiting until after the vote. The total value of property tax rolls had increased 17.5 percent—a remarkable figure considering that only one third of the properties had been reassessed. Assessment increases of 50 to 100 percent on single-family homes were not uncommon. As the news of the new Los Angeles County assessments spread across the state, the tide turned and Prop. 13 coasted to a comfortable victory, with 65 percent of the vote.

Suddenly, people like Gov. Jerry Brown were acting as though they had secretly been for Prop. 13 all the time. As *Fortune* magazine observed, "After opposing 13 during the campaign as a 'rip-off' and a potential 'disaster,' Governor Brown did an instant flip-flop after the proposition passed by a two-to-one margin, and declared his support for a smaller public sector."[14] On election night Brown said, "The people have spoken very clearly. There will be no new state taxes, and we must put a lid on government spending."[15]

The Jarvis-Gann Amendment (now Article XIII A of the California state constitution) went into effect on July 1, 1978. In the three weeks between passage and implementation state and local government officials scrambled to deal with the potential loss of $7 billion in property tax revenue. The state government had a $3.9 billion accumulated surplus on hand to help local governments through the fiscal crunch. It quickly disbursed much of it in a hastily passed bailout. In total the state handed out $4.3 billion. When the dust had settled, California's localities ended up with about 10 percent less revenue than they would have had if Prop. 13 had not passed. Specifically, California's cities lost about 10.5 percent; schools, 10.5 percent; counties, 9.8 percent; and special districts, 6 percent.[16] Compared to fiscal year 1978, aggregate state and local government revenues were only 0.7 percent lower in fiscal 1979.[17]

Virtually no cuts were enacted in "essential" programs, such as welfare, health, public safety, or education (in terms of regular instructional programs). Most of the cutbacks were in the areas of parks and recreation, libraries, cultural activities, summer school and adult education. Even so, the cuts were moderate, rather than being wholesale eliminations. In terms of personnel, only 26,500 public employees statewide lost their jobs as a result of Prop. 13, with 9,500 subsequently rehired. Another 90,000 employees were lost through attrition. Although large, these cuts stand in stark contrast to the pre-election predictions of 300,000 to 450,000 public employee layoffs.[18]

Thus the U.S. General Accounting Office concluded that the major effect of Prop. 13 its first year was to slow the rate of growth of California's local government sector.[19] Similarly, the Federal Reserve Bank of San Francisco has said, "The irony of Proposition 13

—perhaps its redeeming feature—is that it neither drastically reduced the size of government (as desired by many proponents) nor led to statewide economic chaos (as predicted by staunch opponents)."[20] As a result, Howard Allen of Southern California Edison recently said, "If I knew then what I know now, I don't think I would have been one of the leaders in opposition to Proposition 13."[21]

Economically, there is no question that Prop. 13 exerted a highly positive effect on the California economy. Total state employment increased by 760,000 from June 1978 through October 1979. State personal income increased by $35 billion from the second quarter of 1978 to the third quarter of 1979, an increase of 18 percent, compared to 15 percent for the U.S. as a whole. Retail sales in California increased 17.5 percent from the second quarter of 1978 to the second quarter of 1979, compared to about 12 percent nationally. "The numbers so far sure look good," Arthur Laffer recently said. "It's all turning out at least as well as I had expected."[22] The effect would probably have been even greater except for the fact that Prop. 13 simultaneously increased federal income taxes for Californians by about $1.5 billion in fiscal years 1979 and 1980, because lower property taxes meant lower property tax deductions on federal tax returns.[23]

Indeed, the economy reacted so strongly to Prop. 13 that it proved to be almost a textbook example of the Laffer Curve in action. State tax revenues increased so much from the greater level of economic activity that, despite the addition of $4.3 billion in bailout expenditures, the state surplus only declined by $1.2 billion in fiscal 1979. In fiscal 1980 revenue growth will cause the surplus to decline a mere $700 million, despite another $4.9 billion in bailout expenditures. The United States Bureau of Economic Analysis predicts that in fiscal 1981 the state should be able to absorb the bailout expenditures from current revenues, with no reduction in the state surplus, and that by fiscal 1982 the surplus should begin to grow again.[24]

Of course, this estimate does not take into account the possible effects of Proposition 4, initiated by Prop. 13 coauthor Paul Gann and approved on November 6, 1979. Prop. 4 was designed to "finish the job" started by Prop. 13 by putting a cap on state and local government expenditures. It also closed loopholes through which state and local government officials attempted to get around Prop. 13's limit on taxes by imposing numerous "user fees" for previously tax-paid services. Although there is a case to be made for user fees in lieu of taxes, such fees had come to be so pervasive that they threatened to undo the good of Prop. 13.[25] "Politicians always seem to find a way to circumvent tax reductions," said John Hay, executive vice-president of the California Chamber of Commerce. "Since Prop. 13 was

TABLE 1

State of California General Fund Summary ($ in billions)

	Fiscal Year		
	Actual		Estimate
	1978	1979	1980
Accumulated surplus, beginning of year	1.8	3.9	2.7
Receipts	13.7	15.2	19.3
Expenditures	11.6	16.3	20.0
Regular	11.6	12.0	15.1
Proposition 13 bail-out	—	4.3	4.9
Education	—	2.5	3.6
Health and welfare	—	1.0	1.3
Block assistance	—	.9	—
Accumulated surplus, end of year	3.9	2.7	2.0

NOTE: Reported expenditures for fiscal year 1979 are $17.1 billion, and the reported surplus (for the end of 1979 and the beginning of 1980) is $1.9 billion. A $0.8 billion loan fund, part of the bail-out, was removed from the general fund during fiscal year 1979. As of June 30, 1979, it had not been restored to the general fund. In this table, the loans have been removed from expenditures and added to the surplus at the end of the year.

SOURCE: U.S. Department of Commerce, Bureau of Economic Analysis.

passed, we have found all kinds of newly created fees, assessments and hoked-up taxes to the point where we've wound up with the same level of government as we had before."[26] Prop. 4 carried all 58 counties in the state and won 75 percent of the vote.[27]

On June 3, 1980, California voters had another opportunity to vote on across-the-board tax reduction. They voted on Proposition 9, initiated by Howard Jarvis, to cut all personal income tax rates in half and index them thereafter to the rate of inflation. Thus the highest personal income tax rate would fall from 11 percent to 5.5 percent and the lowest rate from 1 percent to 0.5 percent. Once again, state officials and other beneficiaries of government largess voiced predictions of gloom and doom. John F. Henning, executive secretary of the California Labor Federation, forecast nothing short of "absolute disaster for governmental service" under the tax cut. Indeed, it was called "Jaws II" by its foes. Although the state forecast a loss of $5 billion in revenue, Howard Jarvis predicted much less—perhaps $3.2 billion the first year—because "feedback" from increased economic growth will increase revenues. And Laffer said that he expected the positive effects of Prop. 9 to be even greater than those for Prop. 13, because reducing income tax rates directly affects incentive, while reducing property tax rates only creates a wealth effect, giving people more money without encouraging them to work, invest, or produce more.[28] Thus one might say that Prop. 13 was not a true supply-side tax cut, but had its major effect in altering the perception of the economic climate in California. As Irving Kristol put it, the most important effect of Prop. 13 is

> a change in the climate of opinion affecting the issue of economic growth. One has to put the matter in so qualified a way because an awful lot of important people in California who don't like the idea of economic growth believe that Californians would all be happier if only existing "affluence" were more equally shared. . . . The enemies of growth—in high office and out—are still well entrenched in California. They will work very hard to nullify the intent of Proposition 13, since they see larger political and ideological implications in it, with further efforts to restrict the size of the public sector along with further efforts to encourage private savings and investment. I think they are right about this, if about nothing else. That is indeed what Proposition 13 was ultimately about: economic growth in a free society vs. the allocation of income and wealth by government in a stagnant economy.[29]

Such changes in perception are extremely important economically. A recent study by the Harris Bank of Chicago, for example, shows that it is changes in tax burden which are more critical to economic growth, rather than the level of the tax burden itself. Thus, a high-tax state like California, whose tax burden is declining, will fare better than a low-tax state where the burden is rising.[30] Prop. 13, therefore, had its most important impact on the perception that California had changed from a state where the business climate was inhospitable to one which is highly attractive to business expansion and investment.[31]

Following the success of Jarvis-Gann, many states were faced with Prop. 13–style tax or spending limitation initiatives. In November 1978, 13 states had such measures on the ballot. Ten states adopted their proposed tax or spending initiatives, while three—Colorado, Oregon, and Nebraska—defeated theirs.[32] However, within the next year seven states adopted tax and spending limitations by legislative action, including Oregon and Nebraska. At least 25 states enacted some kind of property tax relief, while many indexed tax rates.[33] While it is impossible to say how much influence Prop. 13 had on these actions, it is significant that state and local tax receipts as a percentage of personal income declined from 19.3 percent in 1978 to 18.4 percent in 1979.

In conclusion, there can be little doubt that Prop. 13 initiated a fiscal revolution in America. While it did not lead to a full-scale tax revolt, as some had believed it would, it did give an enormous boost to the tax limitation movement throughout America which will probably continue for years. Perhaps its most long-term effect will have been to show that radical tax reduction need not cripple government

TABLE 2
State & Local Government Receipts ($ in billions)

Year	Tax Receipts	Personal Income	Percent
1977	298.8	1,531.6	19.5
1978	331.0	1,717.4	19.3
1979	354.4*	1,923.1*	18.4

*Partial figures.
SOURCE: National Income and Product Accounts.

services and that spending can be controlled from the revenue side. As Howard Jarvis says, the way to slow the growth of government is to deny it the money.[34]

Unfortunately, we do not yet know what the full economic impact of Prop. 13 will be. Shortly after its passage dozens of organizations, individuals, and foundations announced that major studies of Prop. 13 would be initiated. Yet, as of this writing, none has appeared. It seems that most of these studies were proposed by liberal groups opposed to Prop. 13, who hoped to document the collapse of the California economy. When the collapse did not take place, it appears they lost interest in the subject, not wishing to give ammunition to the other side.

Nevertheless, the positive effects of Prop. 13 are quite evident without the necessity of thorough economic analysis. It is obvious that the California economy is booming and that there has been no significant decline in government services. Although Prop. 9 went down to defeat on June 3, 1980, it does not appear to have been because of dissatisfaction with the results of Prop. 13, but because the selling job for Prop. 9 was inadequate and the opposition more sophisticated. Howard Jarvis has vowed to press onward. Considering that Prop. 13 failed three times before it finally passed, it would be unwise to dismiss his efforts. The success of Prop. 13 is still a powerful selling point.

Notes

1. Howard Jarvis, *I'm Mad As Hell* (New York: Times Books, 1979), pp. 33–39; Frank Levy, "On Understanding Proposition 13," *The Public Interest* (Summer 1979), pp. 68–72.

2. Levy, "Understanding Prop. 13," pp. 73–74.

3. Advisory Commission on Intergovernmental Relations, *Significant Features of Fiscal Federalism, 1978–79 Edition* (Washington: U.S. Government Printing Office, 1979), pp. 56, 61, 62.

4. Jarvis, *Mad As Hell*, pp. 59–60.

5. Lou Cannon, "In California, a Ceiling Is Proposed," *Washington Post* (April 17, 1978).

6. Walter Heller, " 'Meat-Axe Radicalism' in California," *Wall Street Journal* (June 5, 1978).

7. John Quirt, "Aftershocks from the Great California Taxquake," *Fortune* (September 25, 1978), pp. 76–77; Congressional Budget Office, *Proposition 13: Its Impact on the Nation's Economy, Federal Revenues, and Federal Expenditures* (Washington: Congressional Budget Office, July 1978), pp. 8–9.

8. Remarks at the UCLA Business Forecast Conference, March 16, 1978. See also Dr. Jacoby's statement before the Subcommittee on the City of the Committee on Banking, Finance and Urban Affairs, U.S. House of Representatives, July 25, 1978; idem, "A Case For Legal Limits on Government Spending," *Taxing and Spending* (October-November 1978), pp. 28–31.

9. Charles W. Kadlec and Arthur B. Laffer, *The Jarvis-Gann Tax Cut Proposal: An Application of the Laffer Curve* (Boston: H. C. Wainwright & Co., 1978).

10. Milton Friedman, "The Message From California," *Newsweek* (June 19, 1978); Editorial, "The Jarvis-Gann Proposition," *Wall Street Journal* (April 25, 1978); idem, "The June 6 Revolt," *Wall Street Journal* (June 8, 1978).

11. Thomas Mullaney, "Business and the Tax Revolt in California," *New York Times* (April 14, 1978); see also Tom Hazlett, "The Scare Tactics That Backfired," *National Review* (July 21, 1978), pp. 887, 912; Milton Friedman, "Needed: An Investigative Report on Investigative Reporting," *Taxing and Spending* (October-November 1978), p. 15.

12. Jude Wanniski, "The California Tax Revolt," *Wall Street Journal* (May 24, 1978).

13. Richard Reeves, "Will California Send Them a Message on Cutting Taxes?" *Esquire* (May 23, 1978), p. 33.

14. Quirt, "Aftershocks," p. 75.

15. *U.S. News & World Report* (June 19, 1978), p. 17.

16. "States Tackle Tough Fiscal Issues," *Intergovernmental Perspective* (Winter 1979), p. 7.

17. Comptroller General of the United States, *Proposition 13—How California Governments Coped With a $6 Billion Revenue Loss* (Washington: General Accounting Office, 1979), p. 9.

18. Ibid., pp. 19–31; see also Wallace Turner, "Little Impact Seen in Coast Tax Slash," *New York Times* (February 11, 1979); Robert Lindsey, "Dire Predictions on Proposition 13 Have Not Materialized," *New York Times* (March 7, 1979); Lou Cannon and Katharine MacDonald, "Prop. 13 Didn't Sink California After All," *Washington Post* (June 3, 1979).

19. Comptroller General, *Proposition 13*, p. 18.

20. Federal Reserve Bank of San Francisco *Weekly Letter* (September 28, 1979).

21. "California Business: Thriving on 13," *Dun's Review* (August 1979), p. 47.

22. Arthur Laffer, *California Tax Update* (Rolling Hills Estates, CA:

A.B. Laffer Associates, March 28, 1980); John Quirt, "Proposition 13's Stellar First Year," *Fortune* (July 2, 1979), p. 47; "Proposition 13, California's Lucky Number," *The Economist* (January 5, 1980), pp. 18–23.

23. CBO, *Prop. 13*, pp. 11–14.

24. David J. Levin, "Proposition 13: One Year Later," *Survey of Current Business* (November 1979), p. 17.

25. Selma J. Mushkin, "The Case For User Fees," *Taxing and Spending* (April 1979), pp. 16–19.

26. Wallace Turner, "New Campaign Is Begun To Trim California Taxes," *New York Times* (April 1, 1979).

27. Lou Cannon, "California Voters Remain Fiscally Conservative," *Washington Post* (November 8, 1979); see also Editorial, "Pinning Them Down," *Wall Street Journal* (November 5, 1979); Marilyn Chase, "Californians Expected to Vote Tax Curb; It Could Bring Similar Moves Elsewhere," *Wall Street Journal* (October 12, 1979).

28. Kathryn Christensen, "California Voters Appear Sure to Approve Proposition to Slash Personal Income Tax," *Wall Street Journal* (January 30, 1980); Rowland Evans and Robert Novak, "On the California Ballot, 'Jaws II,' " *Washington Post* (March 26, 1980); Laffer, *California Tax Update*.

29. Irving Kristol, "The Meaning of Proposition 13," *Wall Street Journal* (June 28, 1978); see also John Davenport, "Voting For Capitalism," *Fortune* (July 17, 1978), pp. 46–47.

30. Robert J. Genetski and Young D. Chin, *The Impact of State and Local Taxes on Economic Growth* (Chicago: Harris Economic Research Office Service, November 3, 1978).

31. "California Business: Thriving on 13," p. 47.

32. "States Tackle Tough Fiscal Issues," p. 10; Donna Rosene Leff, "States Follow California's Lead," *Taxing and Spending* (October-November 1978), pp. 26–27; Robert Lindsey, "Coast Vote Spurs States to Try to Limit Taxes," *New York Times* (June 26, 1978).

33. "Numerous States Reduce Taxes, Enact Spending, Tax Limits," *Intergovernmental Perspective* (Summer 1979), p. 4; Lawrence Ingrassia and Laurel Leff, "Several States Adjust Income-Tax Brackets To Discount Inflation," *Wall Street Journal* (March 4, 1980); John Herbers, "Nationwide Revolt on Taxes Showing No Sign of Abating," *New York Times* (August 5, 1979).

34. See Anthony H. Pascal, et al., *Fiscal Containment of Local and State Government* (Santa Monica, CA: The Rand Corporation, September 1979).

13

The Capital Gains Tax Cut

A CAPITAL GAIN (OR LOSS) IS THE DIFFERENCE BETWEEN THE purchase price of an asset and its sale price. Until 1969, the maximum tax rate on long-term capital gains was 25 percent. In 1969, however, Congress increased the tax on capital gains, raising the maximum tax rate to almost 50 percent (including the minimum tax). The effect of this tax change was immediate and dramatic. There was a sharp drop in initial common stock public offerings and equity capital raised by companies having net worths under $5 million (see table 1). There was also a drop in capital gains tax revenue to the government. In 1968 the federal government raised $7.2 billion from capital gains taxes on individuals. This fell to $5.9 billion in 1969, as Congress passed the Tax Reform Act of 1969 containing the higher capital gains taxes, and fell to $3.6 billion in 1970, the first year the higher tax rates were in effect. Capital gains tax revenues have never recovered. From 1965 to 1969 capital gains taxes constituted an average of 3.6 percent of individual income tax revenue to the government. From 1970 to 1975, after the increase in rates, capital gains tax revenues have averaged only 2.5 percent of revenues.

By 1978 the negative effects of the 1969 changes in the capital

TABLE 1

Effects of Raising Capital Gains Taxes

YEAR	INITIAL COMMON STOCK OFFERINGS		EQUITY CAPITAL RAISED BY SMALL COMPANIES*	
	Share Value ($ in millions)	Number of Issues	Share Value ($ in millions)	Number of Issues
1969	3,545	1,298	1,366.9	698
1970	1,451	566	375.0	198
1971	1,917	446	550.9	248
1972	3,301	646	896.0	409
1973	1,872	177	159.7	69
1974	117	55	16.1	9
1975	236	25	16.2	4
1976	271	45	144.8	29
1977	276	49	42.6	13
1978†	54	18	1.2	1

*Companies having a net worth of under $5 million.
†First half.
SOURCE: Securities Industry Association.

gains tax had motivated many people to begin working for changes in the law.[1] However, most of the discussion was highly abstract. It was not until Dr. Edwin Zschau of the American Electronics Association presented Congress with hard data on what the capital gains tax was doing to his industry that legislators began to listen.[2]

In testimony before the Senate Select Committee on Small Business on February 8, Zschau said that companies in his association founded during 1971–75 were able to raise only one half as much equity capital on the average as those firms founded during 1966–70. By 1970, the 135 firms founded in the 1966–70 period had raised an average of $1,039,000 in risk capital, while by 1975 the 77 companies founded during 1971–75 had raised only $522,000 per firm. This was even less than the capital companies founded during 1961–65 had been able to raise. The result was that the newer firms were undercapitalized, became overburdened with debt, and became vulnerable to bankruptcy.[3]

Shortly thereafter, the Securities Industry Association released a study by Data Resources, Inc. (DRI), which showed a significant economic impact could be realized by elimination of capital gains taxes. According to DRI, an elimination of capital gains taxes would, over five years, increase GNP by $199 billion, increase business investment by $81 billion, create 3.1 million man-years of employment, and *increase* federal tax revenues by $38 billion. Conversely, adopting President Carter's proposal to treat all capital gains as ordinary income would *reduce* GNP by $115 billion, *reduce* business investment by $73 billion, *reduce* employment by 1.5 million man-years, and *reduce* federal tax revenues by $25 billion, again over five years.[4]

The next important development was publication of a study by Profs. Martin Feldstein and Joel Slemrod of Harvard University which showed that inflation was seriously distorting stock values, causing people to pay enormous taxes on illusory gains. According to Feldstein and Slemrod, in 1973 individuals paid nearly $500 million in extra taxes on corporate stock capital gains because of inflation. In 1973, individuals paid capital gains tax on more than $4.5 billion of nominal capital gains on corporate stock. If the costs of these shares are adjusted for the increases in the consumer price level since they were purchased, the $4.5 billion nominal gain becomes a capital loss of nearly $1 billion. Thus there was no real gain upon which to pay tax.[5]

As a result of these revelations, Republican Cong. William Steiger of Wisconsin introduced a bill on April 13, 1978, essentially to restore the pre-1969 treatment of capital gains.[6] Support for the Steiger bill developed so quickly it caught the administration and the Democrat leadership by surprise. When it became clear that Steiger had close to majority support for his proposal within the House Ways and Means Committee, its chairman, Congressman Al Ullman, was forced to postpone consideration of the president's tax package for a couple of weeks while things were sorted out.[7]

Unfortunately for Steiger's opponents, the evidence in favor of a capital gains tax cut continued to mount. On April 17, Chase Econometric Associates issued a study showing economic effects similar to those shown by DRI's. According to Chase, passage of the Steiger proposal would create 440,000 new jobs by 1985, raise business expenditures for new plants and equipment by a full percentage point per year, and *increase* federal revenues. The federal deficit would be $16 billion less by 1985 with the bill than without.[8]

Shortly afterwards, Merrill Lynch Economics issued another study of the Steiger bill. The Merrill Lynch study showed that, if the tax cut were effective by the third quarter of 1978, it would increase the growth of GNP from 3.3 percent to 3.5 percent by 1980, reduce the unemployment rate from 5.7 percent to 5.5 percent by 1980, and reduce the federal deficit by $2.3 billion in 1980. Merrill Lynch said that these positive effects resulted from the following factors:

1. A reduced capital gains tax will tend to increase current market prices for capital assets.
2. In particular, the prices of financial assets—especially equity—will tend to increase.

3. Increased equity and bond values reduce the cost of capital to the corporation.

4. This reduction in capital costs stimulates investment in plant and equipment.

5. The increased plant and equipment spending stimulates the economy leading to enhanced real GNP growth, more jobs, higher tax revenues via ordinary income and profits taxes, and greater productivity.

6. The decline in the Federal deficit results from increased tax revenues and reduced transfer payments—both effects arising from the stimulated economy.

7. The decline in the capital gains tax rate should be essentially offset, in revenue terms, by the expected increased capital gains realizations accompanying a stronger equities market.[9]

Needless to say, the Steiger bill and these econometric analyses came under heavy attack from the administration and liberals. Treasury Secretary Blumenthal said the bill should be renamed the "Millionaire's Relief Act of 1978," because Treasury's analysis had shown that four-fifths of the benefits would go to those with incomes over $100,000 per year.[10] The *New York Times* called it a "Wall Street version of the free lunch." It suggested that a better way to promote capital formation would be to increase the investment tax credit.[11]

By the middle of the summer, the capital gains tax cut was becoming an issue in congressional races, fueled by the middle class tax revolt which supported Proposition 13 in California.[12] A Harris Survey showed that 66 percent of Americans favored the Steiger bill.[13]

In June, Martin Feldstein produced another study of the capital gains tax, with special reference to the lock-in effect. What Feldstein found was that many people with capital gains were forced to hold on to their assets longer than they wished to, because they did not want to realize their gains and pay tax at the higher rates. The result was a less efficient market and fewer sales of assets, thereby reducing the revenue the government would get at a lower tax rate. Feldstein concluded "that reducing the tax on capital gains would not only encourage a more active market in corporate stock but would also increase tax revenues."[14]

When the vote on reducing capital gains taxes came in the Ways and Means Committee late in July 1978 it won easily. The final vote on the tax package, virtually stripped of all the "reforms" desired by President Carter and containing many other elements favorable to investment, such as the indexing of capital gains to inflation, came on July 27. It was approved 25 to 12. The full House approved the tax bill exactly as it emerged from committee on August 10, by a vote of 362 to 49. The Senate made numerous changes in the bill, but on

October 10 approved a bill even more favorable to capital gains than the House bill, by a vote of 86 to 4. In conference, the House and Senate agreed to a compromise capital gains provision which basically split the difference between the two versions.[15]

In the bill signed into law by the president, individuals were allowed to exclude 60 percent of long-term capital gains from tax. This reduced the maximum tax rate on capital gains from about 49 percent to 28 percent. The Joint Committee on Taxation's explanation of why this change was made is instructive:

> The Congress believed that the present level of taxes applicable to capital gains has contributed both to a slower rate of economic growth than that which otherwise might have been anticipated, and also to the realization of fewer gains than would have been realized if the tax rates had been lower. In some instances, the taxes applicable to capital gains effectively may have locked some taxpayers into their existing investments. Moreover, the Congress believed that the present level of capital gains taxes had contributed to the shortage of investment funds needed for capital formation purposes generally, and especially for new and small businesses. As a result, the Congress believed that changes were required in the tax provisions applicable to capital gains.
>
> The Congress believed that lower capital gains taxes will markedly increase sales of appreciated assets, which will offset much of the revenue loss from the tax cut, and potentially lead to an actual increase in revenues. In addition, the improved mobility of capital will stimulate investment, thereby generating more economic activity and more tax revenue.[16]

Did the capital gains tax cut have the effects predicted by its proponents? The available evidence seems strongly to suggest that it did, although liberals are still fighting the facts.[17] In December 1979 the *New York Times* said:

> Remember all the clamor for a cut in the capital gains tax last year? Its sponsors insisted a reduction would send investors rushing to risk their money on new business plant and equipment, stimulate the stock market and promote economic recovery. . . . Well, it didn't work. The proportion of America's resources devoted to investment has not increased during 1979, and it is expected to decline in the coming recession. Contrary to the predictions about venture capital flowing to new and riskier businesses, there has been no increase in the number of newly incorporated firms. No one knows whether extra capital is flowing into small businesses, but as yet there is no sign that these businesses are expanding plant and equipment. There has been little real economic growth in 1979 and the predictions for 1980 are for recession and decline.[18]

The *Times* had things so wrong about the tax cut that W. R. Grace and Company took a full-page advertisement in that paper a few days later to offer a point-by-point rebuttal to the editorial. The Grace ad pointed out that sponsors of the tax cut were seeking investment incentives, not a rush to the stock market. Nevertheless, real GNP was up by 2.3 percent in 1979—contrary to predictions made in 1978—and business investment was up 7.3 percent in real terms, with its proportion to GNP rising from 10 percent to 10.4 percent. Moreover, new incorporations were up 11.3 percent in the previous 12 months.[19]

Since then, further evidence has become available indicating the positive effects of the tax cut. In particular, venture capital investments increased dramatically following the tax cut. Such investments are typically not made for income but to get capital gains which may return 50 percent or more on an investment. Stanley Pratt, editor of the *Venture Capital Journal,* estimates that private partnership venture capital investments amounted to approximately $22.5 million in 1974. No private funds were committed to venture capital enterprises during 1975. In 1976, such funds amounted to $25.7 million, and in 1977 just $20.2 million was raised. In 1978, private partnership venture capital investments rose dramatically, to $215 million. The bulk of this increase took place in the fourth quarter of 1978, after congressional passage of the capital gains tax cut became imminent. It is believed that the amount of funds allocated to venture capital investments will reach close to $300 million in 1979.[20]

In addition, there have been significant increases in initial public offerings of common stock and equity capital raised by companies with a net worth of less than $5 million. As table 1 shows, initial public offerings of common stock steadily declined from 1972 onward, with only 18 issues having a share value of $54 million being offered in the first half of 1978. In the second half of 1978, however, 40 issues were offered having a share value of $160 million. In 1979, 144 issues were offered having a share value of $592 million—the most since 1973. In terms of companies with less than $5 million in assets, there was just one issue in the first half of 1978, having a share value of $1.2 million. But in the second half of 1978 there were 20 issues having a share value of $128 million. In 1979 there were 29 such issues, with a share value of $183 million.[21]

Further evidence comes from a study by the Opinion Research Corporation. According to this study, of the 516 executives interviewed, one-fourth said that they had made new or increased investments *as a result* of the reduction in the capital gains tax. In addition, 9 percent of the respondents reported selling assets and realizing capital gains which they otherwise would not have done without the tax change. Significantly, of those with investment portfolios of $100,000 or more, 20 percent reported selling investments they would not otherwise have sold without the tax cut.[22]

Lastly, it should be noted that early indications from the Treasury Department are that the capital gains tax cut did increase revenue. As table 2 shows, there was a 23 percent jump in realized capital gains in 1979 over 1978, with a further increase expected in 1980. These increases in realized gains caused 1979 capital gains tax revenue to drop only $1 billion below that of 1978, despite a 30 percent reduction in the effective tax rate. Prior to the tax cut, the Treasury had been predicting a $2.2 billion loss in revenue.[23] As a result, Sen.

TABLE 2

TOTAL CAPITAL GAINS AND THE EFFECTIVE TAX RATE ON CAPITAL GAINS FOR RETURNS WITH NET CAPITAL GAINS ONLY (INDIVIDUAL ONLY), 1955–80

Year	Total Gains* ($ in billions)	Taxes paid on Capital Gain Income ($ in billions)	Effective Tax Rate (percent)
1955	$ 9.9	$1.2	12.0%
1956	9.7	1.1	11.8
1957	8.1	0.9	11.1
1958	9.4	1.1	11.1
1959	13.1	1.6	11.8
1960	11.7	1.4	11.6
1961	16.3	2.0	12.4
1962	13.5	1.6	11.8
1963	14.6	1.7	11.9
1964	17.4	2.2	12.7
1965	21.5	2.8	13.1
1966	21.3	2.7	12.8
1967	27.5	3.9	14.0
1968	35.6	5.2	14.5
1969	31.4	4.4	14.1
1970	20.8	3.0	14.6
1971	28.3	4.3	15.2
1972	35.9	5.6	15.7
1973	35.8	5.3	14.9
1974	30.2	4.3	14.3
1975	30.9	4.5	14.4
1976	39.0	6.2	15.9
1977	45.9	7.3	15.8
1978†	48.0	7.4	15.4
1979†	59.3	6.4	10.8
1980†	63.9	7.0	11.0

*Net long-term gain in excess of short-term loss plus short-term capital gain.
†Estimates.
SOURCE: Office of the Secretary of the Treasury, Office of Tax Analysis, February 13, 1980.

Russell Long, chairman of the Senate Finance Committee, has suggested that the capital gains tax be cut further and that such a cut would not cost any revenue. "We in the Senate Finance Committee," he said, "had concluded two years ago if you cut the capital gains tax down to 21 percent that the Treasury would actually gain revenue, and all indications are so far that the big tax cut we did vote is gaining rather than losing us revenue."[24]

Notes

1. Among the most energetic was Bill Ballhaus, president of Beckman Instruments; see John Cobbs, "The Tax That Is Killing Investment," *Business Week* (January 16, 1978), pp. 14–16.

2. Robert J. Samuelson, "Making Life Difficult For Congress," *National Journal* (March 18, 1978), p. 437.

3. Statement before the Senate Select Committee on Small Business, February 8, 1978; see also statement before the House Ways and Means Committee, March 7, 1978; statement before the Senate Finance Committee, June 29, 1978.

4. See statement of the Securities Industry Association before the House Ways and Means Committee, March 7, 1978; see also Jack Egan, "SIA Sees Tax Cuts Aiding Economy," *Washington Post* (March 3, 1978).

5. Martin Feldstein and Joel Slemrod, *Inflation and the Excess Taxation of Capital Gains on Corporate Stock* (Cambridge, MA: National Bureau of Economic Research, Working Paper No. 234, February 1978); see also Lindley H. Clark, Jr., "Taxing Capital," *Wall Street Journal* (March 28, 1978).

6. H. R. 12111, 95th Cong., 2nd sess.

7. Editorial, "Stupendous Steiger," *Wall Street Journal* (April 26, 1978).

8. Michael K. Evans, *The Economic Effects of Reducing Capital Gains Taxes* (Chase Econometric Associates, Inc., April 17, 1978); see also Evans' statement before the Senate Finance Committee, June 29, 1978.

9. Merrill Lynch Economics Inc., *Economic Impact Analysis of a Capital Gains Tax Reduction* (May 4, 1978); see also statement before the Senate Finance Committee, June 29, 1978.

10. Statement before the Senate Finance Committee, June 28, 1978.

11. Editorial, "How to Unsoak the Rich," *New York Times* (May 19, 1978).

12. Jack Germond and Jules Witcover, "Debate Over Capital Gains Shows True Power of the Middle Class," *Washington Star* (July 7, 1978).

13. Lou Harris, "66 Pct. Favor House Bill to Cut Maximum Tax on Capital Gains," *Washington Post* (August 14, 1978).

14. Martin Feldstein, Joel Slemrod and Shlomo Yitzhaki, *The Effects of Taxation on the Selling of Corporate Stock and the Realization of Capital Gains* (Cambridge, MA: National Bureau of Economic Research, Working Paper No. 250, June 1978); see also Martin Feldstein and Shlomo Yitzhaki, *The Effect of the Capital Gains Tax on the Selling and Switching of Common*

Stock (Cambridge, MA: Harvard Institute of Economic Research, Discussion Paper No. 532, January 1977); Richard Goode, *The Individual Income Tax* (Washington: The Brookings Institution, 1976), pp. 197–206.

15. *Congressional Quarterly Almanac, 1978,* pp. 228, 234–35, 237, 239, 246.

16. Joint Committee on Taxation, *General Explanation of the Revenue Act of 1978* (Washington: U.S. Government Printing Office, 1978), p. 252.

17. C.V. Wood, Jr., "Another Look at a Tax Cut," *New York Times* (June 10, 1979); Editorial, "Snapping Back," *Wall Street Journal* (July 30, 1979); Edward I. O'Brien, "Reduction of Tax on Capital Gains Spurs Investment," *Wall Street Journal* (October 31, 1979).

18. Editorial, "Capital-Gains Cut to Nowhere," *New York Times* (December 4, 1979).

19. The advertisement appeared in the *New York Times* on December 10, 1979.

20. "Removing Tax Disincentives Does Work," *Securities Industry Trends* (December 17, 1979), p. 8; William Bulkeley and Lindley Richert, "Venture Capital Is Plentiful Once More, Partly Due To Change In Capital-Gains Tax," *Wall Street Journal* (June 15, 1979); "Venture Capital Comes Back," *Newsweek* (June 4, 1979), p. 67.

21. Data obtained from the Securities Industry Association.

22. *Executives' Responses to Tax Proposals for Increasing Savings and Investment* (Princeton, NJ: Opinion Research Corporation, January 1980); see also "Further Evidence on Removing Tax Disincentives," *Securities Industry Trends* (March 21, 198); James L. Rowe, Jr., "Tax Cut Effects," *Washington Post* (December 18, 1979); idem, "Capital Gains Tax Cut a Booster for Stocks," *Washington Post* (February 21, 1980).

23. "Cuts, Realizations and Capital Gains Tax Revenues," *Securities Industry Trends* (July 2, 1980), pp. 2–5.

24. Columbia Broadcasting System, "Face the Nation," (March 2, 1980).

14

The Balanced Budget Question

FOLLOWING THE SPECTACULAR SUCCESSES OF 1978, IN WHICH Proposition 13 was overwhelmingly approved in California, in which the Kemp-Roth bill came within a hair of passage, and in which the Congress passed its first supply-side tax cut in 15 years, the leaders of the tax revolt naturally assumed that 1979 would see even greater victories. Unfortunately, the tax revolt got derailed, not by its enemies, but by its ostensible friends in the balanced-budget movement. How did this happen?

The answer, I think, can be found in a dialectical view of the political process. The dialectic envisions the political process evolving through these stages: establishment of a thesis, which gives rise to an antithesis, which ultimately results in establishment of a new synthesis. The synthesis becomes the new thesis and the process starts over again. What has happened to the tax cutters fits perfectly into this pattern.

The thesis and antithesis of our political system are embodied in the philosophies of the two major political parties. For most of this century the Democrats won their elections and established the dominant thesis of our political system with ever-increasing government spending. As the *Wall Street Journal* recently put it: "For almost a half-century the party has used federal spending as its dry martini, its scotch on the rocks; ever increasing spending has enabled the party to woo diverse interest groups and cement them into a political alliance."[1]

Thanks to the economics of Lord Keynes the Democrats could buy their votes with an absolutely clear conscience, in the genuine belief that deficits were good for the economy. This allowed them to, in effect, promise the people something-for-nothing. They could have all the new government programs they wanted and it would not cost a dime, because they were paid for with deficits rather than taxes.

The Keynesian spend-your-way-to-prosperity philosophy was itself a synthesis which grew out of the political contradiction which developed in the 1930s as a result of the Great Depression. Until the Depression, the dominant thesis in the American political system was one of laissez-faire. This did not mean that the government stayed entirely out of the economy, merely that when there was doubt about what the government should do, it tended to do nothing. Therefore, when the Depression hit and there was no clear-cut way to respond to it, the government did nothing (or at least gave the appearance of doing nothing). This gave rise to the antithesis of laissez-faire, which is socialism.

In the 1932 election, when the Socialist Party received almost a million votes, or more than 6 percent of Herbert Hoover's total, the specter of socialism as a threat to the established order was driven home forcefully. Roosevelt, it can now be seen, was at heart a conservative, in the sense that he opposed socialism and radical change.[2] (Anyone who does not believe this should read some of his 1932 campaign speeches or the 1932 platform of the Democratic Party.) But he understood, perhaps more clearly than is possible today, that socialism represented a threat to the system. His response was to move away from laissez-faire toward a more activist role for government in the economy. Roosevelt understood that, unless government was able to deal with the Depression (or at least give the appearance of doing so), socialism might triumph. Although his policies were unsuccessful in ending the Depression—the economy was worse off in 1937 than it was in 1932—Roosevelt was totally successful in conveying the view that government could deal with the situation within the context of capitalist democracy. The socialists were destroyed.

Thus we can see that what happened fits perfectly into dialectical terms. The thesis was laissez-faire, the antithesis was socialism, and the synthesis was New Deal liberalism. The New Deal has been the political model for the Democratic Party and, indeed, the nation ever since.

New Deal liberalism, though dominant thus far, has not been without its antithesis, of course. Until recently, however, the antithesis has not been strong enough to lead to a new synthesis that is significantly different from the dominant thesis. If increasing government spending and deficits were the principal features of New Deal liberalism, then the antithesis was the balanced budget. As one can readily see, if the thesis is that big deficits are good, and the antithesis is that we should balance the budget, then it follows that the synthesis will be somewhat smaller deficits, but deficits nonetheless. And this is precisely what has happened for 30 years; the Democrats push for spending, the Republicans try to balance the budget, and we end up with more and more spending—but at a slower rate.

In the context of the political situation just described, the truly remarkable thing is that the Republican Party survived at all. With Democrats promising something-for-nothing and Republicans proposing austerity, is it any wonder that the Democrats triumphed so regularly—especially when the Republicans' dire predictions about the destruction of our economy if deficit spending continued never took place?

The balanced budget was not always the cornerstone of the Republican fiscal philosophy. Indeed, the only times since World War I when the Republican Party has controlled Congress it did so by running against this philosophy. In its electoral victories following World War I and World War II the dominant theme of the Republican Party was not a balanced budget but across the board tax reduction.

In the 1920s the Republicans totally dominated all levels of government as they slashed tax rates year after year. Had they continued they might have stayed in power, but Herbert Hoover destroyed them when he raised tax rates significantly, in the belief that a balanced budget would pull the nation out of the Depression. Needless to say, Hoover's actions, which doubled and even tripled most tax rates, only exacerbated the economic problem and the Republicans were thrown out of office, as they justly deserved to be.

Although nearly extinguished by the Democrats during the 1930s, the Republicans came back strong after the Second World War, with tax reduction as their major theme again. Republicans won control of Congress in 1946 and the first bill introduced, H.R. 1, was a bill to slash tax rates across the board. It easily passed the House and Senate but was vetoed by President Truman as inflationary. Republicans failed by two votes to override the veto in the House. A second tax cut bill introduced immediately afterwards again passed the House and Senate and was again vetoed by Truman. This time the House voted to override the veto, but it was sustained in the Senate.

It was not until the following year, 1948, that a watered-down version of the original tax cut bill was passed over a third Truman veto.

The Republicans lost control of Congress in the 1948 elections, but regained control in 1952. Once again the first bill introduced was a major tax cut, only this time there was a new obstacle: President Eisenhower, a Republican. Eisenhower opposed a reduction in taxes on the grounds that the budget must be balanced first. The result was that the Democrats won back control of Congress in the 1954 elections.

Since Eisenhower's time, Republicans in general have been wedded to the balanced-budget philosophy. They even opposed the Kennedy tax cut of 1963–64 on the grounds that it would increase the deficit (actually, it increased tax revenues by expanding the tax base just as the Republican tax cuts of the 1920s had done). Predictably, Republicans have also been the minority party in Congress since 1954.

The Republican attitude would be admirable if it were based on sound economic principles. Unfortunately, it is not, because deficits per se are not harmful to the economy. The things that count are the aggregate level of spending, the amount and form of taxation, and the quantity of money. Deficits in and of themselves are not important. As Prof. Milton Friedman argues:

> There is an important point that needs to be stressed to those who regard themselves as fiscal conservatives. By concentrating on the wrong thing, the deficit, instead of the right thing, total government spending, fiscal conservatives have been the unwitting handmaidens of the big spenders. The typical historical process is that the spenders put through laws which increase government spending. A deficit emerges. The fiscal conservatives scratch their heads and say, "My God, that's terrible; we have got to do something about that deficit." So they cooperate with the big spenders in getting taxes imposed. As soon as the new taxes are imposed and passed, the big spenders are off again, and then there is another burst in government spending and another deficit. . . . I would far rather have total spending at $200 billion with a deficit of $100 billion than a balanced budget at $500 billion.[3]

Furthermore, it cannot even be argued that deficits cause inflation. Inflation is basically a monetary phenomenon. If the Federal Reserve wants to pump up the money supply there is going to be inflation regardless of whether the budget is balanced or not. Although the Fed does so, it is not required to purchase the Treasury's bonds, thereby monetizing the debt. If the Treasury covered the deficit by selling all of its bonds to the general public it would merely draw down private savings by that amount and drive up the interest rate.

Crowding out private investors from the market is certainly not a desirable thing, but it is not the cause of inflation. Without an increase in the quantity of money there cannot be any increase in the general price level.

Although Congress has not explicitly raised income taxes since the Vietnam War surtax, it has acquiesced to an implicit tax increase caused by inflation. Inflation increases income tax revenues faster than the rate of inflation because of progressivity. The individual income tax increases roughly 1.67 percent for every one percent increase in the consumer price index. Although Congress has periodically cut taxes, tax rates are left intact, meaning that tax revenues continue to increase. The most serious side-effect of this is that marginal tax rates (the tax on each additional dollar earned) have increased dramatically since 1965. The higher the marginal tax rate, the lower the tradeoff between work and leisure, savings and consumption. The ultimate cost to the economy of even a small increase in average marginal tax rates can be enormous, as shown by the work of Arnold Harberger at the University of Chicago, Michael Boskin at Stanford, and others.

This enormous increase in taxes since the last major tax rate reduction in 1965 set the stage for a new dialectic, which we are presently witnessing.

In 1978 there was a revolution in the Republican Party. For a variety of historical reasons, including almost a complete turnover in membership in Congress since 1974, the party was ready for something new. In this case it turned out to be something old: a return to the tax cutting tradition of earlier Republican congresses. Led by proponents of the Kemp-Roth Bill and its later variations, the Steiger Amendment to slash capital gains taxes, and Proposition 13, the Republicans established a new antithesis to the dominant thesis of New Deal liberalism.

Note what has happened: When confronted with the old antithesis of a balanced budget versus more government spending, the synthesis was government spending at a reduced rate. When the New Deal liberal thesis came up against an antithesis which said, "Forget the deficit, just cut taxes," the synthesis became the balanced budget.

Thus we now see almost everybody talking about balancing the budget—especially Democrats. They fell all over themselves in the 96th Congress trying to pass balanced budget amendments and using the cry of "balance the budget" quite effectively against the tax cutters. As the *Wall Street Journal* observed:

> So why are deficits suddenly alarming to the big spenders? We believe the answer lies in the momentum of the Kemp-Roth-Steiger tax

rate reductions. Just as the conservatives pointed the deficit finger at the growth in spending programs, now that there is a different momentum the big spenders are pointing a deficit finger at the looming tax cuts. What is at issue is not the deficit itself but political power.

A tax cut would reduce the size of government relative to the private sector. It would be an inroad on the power that has been concentrated in Washington, and the prospect of a decline in political clout is not universally cherished. The political careers of many liberals depend on government action replacing private action. Besides, if the tax cut proponents are right and the economy booms, there would no longer be a sluggish economy as one excuse for expanding government.

We would not turn away the truly born again, but before we welcome big spenders to the ranks of the budget balancers we will wait to see if their new-found devotion to smaller deficits applies to restraining spending, or just to preventing tax cuts.[4]

There is no question that the Democrats are scared. The possibility that the Republicans could take control of the Senate in 1980 or 1982 is very real. And there is no question that the Republicans will make significant gains. The critical numbers are these: 23 Democrats running for reelection, 7 Republicans. The last thing the Democrats want is for Jimmy Carter or Ted Kennedy to force a spending issue upon them which is critical to their constituency, like national health insurance.

Meanwhile, the Republicans are so flushed with vindication for their traditional balanced budget position they have almost totally missed the true significance of what has happened and why. If they drop tax reduction as their major theme and fall back on their old balanced-budget position, Republicans will be right back where they were before. Only by keeping up the pressure for across-the-board tax reduction can they hope to establish the balanced budget as a permanent thesis, rather than a transitory synthesis.

There is not much danger that the Democrats can react to the Republican initiatives by coopting the balanced budget position because spending is so critical to their constituency. As Cong. Tom Foley, chairman of the House Democratic Caucus, recently told the *Wall Street Journal:* "Tight budgets strain all the natural fault lines of the Democratic Party. The pressures will intensify as we approach the presidential election year and each group starts pressing its claims. You can see it happening already. Holding this team of wild horses together is a job for the most skilled congressional coachman."[5]

Unfortunately, Republicans seem ready to grasp defeat from the jaws of victory. As they stand on the brink of their greatest electoral success since 1952, some Republicans are arguing for a return to the economics of austerity which put the Republican Party into semipermanent minority status in the first place. Prominent among them is Dr. Herbert Stein, former chairman of the Council of Economic Advisors under President Nixon. Recently, Stein not only emphatically denounced efforts to cut taxes but called for a significant tax increase. As he told the Senate Budget Committee:

> Today's common prescription for raising the growth rate is to reduce taxes. Unfortunately, at a 4 percent growth rate the present tax burden will not quite suffice to balance the budget . . . so there is no room for cutting taxes to get the growth rate up more. . . . I believe, therefore, that we should preserve our present revenue-raising capacity until we are fairly sure that we are not going to need it soon. The simplest way to do this is to keep all existing taxes in place and allow the tax burden to rise as the automatic consequence of economic growth and inflation. This is not a very satisfactory solution. It is undemocratic, in that it does not reflect any explicit decision of the Congress. Its distribution of the added tax burden has no particular logic. . . . We should be looking for revenue sources that can replace some of the revenue automatically yielded by inflation and generate still more revenue if needed.[6]

Stein is a fool if he believes that this kind of talk will do anything except play into the hands of the big spenders. There is no guarantee that the additional revenue raised will go into defense spending, as he wishes. Nor is it clear that an increase in already unprecedented tax levels will leave us with an economy strong enough to fend off the Soviets. He should understand that a strong economy is critical to a strong defense.[7]

Fortunately for the Republican Party, its nominee for president of the United States in 1980, Ronald Reagan, understands the need for tax cuts and a strong defense. One can only hope that people like Stein are not invited to join his administration.

Notes

1. Dennis Farney, "Tip O'Neill's Unpleasant Duty," *Wall Street Journal* (April 5, 1979).

2. See Barton Bernstein, "The New Deal: The Conservative Acheivements of Liberal Reform," in Barton Bernstein, ed., *Towards a New Past: Dissenting Essays in American History* (New York: Random House, Vintage Books, 1969), pp. 263–88; Ronald Radosh, "The Myth of the New Deal," in Ronald Radosh and Murray Rothbard, eds., *A New History of Leviathan* (New York: E.P. Dutton, 1972), pp. 146–87; Arthur A. Ekirch, *Ideologies and Utopias: The Impact of the New Deal on American Thought* (Chicago: Quadrangle, 1969).

3. Milton Friedman, "The Limitations of Tax Limitation," *Policy Review* (Summer 1978), pp. 11–12.

4. Editorial, "Born Again Budget Balancers," *Wall Street Journal* (July 25, 1979).

5. Farney, "Tip O'Neill's Duty."

6. From his testimony before the Senate Budget Committee on March 4, 1980, reprinted in *The AEI Economist* (March 1980).

7. Frank A. Weil, "The Best Defense Is a Good Economy," *Washington Post* (May 25, 1980).

15

The High Cost of
Jimmy Carter

JIMMY CARTER'S MOST REVEALING CAMPAIGN STATEMENT ABOUT what he intended to do as president regarding tax policy was made to the Associated Press in September 1976. He told AP, "I would like to . . . guarantee a truly progressive tax rate, so that the higher income one has, the higher percentage of one's income one pays. . . . The overall effect would be to shift a substantial increase toward those who have the higher incomes and reduce income [taxes] on the lower income and middle income families." When asked what he considered a higher income, Carter replied, "I would take the mean or median level of income. Anything above would be higher, anything below lower."[1]

The median family income in the U.S. in 1976 was $14,958, the mean (average) family income was $16,870.[2] Thus Jimmy Carter was telling us that he planned to increase taxes on those earning above $14,958 to $16,870 and reduce taxes for those below, thereby increasing progressivity. Unfortunately, this is one promise he kept.[3]

On January 31, 1977, shortly after taking office, Jimmy Carter took his first action toward increasing tax progressivity by proposing a $50 rebate for every person in America. Tax credits, by definition, do more to help those with lower incomes than those with upper incomes. (A $50 tax credit would be equal to 0.5 percent of income for someone earning $10,000, but only 0.1 percent of income for someone earning $50,000.)

The idea of a one-shot $50 rebate to pump up aggregate demand was not especially popular on Capitol Hill. Sen. Russell Long, chairman of the Senate Finance Committee, likened it to "throwing a bushel of $50 bills off the Washington Monument on a windy day."[4] Republicans, of course, were even more critical. Former Chairman of the Council of Economic Advisors Paul McCracken called it "a Rube Goldberg contrivance."[5] On April 14, 1977, President Carter withdrew the $50 rebate plan, saying that the economy had improved sufficiently for it to be unnecessary. The stock market immediately shot up.[6]

In retrospect, it appears that what really concerned President Carter was the effective way in which Republicans were able to put forward arguments in favor of a permanent tax cut in lieu of the rebate. The fact is that Republicans were more united on the need for a permanent tax cut than they had been on any major issue for years. For example, the Republican members of the House Budget Committee were unanimous in their opposition to the $50 rebate and in favor of a permanent tax cut. In their minority views to the report on the Third Concurrent Resolution on the Budget for fiscal year 1977 they said:

> Why a temporary rebate to everyone, taxpayer and non-taxpayer alike, rather than permanent tax rate reduction for those who carry the burden of government? Did the advocates of a rebate make a case that rebates would be more effective in reducing unemployment and stimulating the economy in a non-inflationary way than a permanent tax rate reduction? Absolutely not. They stated their case for a rebate explicitly on the grounds that it was a way to stimulate the economy without having to give the taxpayer a permanent tax rate reduction—the aim being to preserve revenues for larger government spending programs in the future. Once again, bigger government takes precedence over the individual taxpayer.[7]

In an effort to build on this unanimous support for permanent tax rate reductions by the Budget Committee Republicans, Cong. Jack Kemp sent a confidential memorandum to all Republican Members of Congress on February 22, 1977. He said:

> With the loss of the Presidency, the national forum of highest visibility available to the Republican Party has been eliminated. For this reason, it is more important than ever for the Republican Members of

Congress to offer constructive alternatives to the programs of the national Democratic Party.

We have to realize now that we can no longer make a political career of just opposing what the Democrats are for. We have to propose a vision and strategy of our own. A strategy for freedom and prosperity that is embodied in the Republican Party's principles and ideals. In short it is time to move the Republican Party from a position of defense to one of offense.

And the upcoming consideration of the Third Concurrent Resolution on the Budget for FY 1977 offers us the opportunity to do so by offering a substitute amendment based on an across-the-board reduction in the tax rates.

On the floor, Cong. John Rousselot offered a substitute amendment for the $50 rebate of a permanent $19 billion tax cut. Although he lost by a vote of 148 to 258, the cohesion of the Republicans was remarkable; only 10 Republicans voted against the Rousselot amendment, while 25 Democrats crossed over. Later, after the president had withdrawn his rebate proposal, he was asked what he would have done had the Congress passed the Republican proposal. Carter said he would have vetoed it, that such action would be "irresponsible" and "not necessary."[8] Nevertheless, this vote proved to be of historical importance, because it clearly reestablished the Republican Party as the party of tax reduction. Afterwards, every budget resolution and every major tax bill became a target for Republican tax cutters. Although they still do not win, they get closer every time. In the process, they are slowly winning Democrat votes and making the people more aware that the Democrats are responsible for high taxes.

Shortly after failure of his rebate plan, President Carter sent to Congress his first major tax increase proposal, the crude oil equalization tax. The purpose of the crude oil tax was to bring the domestically produced price of oil, which had been controlled by the federal government since 1971, up to the world price, with the government taking 100 percent of the difference between the controlled price and the world price. In addition, he proposed a "gas-guzzler" tax on low mileage autos, taxes on industrial use of natural gas, and a standby 50 cents per gallon gasoline tax. The money raised was to be rebated back to taxpayers in some unspecified way.

Carter's energy plan came under immediate attack. Republicans argued that it was just a backhanded way of increasing the overall tax burden on the American people and of raising revenue for new Democrat spending programs.[9] The U.S. Chamber of Commerce revealed that the tax program would cost $377.31 billion between 1978 and 1985, or over $5,390 for every American family.[10] In addition, economists began raising serious questions about the overall effect of the program. Prof. Arthur Laffer, for example, noted that even if 100 percent of the tax money were rebated, output would fall, because the demand effects of the tax would wash out the disincentive effects of the tax on supply would remain.[11] And Dr. Barry Smernoff of the Hudson Institute warned that passage of the energy program would throw the United States into a recession.[12]

The crude oil tax emerged from the House of Representatives relatively intact. This is because Democrat leaders shrewdly moved the entire energy program through the House as a package, using a special Ad Hoc Committee on Energy to write the legislation. The House leadership also severely restricted amendments to the bill from the floor. Nevertheless, Republicans came within 9 votes of defeating the measure, on a motion to recommit the bill which lost by a vote of 203 to 219.

In the Senate, however, the tax fell apart. First, the Senate Finance Committee broke the energy bill into separate pieces. Then the committee voted to scrap the crude oil tax altogether. In conference, the House tried to revive the tax, but by then it was very close to the end of the session and the Senate refused to budge.[13] So ended the crude oil tax. Or did it?

Meanwhile, even as Congress continued work on his massive energy tax proposal, Carter was asking for another massive tax increase to fund social security. He asked for an increase in the social security tax rate, an increase in the earnings base subject to the tax, and some revisions in benefits (primarily to eliminate a congressional error which overindexed social security benefits to inflation).

Needless to say, the proposal came in for heavy criticism from liberals and conservatives alike. Conservatives generally were concerned that the Carter plan did nothing to increase the overall financial soundness of the social security system, calling his plan a "quick fix."[14] Liberals, on the other hand, were concerned about the regressivity of the tax and its effect on employment. As the *Washington Post* put it, "The payroll tax makes labor more expensive to the employer. . . . To accelerate this trend over the coming years, as the emerging social security bill will do, is going to make it harder than ever to push the unemployment rate down."[15]

They were both right, of course. The tax increase which passed Congress in December 1977, which will raise $227 billion by 1987, has done nothing to increase the fundamental soundness of the social security system. Indeed, shortly after passage of the social security tax bill—until then the largest tax increase in American history—the Congress was told that additional tax increases might still be necessary.[16] And the social security tax increase certainly had a detrimental effect on employment, by simultaneously increasing the cost of employment to businesses while reducing the after-tax return to workers.

The fact is that firms hire an employee based, in part, on the total cost to the firm of hiring the employee. The higher the total cost to the firm, the fewer employees it will hire. On the other hand, an employee, in deciding where or whether to work, does not care how much his employment costs the firm. The employee is concerned about how much he personally receives. If nothing else changes, the more an employee receives, the more willing he is to work, and the less he receives, the less willing he is to work. The difference between what it costs a firm to hire an employee and what he gets paid can be considered a wedge. The larger the wedge, the greater the disincentive for employers to hire and employees to work.[17] As one can see from table 1, the social security tax wedge has increased dramatically in recent years.

By contrast, Republicans argued that such a massive increase in social security tax rates was unnecessary. The main features of the Republican alternative were to (1) gradually raise the retirement age at which full benefits are payable from 65 to 68, (2) require the payment of social security taxes by federal, state, and local government employees, (3) remove the earnings limitation for those on social security, and (4) reallocate social security taxes between the Old Age and Survivors Insurance (OASI) and Disability Insurance (DI) Trust Funds. Such changes would have made the social security system financially sound for the next 75 years and would have required no increase in social security tax rates or the wage base before 1982·and only a 1.2 percent increase in tax rates by the year 2000. Nevertheless, despite widespread opposition to the social security tax increase it was approved in the House by a 275 to 146 vote, and in the Senate by a 42 to 25 vote.[18]

Having put the crude oil tax and the social security tax increase behind him, in 1978 President Carter turned to tax reform. Carter had expected to be able to propose his program in 1977 and had begun leaking details as early as February. Early indications were that the program might not be so bad after all. Among the changes proposed were a reduction in the top marginal tax rate on individuals from 70 percent to 50 percent and elimination of the double-taxation of corporate profits, in keeping with Carter's campaign promise to tax all income only once.[19]

On September 2, 1977, the Treasury Department completed a draft of the proposed tax reform package. Although the package contained a reduction in the maximum tax rate to 50 percent and

TABLE 1

HISTORY OF SOCIAL SECURITY TAX RATES

Period	Combined Employee-Employer Tax Rate	Tax Base	Maximum Contribution
1937–49	2.0%	$ 3,000	$ 60
1950	3.0	3,000	90
1951–53	3.0	3,600	108
1954	4.0	3,600	144
1955–56	4.0	4,200	168
1957–58	4.5	4,200	189
1959	5.0	4,800	240
1960–61	6.0	4,800	288
1962	6.25	4,800	300
1963–65	7.25	4,800	348
1966	8.4	6,600	554
1967	8.8	6,600	581
1968	8.8	7,800	686
1969–70	9.6	7,800	749
1971	10.4	7,800	811
1972	10.4	9,000	936
1973	11.7	10,800	1,264
1974	11.7	13,200	1,544
1975	11.7	14,100	1,650
1976	11.7	15,300	1,790
1977	11.7	16,500	1,930
1978	12.1	17,700	2,142
1979	12.26	22,900	2,808
1980	12.26	25,900	3,175
1981	13.3	29,700	3,950
1982*	13.4	32,400	4,340
1983*	13.4	35,400	4,644
1984*	13.4	39,000	5,226
1985*	14.1	42,900	6,049

*Estimated.

SOURCE: Senate Finance Committee, Office of Management and Budget

partial integration of the individual and corporate income taxes, it also contained many tax changes which would clearly be negative for economic growth and investment. The most important of these would be elimination of preferential tax treatment for capital gains. Under existing law, only 50 percent of long-term capital gains was subject to tax. Under Carter's proposal this would have been reduced to 30 percent in 1979, 15 percent in 1980, and zero afterwards. In addition, numerous tax deductions and tax preferences would be eliminated, aimed at increasing the effective tax rate on upper incomes and increasing overall progressivity.[20]

These proposals quickly came in for criticism from both liberals and conservatives. Interestingly, both groups were concerned about how the tax package would impact on business. Liberals thought business was getting too much; conservatives not enough.[21] Indeed, the Wall Street Journal argued that the overall effect of the proposal, even though taxes would be reduced by $25 billion, would be negative—worse than if nothing were done.[22]

When the final tax program was sent to Congress in January 1978, it was apparent that it had undergone considerable revision. The key feature of the plan was elimination of the $750 personal exemption and replacement with a $240 tax credit per person. In addition, tax rates were reduced from the existing range of 14 percent at the bottom and 70 percent at the top, to 12 percent at the bottom and 68 percent at the top. As far as corporations are concerned, the corporate tax rate would have been reduced from 48 percent to 44 percent and the 10 percent investment tax credit made permanent. Most of the rest of the package would have reduced or eliminated a variety of tax preferences and deductions. Deductions for medical expenses and state and local taxes would have been limited. Certain employee fringe benefits would become taxable, business-related entertainment expenses (the infamous "three martini lunch") would be reduced, and numerous tax shelter arrangements would be curtailed. The administration estimated that the package contained $33.9 billion worth of tax reductions and $9.4 billion of tax increases, for a net tax reduction of $24.5 billion.[23]

In its presentation to the Congress, the administration made quite clear that its program would increase progressivity. The change from a personal tax exemption to a tax credit, for example, meant that those below the 29 percent marginal tax bracket got a tax reduction, those above a tax increase. The *Wall Street Journal* pointed out that this meant increasing taxes for single individuals earning more than $12,000 per year and for married couples earning more than $16,000.[24] The *Journal* also made this observation about the tax package:

> The problem with this string of proposals is that they were designed by economists still trapped in a Keynesian framework that does not seem to apply to today's problems. In this view, a tax cut works solely because it will increase the government deficit, and because deficits induce economic expansion by boosting aggregate demand. Thus in this view, it does not matter how you cut taxes; any tax cut will pump up the deficit as well as any other. It is the same thinking that led to the ill-fated $50 rebate.
>
> The problem with today's economy, at least so it seems to us, lies on the supply-side of the equation, not on the demand one. High marginal tax rates have reduced incentives to work and invest. To stimulate production and growth, you need to cut rates where they are highest. In a supply model, putting the tax load on the most productive sector of society leads to less production, more unemployment, more inflation and ultimately lower living standards for everyone—including the low income families that initially got tax breaks.[25]

Soon, academic economists were making much the same point. Arthur Laffer said "by advocating a tax plan designed more to redistribute income than increase incentives to supply goods and services to the economy, the President has sacrificed a major opportunity to reverse, in part, the economic errors of the past decade."[26] Profs. Michael Boskin of Stanford and Jerry Green of Harvard criticized the president for orienting his tax program so heavily toward consumption and away from capital formation, which, they said, is "the most important problem facing the U.S. economy today."[27] Prof. Martin Feldstein of Harvard, president of the National Bureau of Economic Research, said the tax program was based on an incorrect "super-Keynesian approach."[28]

An especially interesting analysis of the president's program by the *National Journal* found that even if the tax reductions were enacted, most people would pay more federal taxes in 1979 than they did in 1977. This is because the administration failed to account for the effect of inflation pushing people into higher tax brackets and the legislated social security tax increases. Taking these factors into account showed that a family with a 1977 income of $6,000 would have its tax bite increased from 2.5 percent in 1977 to 4.5 percent in 1979. A $30,000 per year family would face an increase from 18.4 percent to 20.1 percent. Thus the *Journal* said that "the effect of the new tax system would not be so much progressive as perverse. Taxpayers at both the bottom and the top of the tax scale would pay more; only those in the middle would gain."[29]

Ultimately, the Congress rejected virtually everything in the president's tax package and substituted provisions of its own—provisions shaped very heavily by the specter of Proposition 13 and the tax revolt. In lieu of Carter's tax reform gimmickry and passion for progressivity, the Congress substituted substantial, across-the-board tax rate reductions, an increase in the personal exemption to $1,000, a reduction in the corporate tax rate, and a significant reduction in capital gains taxes. It was, in fact, the first supply-side tax cut since John F. Kennedy. Table 2 shows the extent to which the Revenue Act of 1978 differed from its predecessors.

Early in 1979 Carter returned to the question of energy taxes. In April he announced his plan to begin phased decontrol of domestic crude oil prices with imposition of a windfall profits tax. Whereas his earlier plan would have given the government 100% of the difference between the domestically controlled price of oil and the world price, his new plan gave the government only 50 percent. According to figures given the Congress in May 1979, such a tax would have raised between $3.8 and $5.6 billion over the period 1979–82. In a sense, therefore, it was a compromise between the crude oil equalization tax and decontrol, which was mandated to take place in 1981 by the Energy Policy and Conservation Act.

TABLE 2

PERCENTAGE DISTRIBUTION OF RECENT TAX CUTS

Adjusted Gross Income	1	2	3	4	5
$0 to $20,000	85.5%	82.4%	84.6%	92.4%	32.6%
$20,000 to $50,000	10.5	16.4	14.3	7.3	43.1
$50,000 +	4.0	1.2	1.0	0.2	24.3

1. Revenue Act of 1971.
2. Revenue Adjustment Act of 1975.
3. Tax Reduction Act of 1975.
4. Tax Reduction and Simplification Act of 1977.
5. Revenue Act of 1978.
SOURCE: Joint Committee on Taxation.

The rapidly escalating world price for oil and the wide publicity given to high nominal profits by the major oil companies in 1979 caused the Congress to look much more favorably upon the proposed windfall profits tax than it had on the earlier crude oil tax. The House Ways and Means Committee quickly moved to increase the basic windfall profits tax rate from 50% to 70%, and expanded it to include more catagories of oil. President Carter, sensing that the political climate had changed dramatically from two years earlier, encouraged the committee to increase the tax rate. (Both the president and the committee feared that the Senate Finance Committee, with its high proportion of members from oil producing states, would reduce the tax anyway.)

On the floor of the House, however, Democrat Cong. Jim Jones of Oklahoma and Republican Cong. Henson Moore of Louisiana joined forces to substitute a more moderate tax for the committee version. The Jones-Moore substitute, which was adopted by a vote of 236 to 183, changed the tax significantly. It lowered the tax rate from 70 percent to 60 percent, ended it in 1990, taxed oil from marginal wells at a lower rate, and gave a tax break for tertiary wells (those requiring enhanced production techniques). According to figures calculated in June 1979, President Carter's original tax would have yielded $21.2 billion between 1979 and 1984, the Ways and Means bill $29.1 billion, and the Jones-Moore substitute $23.3 billion.[30]

The Senate Finance Committee did prove to be more concerned about the impact of the tax on production than the House Ways and Means Committee. It quickly began to exempt certain categories of oil from the tax, such as newly discovered oil, and provided lower tax rates for certain high-cost types of production. At one point, in fact, the committee had given away more in tax credits for energy conservation and alternative fuel development than the windfall tax would have raised. But, under pressure from President Carter and the press, the committee quickly moved to increase the revenue take. The Finance Committee bill would have raised $51.6 billion between 1979 and 1984, net of credits (based on different assumptions than those which applied to the House-passed bill, since the OPEC price for oil had increased substantially in the meantime).

On the floor of the Senate the tax was increased. A major change was imposition of a minimum tax on categories of oil which had been exempt, including newly discovered oil. This led to a mini-filibuster by Republicans and oil-state Democrats, which finally resulted in a compromise which set the tax on newly discovered oil at 10 percent and increased the base price from which the tax would be calculated from $17 to $20. The minimum tax raised revenues substantially, by about $40 billion between 1980 and 1990. Thus the Senate-passed bill would have raised $177.8 billion between 1980 and 1990, compared to $276.8 billion for the House bill (based on the same oil price assumptions). The House-Senate conference agreed on a final bill which would raise $227.3 billion before phasing out.

However, the tax take could be much higher depending on what happens to the price of oil. The Congress has assumed that the world price for oil in 1981, after decontrol, will be $30 per barrel and that the price will rise 2 percent per year in real terms afterward. If prices were to rise 3 percent, the tax take would increase to $256.8 billion. If the price in 1981 is $35 per barrel and prices increase 2 percent the tax take increases to $304 billion (between 1980 and 1990).[31]

Even now, after the tax has been enacted, it is still difficult to figure out what the basic justification for it is. As *The Economist* observed, "the tax sets a new principle: that private oil resources, whether existing or potential, are subject to a confiscatory tax whenever the politics of the moment demands it."[32] It may, therefore, represent nothing more than envy and vindictiveness against those who have been successful by those who have not. More likely, it was just a convenient and relatively easy opportunity for the president and Congress to raise some revenue with which to buy votes. As the *Wall Street Journal* argued, the president is caught in a dilemma:

> He is caught between public wrath at high taxes and the inexorable pressures from organized spending constituencies. Even the automatic tax increases generated as inflation pushes everyone into higher tax brackets do not supply enough money to solve the dilemma. To pay off all the promises, another hidden tax is needed. If only you can find a sector of society with both high cash flows and enough popular mistrust, you can try to make it even more unpopular than government and then

use it as a tax collector. What could be more logical than demagoguing the oil industry?

The danger is that Congress, which faces the same dilemma, will come to the same conclusion. But in a real sense you have not decontrolled the oil industry if you expropriate the profits that justify and finance capital investment. To understand the windfall profits tax, you have to see it as a revenue measure in disguise. And the rhetoric surrounding it as a diversion, telling you the oil companies are about to get away with something, and trying to keep you from noticing that the politicians are grabbing a bigger share of the nation's purse.[33]

The *Journal*'s view is confirmed by the the Senate's vote on an amendment offered by Sen. William Roth to the windfall profits tax bill requiring that all of the revenue raised by the bill be returned to the people in the form of tax reduction, so that the overall tax burden will not rise as a result of the windfall tax. But the Senate rejected Roth's proposal.[34] Later, during conference, 60 percent of the revenue was specified to be used for individual income tax reduction. But the House and Senate refused to mandate such reductions, instead leaving the 60 percent figure as an expression of intent for future action.

It is not surprising, therefore, that the president's 1981 budget projects substantial increases in both taxes and spending, even while balancing the budget. It should be noted that if these projections are correct (see table 3), the tax burden will rise to its highest level in American history, never exceeded even during war.

TABLE 3

BUDGET RECEIPTS AND OUTLAYS AS A PERCENT OF GNP ($ in billions)

Fiscal Year	GNP	Budget Receipts	Percent	Budget Outlays	Percent
1977	$1,899	$ 357.8	18.8	$411.4	22.3
1978	2,128	402.0	18.9	461.2	22.4
1979	2,369	465.9	19.7	506.1	21.9
1980	2,567	523.8	20.4	580.3	23.0
1981	2,842	600.0	21.1	633.9	22.9
1982	3,206	691.1	21.5	686.3	21.4
1983	3,619	798.8	22.1	774.3	21.4
1984	4,052	920.5	22.7	838.9	20.7
1985	4,498	1,061.2	23.6	902.6	20.1

SOURCE: *The Budget of the United States Government, Fiscal Year 1981.*

Based on these numbers from the president's budget, the aggregate tax increase on the American people by 1985 will be a staggering $711 billion. This is the cumulative tax increase over and above what it would be if the ratio of tax receipts to GNP had remained at 18.8 percent. This works out to about $3,250 for every man, woman, and child in America.

Considering that output per man hour has fallen from 3.5 percent in 1976 to *minus* 1.1 percent in 1979, that industrial production has fallen from 10.8 percent in 1976 to 4.2 percent in 1979, and that the rate of growth of real GNP has fallen from 5.9 percent in 1976 to 2.3 percent in 1979 as the result of Jimmy Carter's tax policies thus far, one can only imagine what will happen to our economy unless there is a massive reduction in taxes. Nevertheless, Jimmy Carter stands forthrightly against any reduction in taxes, in the belief that this will help in the fight against inflation. Unfortunately, he will find inflation increasing, not decreasing, if he continues to impose disincentives on the economy. Higher taxes do not reduce the quantity of money in circulation; it is merely transferred from the private sector to the public sector. But the higher taxes reduce the incentive to produce, reducing the quantity of goods and services, leading to price increases. This is why the Joint Economic Committee recently argued that a tax cut aimed at increasing productivity and investment would reduce inflation.[35]

Although members of his own party in the House and Senate are slowly shedding their Keynesian dogma in the face of economic reality, there is no evidence that Carter will ever do so, despite his campaign promise to pay closer attention to the supply side of the economy.[36] For the sake of our economy we can only hope that he either becomes a "born again" supply-sider, or that we get a new president, because our economy is not going to hold up under four more years like the last four.

Notes

1. Committee on House Administration, U.S. House of Representatives, *The Presidential Campaign 1976: Volume One, Jimmy Carter* (Washington: U.S. Government Printing Office, 1978), p. 764.

2. U.S. Bureau of the Census, *Statistical Abstract of the United States: 1977* (Washington: U.S. Government Printing Office, 1977), pp. 440, 447.

3. For Carter's promises related to tax policy, see Memorandum from Stu Eizenstat and David Rubenstein to President-elect Carter, November 30, 1976. This memorandum was partially reprinted in the *New York Times* (March 19, 1977). See also *Promises, Promises,* vol. 3 (Washington: Republican National Committee, 1980).

4. John Pierson, "Business Tax Cuts for Investment, Hiring Both Likely to Get Senate Panel's Backing," *Wall Street Journal* (March 14, 1977).

5. Speech before the Economic Club of Detroit, February 7, 1977, reprinted in the *Congressional Record* (February 21, 1977), pp. H 1223-25.

6. "$50 Rebate Dead; Carter Also Cancels Two Business Credits," *New York Times* (April 15, 1977).

7. House of Representatives Report No. 95-12, 95th Cong., 1st sess. (February 8, 1977), p. 83.

8. *New York Times* (April 16, 1977).

9. Edward Cowan, "Republicans Contend Energy Levies Are Designed as General Tax Rise," *New York Times* (April 26, 1977).

10. See Milton Copulos, *Economic Impact of Carter's Energy Program* (Washington: The Heritage Foundation, 1977). See also Editorial, "Repent at Leisure," *Wall Street Journal* (August 1, 1977).

11. U.S. Congress, *The Economics of the President's Proposed Energy Policies: Hearings Before the Joint Economic Committee*, 95th Cong., 1st sess. (Washington: U.S. Government Printing Office, 1978), pp. 14-19; see also Arthur B. Laffer, *The Carter Administration's Energy Program* (Boston: H. C. Wainwright & Co., April 26, 1977).

12. Barry J. Smernoff, *Politics of the Energy Transition: Policy Trade-Offs in an Inflationary Economy* (Croton-on-Hudson, NY: Hudson Institute, September 1977). For the views of other economists on the energy program, see Herbert Stein, "Fairness in the Energy Program," *Wall Street Journal* (June 22, 1977); Paul McCracken, "The Demagoguery Over Energy," *Wall Street Journal* (May 16, 1977); William Simon, "The Energy Policy Calamity," *Wall Street Journal* (June 10, 1977); Milton Friedman, "Energy Rhetoric," *Newsweek* (June 13, 1977); Walter J. Mead, *An Economic Appraisal of President Carter's Energy Program* (Los Angeles: International Institute for Economic Research, 1977).

13. For details, see Richard Corrigan and Dick Kirschten, "The Energy Package—What Has Congress Wrought?" *National Journal* (November 4, 1978), pp. 1760-68; Albert Hunt, "Congress Clears Energy Package That Carter Sought," *Wall Street Journal* (October 16, 1978); *Congressional Quarterly Almanac 1977*, pp. 708-45; *Congressional Quarterly Almanac 1978*, pp. 639-67.

14. Editorial, "Social Security Needs More Than a Quick Fix," *Fortune* (June 1977), p. 97; Editorial, "A quick fix, not a remedy," *Business Week* (May 23, 1977); Editorial, "A Sneaky Fix," *Wall Street Journal* (May 13, 1977).

15. Editorial, "The Tax on Labor," *Washington Post* (December 4, 1977); see also Editorial, "Patching Up Social Security," *New York Times* (May 5, 1977); Tom Wicker, "Payroll Tax—Up, Up, Up," *New York Times* (December 13, 1977).

16. John Pierson, "Despite Big Tax Rise, Social Security System Faces Many Problems," *Wall Street Journal* (December 29, 1977); Christopher Conte, "Financing Squeeze Forces New Assessment of Social Security," *Congressional Quarterly* (March 17, 1979), pp. 442-49; Edward Cowan, "Congress Told Social Security Fund Again Requires Infusion of Money," *New York Times* (August 6, 1979); James Singer, "Social Security's Shaky Financing May Work Against 1980 Tax Cuts," *National Journal* (August 25, 1979), pp. 1413-16. See also Michael Boskin, "The Social Security Deficit," *Wall Street Journal* (December 6, 1979). The actuarial liability of the social

security system on September 30, 1979 was $4.225 trillion, according to the Treasury Department, Bureau of Government Financial Operations.

17. See Arthur Laffer and R. David Ranson, *A Proposal for Reforming the Social Security System* (Boston: H. C. Wainwright & Co., May 19, 1977), p. 9. See also Editorial, "Whoa on Social Security," *Wall Street Journal* (October 10, 1977).

18. See House of Representatives Report No. 95–702, 95th Cong., 1st sess. (October 12, 1977); Editorial, "Serious on Social Security," *Wall Street Journal* (September 13, 1977); *Congressional Quarterly Almanac 1977*, pp. 161–72.

19. Rowland Evans and Robert Novak, "Sweeteners for Business in Tax Reform," *Washington Post* (March 10, 1977); "Carter 'Hopes' to Cut Maximum Tax Rate of Individuals to 50%, Blumenthal Says," *Wall Street Journal* (June 20, 1977); "Jimmy Carter on the U.S. Economy and Business," *Fortune* (May 1976), p. 290; "Jimmy Carter on Economics: Populist Georgia-Style," *Business Week* (May 3, 1976), p. 65.

20. "The Treasury Department's Tax Proposal—An Overview," *Tax Policy and Economic Growth—A National Issues Book* (Washington: Government Research Corp., 1977), pp. 2–6.

21. Art Pine, "House Liberals Urge Carter to Cut Back on Tax Package," *Washington Post* (October 18, 1977); Editorial, "Taxes and Democrats," *Washington Post* (December 1, 1977); Editorial, "Package Number 2," *Wall Street Journal* (September 30, 1977); Editorial, "Delaying the Tax Package," *Wall Street Journal* (October 31, 1977).

22. Editorial, "The Carter Tax Package," *Wall Street Journal* (December 22, 1977).

23. Department of the Treasury, *The President's 1978 Tax Program* (Washington: U.S. Government Printing Office, 1978); *The Administration's 1978 Tax Package* (Washington: American Enterprise Institute, 1978).

24. Editorial, "Mr. Mondale in the Wings," *Wall Street Journal* (January 4, 1978).

25. Editorial, "The Carter Tax Package," *Wall Street Journal* (December 22, 1977).

26. Arthur B. Laffer, "President Carter's Tax Plan," *The Political Economy in Perspective* (Boston: H. C. Wainwright & Co., January 30, 1978).

27. Michael J. Boskin and Jerry Green, "Taxation and Capital Formation: Missing Elements in the President's Tax Program," in Rudolph Penner, ed., *Tax Policies in the 1979 Budget* (Washington: American Enterprise Institute, 1978), pp. 47–54.

28. U.S. Congress, *The President's 1978 Tax Reduction and Reform Proposals: Hearings Before the Committee on Ways and Means, House of Representatives*, 95th Cong., 2nd sess. (Washington: U.S. Government Printing Office, 1978), pt. 9, p. 6279.

29. Joel Havemann and Robert J. Samuelson, "Even Under Carter Tax Plan, Most People Lose," *National Journal* (February 4, 1978), p. 197; see also Art Pine, "Carter Tax Plan Would Mean Rise for Quite a Few," *Washington Post* (February 3, 1978). Much the same point had been made by Sen. William Roth, *Congressional Record* (January 26, 1978), pp. S612–13 (daily ed.).

30. *Congressional Record* (June 28, 1979), pp. H5289–342; *Congressional Quarterly* (June 30, 1979), pp. 1283–85.

31. "Oil Taxes: Uncle Sam Taps Into a Gusher," *Business Week* (February 11, 1980), pp. 35–36.

32. "Landfall for the Windfall Tax," *The Economist* (December 22, 1979), p. 23.

33. Editorial, "A Revenue Measure," *Wall Street Journal* (April 17, 1979).

34. *Congressional Record* (December 10, 1979), pp. S18127–36 (daily ed.).

35. Senate Report No. 96–618, 96th Cong., 2nd sess. (March 4, 1980).

36. Committee on House Administration, *The Presidential Campaign*, p. 144.

16

Taxes in Great Britain

I N 1776, ADAM SMITH LAID DOWN HIS FOUR MAXIMS OF TAXATION.
The fourth and most important of these stated:

Every tax ought to be so contrived as both to take out and to keep
out of the pockets of the people as little as possible, over and above what
it brings into the public treasury of the state. A tax may either take out
or keep out of the pockets of the people a great deal more than it brings
into the public treasury. . . . First, the levying of it may require a great
number of officers, whose salaries may eat up the greater part of the
produce of the tax, and whose perquisites may impose another additional tax upon the people. Secondly, it may obstruct the industry of the
people, and discourage them from applying to certain branches of business which might give maintenance and employment to great multi-
tudes. While it obliges the people to pay, it may thus diminish, or
perhaps destroy, some of the funds which might enable them more
easily to do so.[1]

Unfortunately, Smith's own country, the United Kingdom, has
been one of the worst violators of his maxims, raising taxes to where
they clearly "obstruct the industry of the people." Only with the
election of Margaret Thatcher as Prime Minister in May 1979 were

the first steps taken to lower tax rates and restore some incentive to the British economy. Although she has a long way to go to undo 60 years of socialism and although she has already made some mistakes, she is at least thinking about the problem in the right sort of way, and it is hoped she will be able to turn things around before the Conservative Party must stand for reelection in 1984.

In Britain, as almost everywhere, the greatest growth of government this century took place during World War I. But whereas postwar spending and tax rates were reduced markedly in the United States under the leadership of Pres. Calvin Coolidge and Treasury Secretary Andrew Mellon, in the United Kingdom they never came down. Indeed, they continued to grow. In 1913 the government's share of national income in Great Britain was 15 percent. It rose to 28 percent in 1932 and to over 30 percent in 1938. Then World War II came along, causing another huge boost in government spending and taxation. By 1942 the basic rate of taxation was 50 percent, with surtaxes imposed on incomes above £2,000 (about $10,000), which took the tax rate up to 99 percent. Again, peace brought no reduction in rates. In 1950–51 a married couple with two children and no unearned income paid income and surtaxes at the following rates:

Income	Effective Tax Rate
£1,000	16.8%
2,000	26.4
4,000	42.9
5,000	47.8
10,000	63.2
20,000	77.9
50,000	89.7
100,000	93.6

"The tax situation would have been bad enough had income and surtax been all," wrote C. Northcote Parkinson, "but to these had been added a variety of other taxes, direct and indirect. There was the purchase tax, the national health and insurance contributions and the greatly increased local rates. Tax had been piled on tax; and one result of death duties (amounting to £2,000 million between 1945 and 1957) was so to lessen the number of the rich that the tax burden had increasingly to fall on the poor." Thus, from 1938 to 1949 total taxes on incomes above £1000 increased 171 percent, total taxes on incomes below £1000 increased 615 percent.[2]

Throughout the fifties, sixties and seventies, through both Labor and Conservative governments, the high tax rates remained essentially intact. Between 1949 and 1973 the *pretax* incomes of the top one percent of British households had been cut in half. But the poor did not benefit. In 1949 the lower half of British income classes had 23.7 percent of the pretax income and 24 percent in 1973.[3]

By the mid-1970s the view was widespread that high tax rates were doing the country a great deal of harm. In 1977 it was estimated that as many as 100,000 British executives, middle managers and entrepreneurs had left Britain during the previous three years, largely because of high taxes.[4] Prominent tax exiles included most important British rock singers, among them the Rolling Stones, Rod Stewart, Led Zeppelin, and the Electric Light Orchestra; many of Britain's greatest actors, including Michael Caine, Richard Burton, David Niven, Sean Connery, Peter Sellers, and Peter Ustinov; Nobel Prize–winning scientists Dr. Francis Crick and Dr. Max Perutz; and bestselling authors Len Deighton and Frederick Forsythe. As Forsythe commented: "It is an automatic assumption [in Britain] that any man who has made money has done it by swindling or speculating. . . . In fact, of course, most have done it by sheer hard work, coupled with talent, energy, drive and determination." The revenue loss from tax exiles in 1976 was estimated to be one billion pounds.[5] (In 1978 Sir Geoffrey Howe pleaded for a reduction in high tax rates to keep such people in Britain. The Labor Party backbenchers in Parliament replied by charging such tax exiles with treason.)[6]

A quarter of British business managers surveyed in 1977 said it was not worth accepting a promotion because of the effect of taxes on pay increases. Half of those surveyed considered that lack of financial reward was causing managers to be less efficient in their jobs. And 15 percent admitted they were working less hard than they used to.[7] The result is that British managers, doctors, and other professionals are paid far less than those in the United States. The chairman of Barclays Bank, the nation's largest, with more than $40 billion in assets, was paid only $110,000 in 1978, of which he kept about $31,-000. Sir Derek Ezra, chairman of the National Coal Board, a firm with 250,000 employees, has said he would have been better off managing a single mine in West Germany.[8]

Thus, the high tax rates not only deny people after-tax rewards, they actually discourage people from asking for high salaries in the first place. Consequently, the British government has lost enormous revenues it would have obtained had its tax rates been lower. Typical is the attitude of Andrew Knight, editor of *The Economist,* writing in the *New York Times:*

> Just for the record, I am being paid a pittance by The New York Times for this article. Why did I not chisel The Times for more? Because 83 percent of the money will already go in taxes to pay for other people's

false teeth and spectacles, so why bother? I refuse all freelance, including lucrative television work, for the same reason.[9]

At a lower tax rate people like Andrew Knight would certainly be encouraged to increase their income, generating more revenue to the government.

Of course, Englishmen have not meekly accepted the situation. They have devised numerous methods for increasing their de facto income in nontaxable ways. British executives receive enormous "perks," which give them the benefits of a high income without paying taxes on it. In Britain, for example, managers are almost always supplied with an automobile by their companies for personal use. As many as half of all cars sold in the UK were sold to companies in recent years. In addition, most British executives get their business suits paid for by the company; wives routinely go along on business trips; children may receive scholarships; and some companies even supply their executives with new homes, stereos and antiques to furnish them. Lower-level employees have their perks as well, ranging from free coal for coal miners to cut-rate loans and mortgages for bank employees. And, of course, there is an enormous amount of expense-account eating at Britain's best restaurants.[10]

All of this may mute the effects of Britain's high tax rates, but it deprives people of the freedom to spend their income as they please. There is still no substitute for disposable income. This is why tax cheating is more pervasive in Great Britain than in the United States, despite the fact that the British employ more tax agents than the Internal Revenue Service does, to handle one-fourth the number of tax returns. There is a thriving "subterranean economy" in Great Britain, just as in the United States, with laborers working "off the books" and others "fiddling" their income as best they can.[11]

Unfortunately, this concern over the effects of high tax rates coincided with rising inflation in Great Britain. Between 1973 and 1978 prices in Britain more than doubled. This crisis led even the Keynesians leading the ruling Labor Party to try and cut back on the growth of government expenditures. But it also forestalled any effort to reduce taxes. As Prime Minister James Callaghan told the British Labor Party conference on September 28, 1976:

> We used to think that you could just spend your way out of a recession and increase employment by cutting taxes and raising government spending. I tell you, in all candor, that that option no longer exists, and that it only worked on each occasion since the war by injecting bigger doses of inflation into the economy, followed by higher levels of unemployment as the next step. And we have just escaped from the highest

rate of inflation this country has known. We have not yet escaped from the consequences of high unemployment.[12]

Although both Callaghan of the Labor Party and Edward Heath of the Conservative Party tried wage and price controls during the 1970s to battle the inflation which engulfed Britain, they did not succeed because they did not get at the root of the problem, which was an excessive increase in the quantity of money.[13] The result was that inflation continued, pushing people up into higher tax brackets, exacerbating the inflation by still further reducing the incentive to work and produce. This effect has been described by the *Sunday Times* of London as follows:

Since 1974, inflation has brought hundreds of thousands of the low paid into the income tax net. Many pay taxes at the same time as they are entitled to draw Social Security benefits. As we move up the scale, few of those grossing above-average wages, salaries or earnings have kept up with inflation. But they still pay more tax because the income bands for higher rate tax have hardly moved while prices have nearly doubled. Even the lucky few whose incomes have kept up with prices still find themselves worse off due to taxation.

Just as the poor now pay taxes that were never intended, so managers, professionals and small businessmen now find themselves—quite unintentionally—treated as plutocrats whose pay should be confiscated as much for the sake of social justice as raising revenue. Those who were well off in 1974 now face 83 percent top rates on earned income or 98 percent on profits from a business at ridiculously low levels in relation to any comparable country. The rich employ accountants, lawyers and insurance brokers to avoid tax legally—or if they cannot, flee the country to become unwilling tax exiles. The poor moonlight for cash on the side to evade tax illegally—or, if they are honest, just suffer. . . . This is the effect of Denis Healey's long and unhappy four years as Chancellor of the Exchequer.[14]

By 1979 the economic situation had become so bad the British people threw the Labor Party out and put the Conservative Party back in power. However, the Conservatives were no longer led by the moderate Edward Heath, who had led the Conservatives to defeat in 1974, but by Margaret Thatcher, who campaigned strongly on the promise to cut tax rates across the board and stop inflation by controlling the money supply. In winning a substantial majority in Parliament on May 3, 1979, the Conservatives even managed to attract union votes, the backbone of the Labor Party.[15]

On June 12, 1979, Thatcher came through on her promise to radically alter British economic policy, by proposing a budget with substantial income tax cuts. "Excessive rates of income tax bear a heavy responsibility for the lackluster performance of the British economy," Sir Geoffrey Howe, chancellor of the exchequer, told the House of Commons. "We have to compete in attracting and retaining the talent required to run our industry efficiently and profitably."[16] Former Prime Minister Callaghan called the budget "a reckless gamble with our economic future," producing "dire industrial consequences."[17]

Unfortunately, at the same time the Conservatives cut income tax rates they raised the value-added tax from 8 percent on some goods and 12 percent on others to 15 percent on everything except food, heating, light, public transportation, children's clothes, and medicine. This was done to recapture the revenue lost through the income tax cuts. But the effect was to raise the effective rate of taxation for many British workers. For this reason, Mrs. Thatcher's budget came under heavy attack from Arthur Laffer:

> The Thatcher budget lowers tax rates where they have little economic consequence and raises tax rates where they affect economic activity directly. The result is a substantial increase in the effective rate of taxation in the UK. . . . Mrs. Thatcher's tax restructuring has lowered direct taxation but has taken even more away through indirect taxation. . . . A consumption tax of the U.K. variety is just as damaging to private incentives as is the equivalent income tax. The objective of work and savings is ultimately consumption. Irrespective of the stage at which the resources are obtained, people supply capital and effort to acquire net purchasing power.[18]

For this reason, Laffer said, people should not associate the Thatcher government with a resurgence of classical incentive economics. "As it turns out, nothing could be further from the truth," Laffer says.[19]

The Laffer argument was rebutted by Dr. Norman Ture, another economist associated with supply-side economics. Ture said that Laffer was ignoring his own theories by concerning himself with effective (average) tax rates, when it is the marginal tax rate (the tax on each additional dollar earned) which counts. And the Thatcher budget clearly cut marginal tax rates.[20] Table 1 shows what the Conservatives have done to marginal tax rates in two years:

Despite these important cuts in marginal tax rates, however, the British economy has continued to languish—supporting Laffer's view.[21] The Thatcher government responds to criticism about its economic performance by saying that things could not be expected to turn around overnight. "We did not promise you instant sun-

TABLE 1

SHRINKING PROGRESSIVITY OF THE BRITISH TAX CODE

MARGINAL TAX RATES (PERCENT)	TAXABLE INCOME (IN POUNDS)		
	1978–79	1979–80	1980–81
25	0–750	0–750	—
30	—	750–10,000	0–11,250
33	751–8,000	—	—
40	8,001–9,000	10,001–12,000	11,251–13,250
45	9,001–10,000	12,001–15,000	13,251–16,750
50	10,001–11,000	15,001–20,000	16,751–22,250
55	11,001–12,500	20,001–25,000	22,251–27,750
60	12,501–14,000	Over 25,000	Over 27,750
65	14,001–16,000		
70	16,001–18,500		
75	18,501–24,000		
83	Over 24,000		

SOURCE: *The Economist* (March 29, 1980), p. 26.

shine," Mrs. Thatcher has said. "We pointed out over and over again that a nation cannot accelerate downhill for years and then jam the brakes on and suddenly return to prosperity, as though the past had never happened. We had to start by slowing down before turning around and trying the long, slow climb up the hill to recovery."[22]

This may be true, but it is also true that the Thatcher government raised taxes its first year, thus negating most of its tax cuts, and again in its second year, by raising the lowest marginal rate from 25 percent to 30 percent, increasing sales taxes on liquor, cigarettes, and gasoline, and increasing taxes on North Sea oil production. Thus, although there has been a substantial shift in the composition of the British tax structure, making it less progressive, there has yet to be an overall reduction in the tax burden.[23]

In addition, although there has been much talk about monetarism and controlling the money supply, the quantity of money continues to grow at a rate faster than the real growth of the economy. This is partly due to the fact that government spending has yet to be cut significantly. As *The Economist* recently noted, "Ministers have reverted quickly to departmental type: it is no fun being a minister for the arts and jeered at by actors, a health minister abused by doctors, a social services minister telling the disabled they must suffer along with the rest of Britain from its new poverty."[24]

Moreover, the power of the labor unions remains unchecked. Many have argued that the rest of Britain's economic problems are trivial compared to those caused by excessive labor union power. Although Mrs. Thatcher made early promises to end secondary boycotts and other union pressure tactics, she has yet to move on this front.[25]

It may be that all these things will be taken care of in time. The problem is that many people in the United States and elsewhere are closely watching the British experiment and their actions will depend on the outcome of it. "What happens here in Britain will have a very important influence in the U.S.," Milton Friedman recently said during a visit to the UK. "If Thatcher succeeds, it will be very encouraging. It is a fascinating experiment, and a good deal depends on it."[26]

Notes

1. Adam Smith, *The Wealth of Nations* (New York: Random House, 1937), pp. 778–79.

2. C. Northcote Parkinson, *The Law and the Profits* (Boston: Houghton Mifflin, 1960), pp. 74–76.

3. Leslie Lenkowsky, "Welfare in the Welfare State," in R. Emmett Tyrrell, Jr., ed., *The Future That Doesn't Work: Social Democracy's Failures in Britain* (Garden City, New York: Doubleday, 1977), p. 155.

4. "Britain: The Alarming Exodus of Business Talent," *Business Week* (May 23, 1977), p. 46.

5. Anne Rubinstein, "Britons Fleeing Taxman," *Philadelphia Enquirer* (April 24, 1977).

6. Roy Reed, "Britain Acts to Reduce High Taxes," *New York Times* (May 12, 1978).

7. Robert Prinsky, "Britain's Onerous Tax System," *Wall Street Journal* (March 28, 1977).

8. Rudolf Klein, "Professional Pay Factor in British Decline," *Washington Post* (April 17, 1977); Robert D. Hershey, Jr., "Britain's High Taxes Seen as Factor in Stagnation," *New York Times* (March 13, 1978).

9. Andrew Knight, "Tax Me, I'm British," *New York Times* (March 8, 1978).

10. Richard F. Janssen, "In Britain, High Taxes Yield High 'Perks,'" *Wall Street Journal* (April 19, 1978).

11. "Exploring the Underground Economy," *The Economist* (September 22, 1979), pp. 106–7; Robert Prinsky, "Income-Tax Cheating Is On the Rise in Britain as Prices Outstrip Pay," *Wall Street Journal* (October 10, 1977).

12. "Mr. Callaghan Talks Business," *New York Times* (October 10, 1976).

13. William Rees-Mogg, "How a 9.4% Excess Money Supply gave Britain 9.4% Inflation," *The* [London] *Times* (July 13, 1976).

14. "The Healey Effect: How Our Absurd Income Tax Must Be Cut—in Everyone's Interest," *The Sunday Times* (March 19, 1978).

15. Robert D. Hershey, Jr., "Car Workers Show Swing to Tory Side," *New York Times* (May 15, 1979).

16. Leonard Downie, Jr., "Thatcher Offers Bold Budget That Cuts Government Role," *Washington Post* (June 13, 1979); Walter Eltis, "The Tory Government's Budget," *Wall Street Journal* (June 14, 1979).

17. Leonard Downie, Jr., "Thatcher's Economic Turnabout: A Gamble for High Stakes," *Washington Post* (June 14, 1979).

18. Arthur Laffer, "Margaret Thatcher's Tax Increase," *Wall Street Journal* (August 20, 1979). .

19. Ibid.; see also Arthur Laffer, *Margaret Thatcher's Tax Increase* (Boston: H. C. Wainwright & Co., 1979).

20. "Taxation in Britain," *Wall Street Journal* (September 7, 1979).

21. "Economy in Britain Is Seen Worsening in 4 Separate Studies," *Wall Street Journal* (March 4, 1980); "Two Terms Into One Won't Go," *The Economist* (February 2, 1980), pp. 63–65.

22. Leonard Downie, Jr., "Thatcher Orders Bitter Medicine for Ailing British Economy," *Washington Post* (March 16, 1980).

23. "Britain's Budget," *The Economist* (March 29, 1980); Philip Revzin, "Britain Slates Tax Changes, Spending Cut," *Wall Street Journal* (March 27, 1980).

24. "Don't Look Now, But You Just Made a U-turn," *The Economist* (February 9, 1980), p. 19; Editorial, "London Fog," *Wall Street Journal* (March 28, 1980).

25. Sterling Slappey, "Making Britain Great Again," *Nation's Business* (March 1980), pp. 49–54; Paul Johnson, "Towards the Parasite State," *New Statesman* (September 3, 1976).

26. Leonard Downie, Jr., "Britons Deflate U.S. Economist," *Washington Post* (March 4, 1980).

17

Supply-Side
Economics Abroad

SURELY THE MOST AMAZING STORY IN WORLD ECONOMIC HISTORY
since World War II is the remarkable resurgence of West Germany and Japan as world economic powers, following the almost total destruction of their economies by war. In large measure, their success can be attributed to tax policies which encouraged growth. Moreover, the poverty of Third World nations and their restrictive tax policies stand in stark contrast to the successes of Germany and Japan. Although the United States has given away billions of dollars in foreign aid since World War II, it has failed as a means of alleviating world poverty. The only way that can be done is by encouraging poor nations to reduce high tax rates and adopt policies which encourage economic growth.

When the war ended and Germany became occupied by Britain, France, the Soviet Union, and the United States, the nation became split between East and West—a division that continues to this day. The eastern half, under Soviet occupation, was turned into a Communist state, with total state control of the economy. West Germany, by contrast, developed a free economy under the leadership of Konrad Adenauer and Ludwig Erhard. However, it was an uphill struggle. When the Western Allies occupied Germany, they inherited and continued in operation all the existing taxes and economic controls. Due to differences among themselves as to what actions should be taken with respect to the economy, the allies decided to simply continue the status quo.[1]

Erhard, who was economic minister, apparently hit upon a ploy to unleash the German economy. He surmised that although he was prohibited from making any changes in the existing controls without approval of the occupying powers, there was no law that said he could not abolish controls. According to Erhard:

> It was strictly laid down by the British and American control authorities that permission had to be obtained before any definite price changes could be made. The Allies never seemed to have thought it possible that someone could have the idea, not to alter price controls, but simply to remove them.[2]

Simultaneously, Erhard instituted currency reform, which halted the rampaging inflation, and moved to cut taxes and restore freedom throughout the economy.[3] Until the middle of 1948 a 50 percent marginal tax rate on personal income became applicable as soon as an individual's income passed the 2,400 Reichsmark level (about $600), and a 95 percent rate was applicable to income exceeding 60,000 Reichsmarks (about $15,000). It was noted that without a thriving black market, outside the reach of tax authorities, combined taxes on income and property might have equalled or exceeded total income. Indeed, it was estimated that half of total income taxes went unpaid.[4]

Beginning in 1948, West Germany began steadily reducing tax rates and instituting special tax incentives for saving and investment. As table 1 shows, the highest marginal tax was reduced from 95 percent to 53 percent, while the personal exemption was increased and the threshold income at which the 50 percent marginal rate was reached steadily increased.[5]

The result is that West Germany now has the fourth largest GNP of any nation in the world, amounting to $640 billion in 1978, and a per capita GNP significantly larger than the U.S.

It is generally believed that the Marshall Plan was a significant factor in Germany's rise. However, it should be noted that the German recovery began before Marshall Plan aid arrived.[6] Moreover, Germany got significantly less aid than did France or the United Kingdom.[7] Consequently, one must say that while the Marshall Plan was helpful, it was not necessary for Germany's recovery.[8]

Lastly, it should be noted that although the German revival took place during the heyday of Keynesian economics, Keynesian princi-

TABLE 1

INDIVIDUAL INCOME TAX RATES IN WEST GERMANY, 1946–66
(REICHMARKS OR DEUTCHMARKS)

Period	Personal Exemption	Income at which Marginal Rate Reaches 50%	Highest Marginal Tax Rate	Income at Which Reached
1946–mid-1948	600	2,401	95	60,000
mid-1948–1949	750	9,001	95	250,000
1950–52	750	20,001	95	250,000
1953	750	36,001	82.25	220,000
1954	800	45,001	80	220,000
1955–57	900	125,001	63.45	605,001
1958–66	1,710	78,420	53	110,040

SOURCE: Karl Hauser, "West Germany," in *Foreign Tax Policies and Economic Growth* (New York: Columbia University Press, 1966), p. 147.

ples were explicitly repudiated by Erhard and the other German policymakers. As one observer has said, "West Germany's impressive recovery took place under policies that were in many respects the direct antithesis of post-Keynesian prescriptions for rapid economic growth."[9]

The situation in Japan was different, of course, not only because of its different history and culture, but because it was under the sole occupation of the United States, with General Douglas MacArthur holding almost total control of the country following the end of war.

During the initial occupation period, 1946–49, the principal problem was halting the spiraling inflation. Unfortunately, the initial tax reforms imposed by the occupation authorities were totally unsuited to an inflationary environment. Among these initial reforms were (1) higher and more progressive individual income tax rates and lower exemptions, (2) higher corporate and excess profits taxes which did not allow taxpayers to adjust depreciation allowances for inflation, (3) a heavy capital levy on wealth, and (4) an increase in the number of sales and excise taxes, including a turnover, or VAT, tax.[10]

These disastrous tax changes soon led to a breakdown of the tax-payment system. Tax evasion was widespread, tax collectors became as hated as the prewar secret police, businesses were falling apart because they could not replace capital, and revenue was seriously lagging behind expectations. It was these factors which led General MacArthur to invite a distinguished group of American tax specialists to come to Japan and rewrite its tax system. The group became known as the Shoup Mission, after its leader, Prof. Carl Shoup of Columbia University.

The first thing recommended by the Shoup Mission was a drastic reduction in tax rates and an increase in exemptions. The top bracket was brought down from 85 percent to 55 percent, the personal exemption raised from 15,000 to 24,000 yen, and a tax credit for dependents of 12,000 yen per dependent was instituted. With regard to business, the main contribution of the Shoup Mission was in revising depreciation schedules for inflation. In addition, the excess-profits tax was eliminated and the corporate tax rate reduced to 35 percent. Lastly, an enormous number of technical and administrative reforms were proposed and carried out. At its conclusion, the Shoup Mission declared that Japan now had one of the best tax systems in the world.[11]

The Shoup Mission reforms gave Japan's economy a big boost. Since then, the Japanese government has carried forward the growth-oriented tax policies instituted by Shoup. Because of the enormous Japanese economic growth of the postwar era—which has given Japan the third largest GNP in the world: $969 billion in 1978 —the government has received an enormous influx of tax revenue. However, the Japanese government has not used this revenue to boost the size of the public sector, but instead returned this "fiscal dividend" to the people in the form of tax reduction, which in turn stimulated further economic growth. Between 1954 and 1974, individual income tax exemptions were increased every year but three, individual income tax rates were reduced eleven times, and corporate tax rates were reduced six times.[12] Table 2 illustrates these changes.

One last point. Japan's remarkable postwar economic performance is all the more amazing when one considers its small size (143,000 square miles—about the size of Montana), its enormous population (114 million in 1977—793 people per square mile), and its almost total lack of natural resources, particularly energy. The only thing which detracts from Japan's record is the even more amazing performance of its Asian neighbor, Hong Kong.

In many respects, Hong Kong is the greatest example of the success of the free market in action the world has ever seen. The British crown colony occupies a mere 404 square miles, with most of its 4.5 million population crammed into 12 percent of that area. Population density exceeds 400,000 people per square mile in many areas. And the colony must import 85 percent of its food, most raw materials, and all capital equipment. Nevertheless, between 1948 and 1977 the per capita income of Hong Kong increased from $180 per year to $2,600 per year. Between 1960 and 1976 its real per capita GNP increased by an amazing 6.4 percent per year (compared to just 3.3 percent per year for West Germany and 2.4 percent per year in the U.S.).

One important reason for Hong Kong's success is its extremely low taxes. The maximum tax rate on profits is 17 percent and the maxi-

TABLE 2

ESTIMATED ANNUAL TAX CHANGES IN JAPAN, 1950–74 (YEN IN BILLIONS)

Fiscal Year	INDIVIDUAL INCOME TAX				CORPORATE		
	Exemptions	Rates	Special Tax Changes	Total	Rates	Other	Total
1950–53	−272	−86	−28	−386	+31	−56	−25
1954	−29	0	−2	−31	0	−3	−3
1955	−23	−13	−18	−53	−14	+2	−12
1956	−23	0	0	−23	0	+14	+14
1957	−40	−85	+15	−110	−2	+24	+22
1958	0	0	−6	−6	−20	−2	−22
1959	−28	−12	+17	−23	0	−4	−4
1960	0	0	0	0	0	0	0
1961	−38	−23	+5	−56	0	−40	−40
1962	−25	−23	−2	−50	0	−1	−1
1963	−32	0	−35	−67	0	+13	+13
1964	−66	0	−8	−75	−5	−54	−59
1965	−92	0	+26	−65	−28	−28	−57
1966	−101	−53	−4	−158	−50	−49	−99
1967	−142	+11	+38	−93	0	−30	−30
1968	−135	−11	0	−125	0	0	0
1969	−142	−41	0	−183	0	+2	+2
1970	−173	−131	+15	−289	+97	−22	+75
1971	−286	−107	−22	−415	0	+12	+12
1972	0	0	−32	−32	0	+31	+31
1973	−335	0	−40	−375	0	+27	+27
1974	−1,467	−260	−56	−1,783	+424	−72	+352

NOTE: Totals may not add due to rounding.

SOURCE: Joseph A. Pechman and Keimei Kaizuka, "Taxation," in Hugh Patrick and Henry Rosovsky, eds., *Asia's New Giant: How the Japanese Economy Works* (Washington: The Brookings Institution, 1976), p. 325.

mum tax on individual incomes is 15 percent. There is no tax withholding in Hong Kong, and the estate tax has a maximum rate of only 18 percent on estates of over $3 million.[13] Thus Alvin Rabushka writes:

> Hong Kong has, to my knowledge, the lowest standard rate of tax on earnings and profits of any industrial state. . . . The official line is Gladstone reincarnated: a narrow tax base and low standard rates of direct taxation facilitate rapid economic growth which generates high and ever-increasing tax yields. These revenues, in turn, finance an extremely ambitious program of public expenditure on housing, education, health, and welfare services, and on other forms of social and community services, with virtually no need to resort to loan finance.[14]

In short, Hong Kong is an almost perfect example of the Laffer Curve in action—low tax rates generate high rates of real economic growth, leading to increased revenues which can be used for social welfare while maintaining low tax rates.

Conversely, one finds that welfare states which rely on high tax rates are invariably experiencing serious economic difficulties, imperiling existing social welfare programs. A perfect example is Sweden, the welfare state par exellence.

For many years Sweden was considered by American liberals to be something of an ideal state. It seemed to be living proof that individual liberty, a high rate of economic growth, and a wide range of social welfare benefits could coexist.[15] However, in the mid-1970s it all began to fall apart. The enormous tax burden, which consumes more than 60 percent of Sweden's gross domestic product, inflation, and collapse of the social contract which kept Sweden's labor unions in line for 40 years, all worked together to slow its economic growth to a standstill. In 1977 Sweden's GNP actually declined 2.5 percent.[16]

The Swedish Employer's Confederation recently estimated that a family of four with an earned income of $4,600 per year in 1978 would net $14,117 when all the government welfare benefits were added. On the other hand, a family of four with an earned income of $23,000 would also net $14,117 after taxes were subtracted. Thus, increasing one's income from $4,600 to $23,000 would have absolutely no effect on the family's net income—an implied marginal tax rate of 100 percent. Such incredibly high taxes cannot help but seriously diminish the incentive to work. As a result, Sweden's Nobel laureate in economics, Gunnar Myrdal, an architect of the Swedish welfare state, recently suggested a complete overhaul of the tax system, with a drastic reduction in personal income tax rates and replacement by higher sales taxes. Myrdal writes:

> My main conclusion is the income taxes are bad taxes from several points of view. . . . For the majority of people . . . a high and progressively increasing marginal tax rate must decrease the willingness to work more than necessary. . . . Through the lowering of the income tax, the irrational direction of investment from production to durable consumption goods would not be so severe. . . . The fact that the consumption tax is a tax on living standard instead of income, and therefore puts a premium on saving and capital accumulation, should be liked by most everyone, especially in these times.[17]

Of course, Sweden would have killed its economy long ago had it not adopted some tax policies favorable to growth. It draws very high taxes from individuals, but it leaves its industrial concerns relatively alone and motivates them highly. Sweden gives businesses very generous depreciation allowances, it taxes inventory profits lightly, it eliminated the double-taxation of corporate dividends, and generally taxes corporations less than in many other countries. In 1972, for example, Sweden collected 3.9 percent of its tax revenue from company income taxes, compared to 7.1 percent in Great Britain and 11.2 percent in the U.S.[18] However, it is not enough just to be lenient on corporate income. At some point, there must also be some compensation for individual incentive, because individuals, not corporations, are ultimately the driving force in any economy.

Unfortunately, many Third World countries attempt to duplicate the tax systems of countries like Sweden without realizing that Sweden's system only works because it already had a well-developed capital structure, a highly skilled and disciplined work force, and was able to capitalize on some fortuitous circumstances, such as remaining neutral in World War II while making a fortune on sales of raw materials to the Nazis.[19] Thus these Third World countries impose tax systems designed for modern industrial states on subsistence economies and then wonder why no growth occurs and no revenue is raised. When they turn to "development experts" for advice, they are invariably told that high, progressive income taxes are just the thing. As one such expert, Barbara Ward, recently wrote, "No nation has even half-way peacefully entered the modern world without a progressive income tax."[20]

Jude Wanniski has pointed out that the existence of highly progressive tax structures is doubly harmful because worldwide inflation ends up making already high marginal tax rates even higher. He therefore argues that most of the Third World is high on the upper end of the Laffer Curve, with a few exeptions. He points to the Ivory Coast, where the highest marginal tax rate is only 37.5 percent, and Venezuela, where the highest rate is 25 percent, as success stories.[21] However, the two greatest successes in recent years among underdeveloped countries experimenting with the free market must be Chile and Puerto Rico.

Since the overthrow of President Salvador Allende by a military junta led by General Augusto Pinochet, Chile has been treated as an outcast among nations. Unfortunately, this has led people to ignore or dismiss the remarkable economic experiment taking place in Chile.

When the junta took over in 1973, inflation was 1,000 percent a year and the country was virtually bankrupt. In March 1975 President Pinochet was approached by his government economists. They told him that the collapse in world copper prices would cost Chile $1 billion a year in lost export earnings, that the increase in world oil prices would cost Chile some $300 million in higher imports, that this would reduce Chile's GNP by 13 percent, and that if he attempted to spend his way out of trouble inflation would exceed the Allende years. With Chile's considerable foreign debt it could not expect outside help.

Pinochet decided to adopt an austere economic policy and appointed a group of University of Chicago–trained economists—dubbed the "Chicago Boys"—to run the show. They put the brakes on the money supply to stop inflation, took controls off interest rates to encourage saving, ended capital controls, cut taxes and indexed them to inflation; and eliminated all existing tariffs—which averaged 100 percent—and substituted a flat 10 percent duty.

There was considerable doubt that this program would work. Many of Chile's businesses needed high tariffs to survive. When forced to compete, a lot of them went under. But those that survived and learned to compete prospered. Chile's largest appliance manufacturer tells this story: "In 1974 we had 5,000 workers and a productivity of only $9,000 a year per worker. Now we have 1,860 workers and a productivity of $43,000 per worker, and we are finally showing a profit."

Some $5 billion in foreign investment has flowed into Chile in the last five years. The public sector's share of gross domestic product has fallen from 43 percent in 1973 to about 30 percent in 1979. Four-fifths of the companies nationalized by Allende have been sold back to the private sector, and those nationalized industries that are left are more tightly managed and beginning to show profits. Inflation is down from 1,000 percent to about 30 percent.[22] Thus a recent report by the U.S. Embassy in Chile says:

> In its reliance on market economics, Chile appears in the vanguard of a world-wide neo-conservative response to the menace of growing inflation. . . . Inflation remains Chile's major economic problem, however the three interrelated problems of unemployment, high interest rates and low fixed capital investment are on the way to being solved. . . . Most U.S. private-sector observers are inclined to believe that the current military regime will be followed within 10 years by a stable, middle-of-the road government reasonably favorable to free enterprise and foreign investment. It has been noted that the constituency for the current liberal economic program is growing.[23]

Of course, Chile continues to have a repressive policy toward political dissension, and many freedoms that are taken for granted in the U.S. and Western Europe are denied. However, the criticism of the Chilean regime generally misses a critical point: it is possible to have a free-market economy without political freedom, but the converse is not true; you cannot have political freedom without a free economy. Thus, while Chile may be a long way from being a liberal state, it is at least half-way closer than the vast majority of other nations, which have neither political freedom nor economic freedom.[24]

Puerto Rico is a "purer" example of the Laffer Curve in action because its success stemmed directly from Laffer's influence. During the 1970s Puerto Rico's economy stagnated, its growth in real GNP going from a 13 percent increase in 1969–70 to a 2.5 percent contraction in 1975–76. Unemployment rose and private saving was nonexistent. In 1974 Gov. Hernandez Colon invited liberal Keynesian economist James Tobin to come to Puerto Rico and offer economic advice. Tobin advised an expansion of government spending financed by higher taxes. Colon then proposed a 5 percent surtax on Puerto Rican incomes, which the islanders dubbed *La Vampirita*, or "Little Vampire."[25]

In 1976 Romero Barcelo of the New Progressive Party was elected governor, ending almost 40 years of rule by the Popular Democratic Party. Romero's principal campaign promise was elimination of *La Vampirita*, which ended in January 1977. He also promised further tax cuts and growth-oriented policies. As Treasury Secretary Cesar Perez commented, "We cannot talk about raising taxes; we must raise revenues by restoring prosperity."[26]

In 1978 Laffer was invited to Puerto Rico to study the island's fiscal system and offer recommendations. Laffer recommended income tax rate reductions to get the top marginal tax rate down to 50 percent, a reduction in the corporate tax rate from 45 percent to 25 percent, a reduction in expenditures as a percentage of GNP, and other economic reforms.[27]

In 1978 the 5 percent World War II victory tax was eliminated. In 1979 there was a flat 5 percent reduction in income taxes. By early 1980 these cumulative tax reductions had so expanded Puerto Rico's economy that tax collections in 1980 were running 13.5 percent ahead of 1979. "It is extremely difficult to say it is all due to the tax cuts," Governor Romero said, "but the things Laffer told us would happen are happening. In fact, he guaranteed it would happen."[28]

Based on the success so far of a 15 percent cumulative tax reduction, Puerto Rico enacted another 15 percent income tax reduction, to take place between 1980 and 1982. In defense of the new program, Governor Romero said, "I'm sold that the [Laffer] theory is correct. He wanted me to take a much bigger step initially but I couldn't. I felt I was charged with the responsibility of balancing the budget and I couldn't gamble on a 15% cut in one chunk. I said if it is going to show results with 15% it will show results with 5%."[29]

Interestingly, there are more than 100,000 more taxpayers on the rolls in 1980 than in 1979, the result of lower tax rates which discouraged taxpayers from cheating. This evidence must, therefore, strongly support the Laffer view that tax rates can reduce revenues by discouraging work and encouraging tax cheating.

TABLE 3

PUERTO RICO TAX CUT CHRONOLOGY

Year	Percent of Cut	Tax Change
1977	5	*La Vampirita* eliminated
1978	5	World War II victory tax eliminated
1979	5	Flat rate reduction with withholding tables unchanged
1980	5	Flat rate reduction with new withholding tables reflecting 1979–80 cuts
1981	5	Flat reduction approved in May, 1980
1982	5	Flat reduction approved in May 1980

These examples support the view that the best thing the industrialized countries can do to help the Third World is to encourage them to adopt free market policies, rather than promoting more foreign aid programs. As David McCord Wright put it:

> We must remember, first, that the whole social surplus of Europe, Russia, and America could not make more than the tiniest dent on the poverty of the world. To a large extent, therefore, our aim must be not to give people goods, but to help them toward a situation in which they can improve their own productivity. . . . The main issue is not building a few projects, but transmitting to the underdeveloped nations something of Western dynamism and democracy. The astounding feature of the last two centuries has been the sustained rise and spread of the ideas of economic growth and the ideas of personal freedom and democratic government. . . . Here is a growth impulse that has not lasted merely for the lifetime of one or two great rulers, not been confined to a small clique, and is still going. Can we assert categorically that there are many roads to such a result?[30]

Some have actually argued that foreign aid is detrimental to growth. They assert that because foreign aid is invariably a government-to-government transfer, the main effect of it is to strengthen the public sector in underdeveloped countries—the opposite of what would actually do some good. "Foreign economic aid," writes Milton Friedman, "far from contributing to rapid economic development along democratic lines, is likely to retard improvement in the well-being of the masses, to strengthen the government sector at the expense of the private sector, and to undermine democracy and freedom."[31]

The common thread running through all the economic success stories of the postwar era is a heavy reliance on the private sector and a government which cut taxes and allowed free markets to operate. Socialist and Keynesian policies have not proven effective. Thus Gottfried Haberler writes:

> In all developed industrial countries policies of economic recovery, stabilization, and growth have been much more successful after the second World War than after the first. But it is difficult to attribute this to the spread of Keynesian thinking. It so happens that none of the economists and economic statesmen who were largely responsible for all the assorted postwar economic miracles can be called a Keynesian: not Camille Gut in Belgium, nor Luigi Einaudi in Italy, nor Ludwig Erhard in Germany, nor Reinhard Kamitz in Austria, nor Jacques Rueff in France. The greatest economic miracle of all, the Japanese, seems to have been performed by conservative Japanese governments and statesmen with the help of some ultraconservative American advisors, while the numerous Keynesians and Marxo-Keynesians had to look on in impotent opposition.[32]

There seems to be no escaping the conclusion that the best path to economic growth lies in low taxes and free markets. The successes of Japan, West Germany, Hong Kong, Chile, and Puerto Rico are living testaments to this fact.

Notes

1. See Henry Hazlitt, "The German Paralysis," *Newsweek* (April 21, 1947), p. 82; John Davenport, "New Chance in Germany," *Fortune* (October 1949), pp. 72–76.

2. Ludwig Erhard, *Prosperity Through Competition* (New York: Praeger, 1958), p. 14.

3. Ibid., pp. 10–20; see also F. A. Lutz, "The German Currency Reform and the Revival of the German Economy," *Economica* (May 1949), pp. 122–42; Jacques Rueff, *The Age of Inflation* (Chicago: Regnery, 1964), pp. 86–105.

4. Karl Hauser, "West Germany," in *Foreign Tax Policies and Economic Growth* (New York: Columbia University Press, 1966), p. 113.

5. Ibid., pp. 114–28; see also Walter Heller, "The Role of Fiscal-Monetary Policy in German Economic Recovery," *American Economic Review, Papers and Proceedings* (May 1950), p. 543.

6. Konrad Adenauer, *Memoirs, 1945–53* (Chicago: Regnery, 1966), p. 165.

7. Egon Sohmen, "Competition and Growth: The Lesson of West Germany," *American Economic Review* (December 1959), p. 988.

8. Wilhelm Röpke, "European Prosperity and Its Lessons," *South African Journal of Economics* 32 (September 1964), p. 190.

9. Sohmen, "Competition," p. 989.

10. Martin Bronfenbrenner and Kiichiro Koqiku, "The Aftermath of the Shoup Tax Reforms, Part I," *National Tax Journal* 10 (September 1957), pp. 236–54.

11. Ibid.

12. Joseph A. Pechman and Keimei Kaizuku, "Taxation," in Hugh Patrick and Henry Rosovsky, eds., *Asia's New Giant: How the Japanese Economy Works* (Washington: Brookings Institution, 1976), p. 324.

13. Alvin Rabushka, *Hong Kong: A Study in Economic Freedom* (Chicago: University of Chicago Press, 1979), pp. 70–72.

14. Ibid., p. 55.

15. See Paul A. Samuelson, "A Good Life," *Newsweek* (January 18, 1971), p. 66.

16. "Sweden's English Disease," *Time* (May 1, 1978), p. 51; Leonard Silk, "The 'Swedish Sickness': Gloomy Economic Picture," *New York Times* (November 10, 1977); Richard Janssen, "Trouble on the Road to Utopia," *Wall Street Journal* (November 10, 1977); Robert L. Bartley, "Sweden Faces a Cloudy Future," *Wall Street Journal* (February 21, 1979); Leonard Downie, "Scandanavian Inflation Imperils Welfare State," *Washington Post* (May 10, 1980); idem, "More Swedes Find Welfare State Too Taxing," *Washington Post* (September 2, 1979).

17. Quoted in Melvyn B. Krauss, "The Swedish Tax Revolt," *Wall Street Journal* (February 1, 1979).

18. Robert L. Bartley, "Sweden: The Closet Capitalists," *Wall Street Journal* (June 5, 1975).

19. Ludwig von Mises, *Human Action* (New Haven: Yale University Press, 1949), p. 793.

20. Barbara Ward, "Taxing the Rich Countries To Aid the Poor," *Washington Post* (December 18, 1977).

21. Jude Wanniski, *The Way the World Works* (New York: Basic Books, 1978), pp. 238–75.

22. See "Chile's Counter-Revolution: A Survey," *The Economist* (February 2, 1980), pp. 17–22; "An Odd Free Market Success," *Time* (January 14, 1980), p. 62; Everett G. Martin, "The Chicago Boys in Chile," *Wall Street Journal* (October 5, 1979); "Monetarism, Chilean Style," *Business Week* (November 26, 1979), pp. 127–30; Robert M. Bleiberg, " 'The Chicago Boys,' " *Barron's* (February 18, 1980), p. 7; Norman Gall, "How the 'Chicago Boys' Fought 1,000% Inflation," *Forbes* (March 31, 1980), pp. 75–80.

23. Quoted in Juan de Onis, "Chile's Regime Sees New Economic Hope," *New York Times* (February 24, 1980).

24. For a discussion of this point, see the symposium on capitalism, socialism and democracy in *Commentary* (April 1978).

25. Wanniski, *Way the World Works*, pp. 288–91.

26. Quoted in Dana Thomas, "Fifty-First State? Puerto Rico Puts Economics Ahead of Politics," *Barron's* (March 28, 1977), p. 12.

27. Arthur Laffer et al., *Report to the Governor: Recommendations for Economic Reform* (Boston: H. C. Wainwright & Co., January 1979).

28. John Simon, "Revenue Increase Bolsters Romero Tax-Cut Policy," *San Juan Star* (May 25, 1980).

29. Ibid.

30. David McCord Wright, "True Growth Must Come Through Freedom," *Fortune* (December 1959), pp. 209–12.

31. Milton Friedman, "Foreign Economic Aid: Means and Objectives," *The Yale Review* (Summer 1958), p. 516; see also P. T. Bauer, *Dissent on Development* (Cambridge, MA.: Harvard University Press, 1972); idem, "Foreign Aid, Forever?" *Encounter* (March 1974), pp. 15–28; idem, "The Harm That Foreign Aid Does," *Wall Street Journal* (June 9, 1980); Francis Moore Lappe and Joseph Collins, "Aid As Obstacle," *New York Times* (February 15, 1980).

32. Robert Lekachman, ed., *Keynes' General Theory: Report of Three Decades* (New York: St. Martin's Press, 1964), p. 295; see also Milton Friedman, "Economic Miracles," *Newsweek* (January 21, 1974), p. 80.

18

Economic Policies for
the Eighties and Beyond

THE GREATEST CHALLENGE OF THE 1980S WILL BE TO PREVENT
supply-side economics from being perverted into an industrial
policy, which would substitute government subsidies and tariffs for
tax reduction or regulatory reform and put the United States on the
road to centralized economic planning.

Such a program has great attraction for liberals. They know that
America's industrial base is deteriorating, the result of years of excessive taxation, overregulation, and inflation. But they are unwilling to
cut taxes in a meaningful way because it would require giving some
benefits to the "rich," seriously cut back the power of the regulatory
agencies which they created, and likely cut government spending.
A policy of "reindustrialization" would allow them to have their cake
and eat it too. They could support business without giving up any
government power. And because the aid would come with strings
attached, it would be a powerful tool for government economic planning. Another benefit of such a policy is that most of the industries
which would be the principal recipients of aid for reindustrialization
—steel, autos, textiles—are based in the Northeast and upper Midwest, strongholds of the Democratic Party.

Of course, there is much truth in what the reindustrialists have to say about what is wrong with the American economy. They have accurately pointed to lagging productivity, the falloff in innovation, distortions in our process of capital formation, the loss of global competitiveness, overconsumption, and underinvestment in our nation's industrial base.[1] However, as Sen. William Proxmire has noted, "There is one common denominator in all this so-called reindustrialization. Every measure would try to assist American industry. And each measure would do so by using federal resources. Reindustrialization would strengthen American business by using the federal taxing, spending, and lending power to do so."[2]

The most common vehicle discussed for aiding reindustrialization is reestablishment of the Reconstruction Finance Corporation (RFC). New York banker Felix Rohatyn has been calling for a new RFC for years.[3] Now, however, people appear to be listening. In August 1980 New York's Sen. Daniel Patrick Moynihan introduced legislation to reestablish the RFC with $3 billion in capital and authority to borrow another $30 billion. Its purpose would be to "serve as a lender of last resort to financially-troubled businesses and municipalities, providing a safety net for them in times of fiscal crisis."[4] Although there is language in the legislation about forcing municipalities to straighten out their finances and aiding the liquidation of firms that cannot succeed, it is hard to see how the RFC would avoid doing anything except bailing out losers at taxpayer expense. This is inevitable, because "winners" do not need government help, while the politically appointed directors of the RFC—no matter how "independent" they may proclaim to be—will be under enormous pressure to put their aid where the votes are. As Senator Proxmire put it:

> Money will go where the political power is. . . . It will go where union power is mobilized. It will go where the campaign contributors want it to go. It will go where the mayors and governors as well as congressmen and senators have the power to push it. Anyone who thinks government funds will be allocated to firms according to merit has not lived or served in Washington very long.[5]

The experience with the original RFC, which was established in 1932 and liquidated in the early 1950s, confirms Proxmire's view. For example, a Senate Banking Committee investigation in 1951 showed that two of the RFC's five directors were involved in influence-peddling activities. Other examples of questionable practices included RFC loans to the Lustron Corporation and the Kaiser-Frazer Corporation. In the Lustron case, Carl Strandlund, the president and principal owner of Lustron, charged that one of the RFC directors repeatedly tried to transfer control of the corporation to some friends and associates. Evidence also indicated that Edgar Kaiser of the Kaiser-Frazer Corporation had been approached by RFC influence peddlers on several occasions. In any case, the record shows that many loans were made to gambling casinos, bars, breweries, and other establishments that hardly seemed to fit the criteria for aid.[6]

The view seems to exist that an RFC would not actually subsidize business operations. However, as the Chrysler case clearly shows, even if loans are made at market interest rates an implied subsidy is involved because risk has been shifted from the private sector to government. Moreover, it should be made clear that an RFC or any type of government loan or loan guarantee program can do nothing to increase the total supply of capital. It merely shifts funds from one potential borrower to another. This tends to raise the general level of interest rates as those firms unable to get government-supported loans must compete for a smaller supply of capital.[7]

Because capital is such a scarce commodity, a government agency with the power to direct its flow can exert effective control over much of the economy. Thus, it would be a powerful tool for national economic planning even in the absence of direct government controls over the economy. For years liberals have sought a means by which the government would centrally direct the economy. They feel that the free market is chaotic, inefficient, and unable to achieve national goals in areas such as employment, housing, and urban development. However, as Friedrich Hayek has made clear, government planning would only make matters worse:

> Implied in the argument for government planning of industrial and commercial activity is the belief that government (with an appropriately increased bureaucracy, of course) would be in a better position to predict the future needs of consumer goods, materials, and productive equipment than individual firms. But is it really seriously contended that some government office (or worse, some politically sensitive plan-making committee) would be more likely to foresee correctly the effects of future changes in tastes, the success of some new device or other technical innovation, changes in the scarcity of different raw materials, etc., on the amounts of some commodity that ought to be produced some years hence, than the producers or professional dealers of those things? Is it really likely that a National Planning Office would have a better judgement of "the number of cars, the number of generators, and the quantities of frozen foods we are likely to require in, say, five years," than Ford or General Motors, etc., and, even more important, would it even be desirable that various companies in an industry all act on the same guess? Is it not the very rationale of the method of competition that we allow those who have shown the greatest skill in forecasting to make preparations for the future?[8]

By way of illustration, Charles Schultze, chairman of the Council of Economic Advisors, recently put together a list of the 20 products and industries that grew fastest during the 1970s—the "winners." Of those 20, 5 might reasonably have been predicted—plastics, oil and gas drilling equipment, semiconductors, and small cars. But number 2 on the list is "utility vehicles." Vacuum cleaners placed number 9, construction glass number 13, cheese number 18, and tufted carpets number 19. Schultze goes on to point out that the highest productivity increase in the past generation occurred in poultry and turkey rearing. What government planning agency would have ever picked that as a "winner"?[9]

Given the impossibility of planning being able to improve upon the performance of the free economy, why do people continue to press for it? One reason is that businessmen desire it. Historically, it has been industry that pushed for establishment of the regulatory agencies. The railroads pushed for the ICC, the bankers pushed for the Federal Reserve, and airlines pushed for the CAB.[10] Thus, economist George Stigler writes, "As a rule, regulation is acquired by the industry and is designed and operated primarily for its benefit."[11]

The reason is simple: businessmen—especially big businessmen—hate competition. They hate having constantly to keep looking over their shoulders to see which competitor may be gaining on them. They hate the uncertainty of the market and the fickle tastes of consumers. They want stability and predictability. "I sometimes suspect that many American capitalists actually distrust the market as much as capitalism's enemies do," Henry Ford II recently remarked. "There are whole industries today that prefer to escape the market's discipline."[12] And Gov. Jerry Brown of California recently said, "Sometimes businessmen almost operate as though they'd feel more comfortable in a Marxist state where they could just deal with a few commissars who would tell them what the production goals were, what quota they had as part of the overall mix. . . . I really am concerned that many businessmen are growing weary of the rigors of the free market."[13]

Although most businessmen publicly proclaim their devotion to the free market, they always do so with a big "but." The "but" is usually followed by some explanation about how their situation is different, about how they are faced with "unfair" competition, or how the "national interest" demands that they receive government help. Former Treasury Secretary William Simon tells how such pleadings for government aid by businessmen were a constant source of irritation to him:

> During my tenure at Treasury I watched with incredulity as business-
> men ran to the government in every crisis, whining for handouts or

protection from the very competition that has made this system so productive. I saw Texas ranchers, hit by drought, demanding government-guaranteed loans; giant milk cooperatives lobbying for higher price supports; major airlines fighting deregulation to preserve their monopoly status; giant companies like Lockheed seeking federal assistance to rescue them from sheer inefficiency; bankers, like David Rockefeller, demanding government bailouts to protect them from their ill-conceived investments; network executives like William Paley of CBS, fighting to preserve regulatory restrictions and to block the emergence of competitive cable and pay TV. And always, such gentlemen proclaimed their devotion to free enterprise and their opposition to the arbitrary intervention into our economic life by the state. Except, of course, for their own case, which was always unique and which was justified by their immense concern for the public interest.[14]

Thus, in recent months we have had the Chrysler bailout, in which Congress voted $1.5 billion in loan guarantees to the company because its financial condition was so grave that no bank would loan it any money. We have had Ford and General Motors calling for restrictions on imports of Japanese autos, while the steel industry successfully got restrictions on imports of Japanese steel. And small oil refiners are now before Congress asking for subsidies to protect them from the loss of a special allocation program which gave them access to low-cost domestic crude oil—a program which ends when the price of oil becomes fully decontrolled in late 1981.

What American business desperately needs is not more government intervention in the economy to compensate for prior intervention, but *a radical reduction in the overall burden of government.* Instead of tariffs we should have regulatory reform. Instead of subsidies we need across-the-board tax-rate reduction. Instead of loan guarantees we need a cut in government's share of GNP. A program which would truly aid in the reindustrialization and revitalization of the American economy would begin with the following steps:

Index the tax code to inflation. Although it would be preferable to just stop inflation, in the present political climate it is unlikely this will happen soon. In the meantime it is extraordinarily harmful to the economy to have individuals continually pushed up into higher and higher tax brackets, corporations being hit for overstated profits and understated depreciation costs, and both individuals and corporations being forced to pay taxes on nonexistent capital gains. Those who argue that indexation of the tax code will eliminate the pain of inflation were strangely silent when almost every major *spending* program was indexed to inflation.

Cut tax rates across the board. Although indexing should be the first priority it does not go far enough. It only keeps things from getting worse. To actually get the economy moving again we must increase the incentive to work, save, and invest. A good place to start would be adoption of the Kemp-Roth bill, which would reduce the highest income tax rate to 50 percent and the lowest rate to 8 percent. This would put individuals into approximately the same relative tax position they were in in the mid-1960s following the Kennedy tax cut. Corporate tax rates should also be slashed. So should taxes on capital gains. Eventually, the corporate income tax should be abolished and taxes on interest and capital gains eliminated.

Cap government spending. It is now widely recognized that the federal budget is out of control. A balanced-budget amendment to the Constitution has been suggested as a solution. Unfortunately, because the budget can be balanced by raising taxes as well as by reducing spending, this is not the answer. If some politically feasible way were found to hold government's share to a fixed percentage of GNP this might help, although the problem of enforcing such a restraint has proven to be difficult. In any case, the burden of government ultimately involves the total amount of resources it commands. This burden must be reduced, which means that cutting taxes is not enough; spending must be cut too.

Reduce regulations and government credit activities. Along this same line, government commands much of its resources in ways that do not show up in the budget. If a company is forced to spend money it would not otherwise spend this is really no different economically than the imposition of a tax. And if government directs capital into one area instead of another, this is no different from government spending. So regulations must be cut back and government loan guarantees and other credit programs cut back as well.

If these things were done, there would be no need for a reindustrialization policy. Our economy would take off on its own. This is the essence of supply-side economics.

Notes

1. See "The Reindustrialization of America," *Business Week* (June 30, 1980), pp. 56–142; "Reviving Industry: The Search for a Policy," *New York Times* (August 18–22, 1980); "The 'Reindustrialization' of America?" *Dun's Review* (July 1980), pp. 34–43; Amitai Etzioni, "Why U.S. Industry Needs Help," *Forbes* (August 18, 1980), 120–21; idem, "Rebuilding Our Economic Foundations," *Business Week* (August 25, 1980), p. 16; idem, "Reindustrialization: View From the Source," *New York Times* (June 29, 1980).

2. *Congressional Record* (August 1, 1980), p. S10513 (daily ed.).

3. Felix Rohatyn, "A New R.F.C. Is Proposed For Business," *New York*

Times (December 1, 1974); idem, "Reconstructing the RFC," *Washington Post* (June 20, 1980).

4. S. 3037, 96th Congress, 2nd sess.; *Congressional Record* (August 6, 1980), pp. S11007–12 (daily ed.).

5. *Congressional Record* (August 1, 1980), p. S10513 (daily ed.).

6. Jules Abels, *The Truman Scandals* (Chicago: Henry Regnery Co., 1956).

7. See Murray L. Weidenbaum and Reno Harnish, *Government Credit Subsidies for Energy Development* (Washington: American Enterprise Institute, 1976), pp. 9–20.

8. F. A. Hayek, "The New Confusion About 'Planning,' " *Morgan Guaranty Survey* (January 1976), p. 9.

9. See James Fallows, "American Industry: What Ails It, How to Save It," *Atlantic Monthly* (September 1980), p. 50.

10. See Gabriel Kolko, *Railroads and Regulation, 1877–1916* (New York: Norton, 1970); idem, *The Triumph of Conservatism* (Chicago: Quadrangle, 1967); James Weinstein, *The Corporate Ideal in the Liberal State, 1900–1918* (Boston: Beacon Press, 1968); William A. Williams, *The Contours of American History* (Chicago: Quadrangle, 1966); Ronald Radosh and Murray Rothbard, eds., *A New History of Leviathan* (New York: E. P. Dutton, 1972).

11. George Stigler, *The Citizen and the State* (Chicago: University of Chicago Press, 1975), p. 114.

12. Quoted in the *Wall Street Journal* (July 11, 1979).

13. Quoted in *Barron's* (June 6, 1977).

14. William Simon, *A Time for Truth* (New York: McGraw-Hill, 1978), p. 196.

Epilogue

On January 20, 1981, Ronald Reagan became the fortieth President of the United States, following a smashing victory over incumbent President Jimmy Carter on November 4, 1980. Throughout his campaign Reagan made the economy his principal issue. He pointed out that the inflation rate had been only 3.7 percent in 1976 and had risen under the Carter Administration to 11.8 percent in 1980. Similarly, the prime interest rate had risen from 6.8 percent in 1976 to 15.3 percent in 1980, while average weekly earnings for workers had declined by 7.5 percent in real terms. Reagan argued that we could do better. He promised that his first priority upon taking office would be to propose a comprehensive economic program to get the economy moving again.[1]

On February 18, 1981, President Reagan addressed a joint session of Congress to outline his program. It involved four components: (1) reductions in personal tax rates and business taxes; (2) spending cuts and other measures to reduce government spending as a share of gross national product; (3) reductions in the burden and the intrusion of federal regulations; and (4) a new commitment to a stable monetary policy.

Reagan's tax package called for a 10 percent reduction in all individual income tax rates in each of three years, beginning on July 1, 1981, combined with a total revision of business depreciation allowances so that structures could be written off in 10 years, equipment in 5 years, and trucks and autos in 3 years. His budget package called for $47.1 billion in spending reductions for fiscal 1982, with the goal of reducing the federal government's share of GNP from about 23 percent in fiscal year 1981 to 19.3 percent in 1984. Reagan imposed a freeze on new regulations and rescinded many enacted during the last days of the Carter Administration, while instituting new procedures for reviewing the economic impact of government regulations. Finally, Reagan asked that the Federal Reserve maintain slow, steady growth of the money supply, with the goal of gradually reducing the rate of money growth to a level equal to the rate of real economic growth.[2]

From the beginning many doubted that Reagan or any President could make such fundamental changes in national economic policy. First, they pointed out, the constituencies in favor of spending were well organized and powerful, while those in favor of lower spending and taxes were diverse and disorganized. Second, they noted, the House of Representatives remained under control of the Democratic Party, whose leaders had been responsible for enacting many of the programs President Reagan was proposing to cut. Virtually no one expected the President to get more than a fraction of his program enacted.

They underestimated the resolve and determination of President Reagan and his administration concerning their program. They also underestimated the ability of the President to mobilize public opinion in support of his goal. And they failed to understand that the Congress had changed, both in the nature of its membership and in its procedures, in ways that substantially aided the chances for enactment of Reagan's economic program.

At the base of Reagan's success was a strong belief that big government and high taxes have destroyed the incentive to work, save and invest, and that this diminution of incentives lies at the root of our economic malaise. As he pointed out many times during the presidential campaign, when he was an actor Hollywood was virtually a laboratory for supply-side economics. Reagan told an interviewer:

> When I was in the movies, I'd reach a point each year where after the second movie I'd be in the 90 percent bracket. So I wouldn't make any more movies that year. And it wasn't just me, but Bogart and Gable and the others did the same. We weren't the ones who were hurt. The people who worked the props and the people who worked the yard, they were the ones who were hurt.[3]

* * *

This commitment to supply-side economics was shared by his principal staff and cabinet officers.

When a President has no ideology, the machinery of government is dependent upon the personal involvement of the President in every aspect of policymaking. Since a President without an ideology may come down differently on every issue, one can never act without first clearing one's position with the President. This obviously creates enormous inefficiency and robs the President's supporters of the vital strength that comes from an ideological commitment to goals rather than mere personal loyalty. Because Reagan's position was clear, it was not necessary for every day-to-day matter to be referred to him personally. He concentrated on using his time and his office to achieve political success for his program, rather than wasting precious effort on formulating an initial position.

Since the ideological direction of the Reagan administration was defined from the start, it was possible to formulate a specific program very quickly, allowing Reagan to use the political capital accumulated by his enormous victory over Jimmy Carter to maximum benefit.[4] The broad outline of his program—a reduction in spending as a percentage of GNP, an across-the-board tax rate reduction, and a severe curtailing of government regulation—was laid out by Reagan. His staff was given a more or less free rein to work out details. David Stockman, director of the Office of Management and Budget, took charge of the spending cuts; Treasury Secretary Donald Regan led the fight on tax cuts; and Vice President Bush coordinated a low-key but extremely significant reform of government regulatory policy.

Working closely with their allies in Congress, the Reagan men exploited with startling success an obscure provision of the Budget Act of 1974 known as reconciliation,[5] and split Democratic ranks by working with disaffected conservative southern Democrats. By using reconciliation, it was possible to move the budget cuts through Congress as a package, disarming the organized constituencies favoring each particular program while drawing on the existing broad support for budget control. With the help of conservative Democrats like Congressman Phil Gramm, Congressman Charles Stenholm, and Congressman Kent Hance (all from Texas), Reagan was able to forge a bipartisan coalition. At each critical juncture, Reagan made the case for his approach over national television.

Before the final House vote on the budget cuts, the Democratically controlled committees attempted to sabotage the package by making excessively deep cuts in certain areas and none at all in others.[6] Although House Speaker Tip O'Neill argued that Reagan was getting most of what he had asked for, Reagan opted for a hastily written alternative sponsored by Congressman Gramm and Congressman Del Latta of Ohio. In an unprecedented defeat for the House leadership, the Gramm-Latta substitute was approved by the full House.[7]

When the tax bill came up for a vote, the House leadership adopted a new tactic: this time they would try to outbid the President. Thus it was the Democrats on the House Ways and Means Committee who first pushed for immediately dropping the top tax rate on individuals from 70 percent to 50 percent; it was the Democrats who first pushed for additional savings incentives, estate tax reform, and reductions in the so-called windfall profits tax on oil companies; and it was even the Democrats who came up with a clearly superior business tax cut, which combined reductions in the corporate tax rate with writing off all investments in new plant and equipment in one year.[8]

The President, who initially favored a "clean" tax bill involving a simple across-the-board tax rate reduction for individuals and a reform of business depreciation, was happy to enter this bidding contest by accepting those Democratic proposals that fit in with his supply-side approach to tax cutting. At the end, Chairman Dan Rostenkowski of the Ways and Means Committee could legitimately claim that his bill contained 90 percent of Reagan's requests. Nevertheless, Reagan decided to fight for 100 percent and went again to the people in a nationwide broadcast. Although the vote was in doubt up to the last minute, the response of the American people, demanding that their representatives support the President's plan, proved decisive. The final vote on a substitute offered by Democratic Congressman Kent Hance and Republican Barber Conable gave Reagan a comfortable victory.[9]

The Economic Recovery Tax Act of 1981 is the best piece of tax legislation, from an economic point of view, passed by the United States Congress since at least the early 1960s, and probably since the 1920s. It will go a long way toward correcting the tax-inflicted economic problems our nation has experienced in recent years and is solidly based on the principles of supply-side economics. Its only weakness is that it does not go far enough. As a result of bracket-creep and previously legislated social security tax increases, the enacted tax bill just barely keeps the overall tax burden from rising.

It is worth remembering that the first version of the Kemp-Roth bill introduced by Congressman Kemp in 1977 called for a 30 percent reduction in individual income taxes *in one year*.[10] And this was at a time when inflation was lower and Congress had not yet enacted the enormous increase in social security taxes. It is also worth remembering that President Reagan originally wanted the tax cut to take effect on January 1, 1981. Concern over revenue loss caused him to move this forward to July 1, 1981. Later, Congress forced him to reduce the first phase of the tax cut from 10 percent to 5 percent and to push it forward to October 1, 1981. Had there been a full 10 percent income tax cut for all of 1981, the recession could well have been avoided.

Nevertheless, the Economic Recovery Tax Act of 1981 is a very good piece of supply-side tax legislation:

(1) It was written almost exclusively with an eye toward the impact of tax policy on economic growth, in contrast to most tax bills enacted in recent years, which emphasized redistribution of income.

(2) It focused on the long term, rather than on short-run economic and political cycles.

(3) To a large extent it focused on incentives rather than aggregate dollar size, which has no meaning outside the context of Keynesian economics.

(4) It indexed the tax code to inflation beginning in 1985, so that taxpayers would no longer be pushed into higher income tax brackets by inflation.

(5) The tax-rate reductions were applied across the board, not targeted toward specific income groups.

(6) The bill partially reduced the tax bias against personal saving by authorizing financial institutions to issue certificates that allow taxpayers to earn up to $1,000 in interest ($2,000 for a joint return), exempt from federal taxation; by allowing taxpayers to exclude up to 15 percent of net interest from taxation after 1985 (up to $3,000 for an individual and $6,000 for a couple);[11] and by substantially expanding the use of Individual Retirement Accounts (IRAs) and Keogh Plans.

(7) It reduced top marginal income tax rate for individuals from 70 percent to 50 percent on January 1, 1982.

(8) Business depreciation allowances were reformed along a 15-5-3 basis.

(9) The tax bias against Americans working overseas was substantially reduced.

(10) A tax credit was instituted for research and development expenditures.

(11) Oil producers received tax credits and exemptions from the so-called windfall profits tax.

(12) It reduced the corporate tax rate for small firms.

(13) It reinstated capital gains treatment for stock options that meet certain conditions.

(14) And it substantially reduced the estate and gift tax, a move that will aid capital formation and help preserve family farms and businesses.[12]

As Congress left for its August recess, President Reagan signed into law the tax and budget cut legislation, completing final action on his initiative. As the senators and congressmen left town, the one question that members of both parties pondered was "Will it work?" Some Republicans, no doubt, never believed it would work but went along for the sake of party unity, while some Democrats were certainly praying that it wouldn't work, so that they could pick up the pieces in 1982 or 1984. But the vast majority of congressmen and senators really wanted the program to work and would do their best to see that it did.

During August, however, opposition to the Reagan program seemed to grow. While Reagan was on his ranch in California and members of Congress were back in their states and districts, the Washington press spent its time searching out critics of supply-side economics. It found many of them on Wall Street, among conservative Keynesians like Henry Kaufman of Salomon Brothers and Albert Wojnilower of First Boston Corporation. The gist of their criticism was that taxes had been cut too much and spending not enough, resulting in continued deficits, leading to high interest rates and slow economic growth. Soon there was a panic atmosphere in Washington, as members of Congress returned to Washington demanding emergency action on the deficit. On September 24, President Reagan proposed additional spending cuts, to address his critics in Washington and on Wall Street. However, quick action by Congress was not forthcoming.

It is unfortunate that Reagan debated his critics on their own terms. By agreeing that the deficit was the critical problem, Reagan undermined his own supply-side economic program. Before long, even members of his own party were calling for rescinding the personal income tax rate reductions or enacting new taxes to balance the budget. Eventually, even his own budget director, David Stockman, said that Reagan's critics were right to blame the deficit for our economic problems.[13]

The trouble with this analysis is that the critics do not seem to care whether the budget deficit results from an increase in government spending or from a reduction in tax revenue. Moreover, they seem obsessed by the dollar size of the deficit, without making any effort to put it in the context of overall spending, saving or GNP. Finally, they do not seem to care that the deficit was rising not because of congressional action, but because the nation was slipping into a recession.

Quite obviously, this attitude is wrong. Whether a budget deficit results from an increase in spending or from a tax cut makes all the difference in the world, and the type of tax cut is at least as important as its aggregate dollar size. When spending is increased, the government preempts from the private sector more goods and services, which are paid for by draining money out of capital markets, causing "crowding-out" and higher interest rates. However, a cut in tax rates has entirely different consequences, because the government is not expropriating more goods and services, but financing their purchase in a different way. Instead of paying for spending programs with tax money, the government borrows the money.

If, in either case, the increase in the deficit were to be financed by the Federal Reserve, then inflation would obviously result. However, if the increased deficit were not monetized, then the only result would be lower private saving. But a tax cut returns additional resources to the private economy, while increased spending does not. Conversely, a tax increase designed to close the deficit will not necessarily relieve pressure on financial markets, because taxes crowd out investment, just as borrowing does. Thus, a tax cut partially provides its own financing and will not affect financial markets like increased spending.

The degree to which a tax cut is self-financing depends on the type of tax cut. Tax rebates do very little to finance themselves, since they merely increase disposable income. However, a tax rate reduction, especially a marginal tax rate reduction, sets in motion dynamic forces because relative prices are altered—in particular, the price of work relative to leisure, and saving relative to consumption.

First, even in the short run, a tax rate reduction will stimulate real economic growth and employment. This broadening of the economic base of taxation will recapture some of the revenue. How quickly the tax base expands depends on many factors, such as the former height of the tax rates and the nature of the tax. In the case of the 1978 cut in capital gains taxes, for example, recent evidence indicates that the cut paid for itself entirely the first year.[14] Across-the-board tax rate reductions also create revenue feedback. Even the heavily Keynesian Congressional Budget Office admits that a tax cut produces 35 percent to 55 percent revenue reflow in the long run.[15]

Second, a tax rate reduction will cause the underground

economy to shrink. Estimates of the size of the underground economy—economic transactions that are not measured by official GNP statistics and are not taxed—vary from $100 billion per year to $200 billion. Since much of this economic activity clearly results from high tax rates on individuals and businesses, it is reasonable to assume that a tax rate reduction will reduce somewhat the incentive to hide income from the tax collector and risk being caught, and will therefore produce some revenue.

Third, there will be a reduction in tax-sheltered investments. About a third of all taxpayers itemize deductions and about 5 percent of all taxpayers are in 50 percent or above tax brackets, considering only federal income taxes. These individuals have a powerful incentive to seek tax-sheltered investments such as municipal bonds. Obviously, if one is above the 50 percent tax bracket, it is more profitable to save a dollar of taxes than to earn a dollar of income. However, if marginal tax rates are cut, then the relative attractiveness of tax shelters automatically declines. This will produce revenue reflow as individuals shift their investments from tax shelters to conventional investments.

Fourth, a tax rate reduction will reduce incentives for non-productive investment in such things as gold, paintings, rare stamps and antiques. The advantage of such investments has been that during periods of inflation they tend to hold their value while producing nontaxable pleasure for their owners. While inflation has been the major impetus for such investments, tax considerations have also been a factor. One important reason why capital gains tax revenue went up after the capital gains tax rate was cut is because people disposed of such assets and realized their gains.

Fifth, a tax cut will increase savings, which will help absorb additional federal borrowing without producing crowding-out or raising interest rates. Thus, in countries like Japan and West Germany the government frequently runs deficits that are a much higher percentage of GNP than those of the United States without producing crowding-out, because the rate of saving is much higher. It is higher because the tax bias against saving is considerably lower in these countries than in the United States.[16] A tax rate reduction will increase the return to saving, and more saving will not only increase our nation's capital base, creating higher real economic growth, but will help finance the deficit as well.[17]

Last, a tax cut will produce some automatic spending cuts. When an economy is stagnating, as ours is, people become unemployed and real standards of living decline, causing individuals to make claims on government. When an individual is employed, he is a source of government revenue; when he is unemployed, he becomes a consumer of government revenue, through such programs as unemployment compensation, trade adjustment assistance, food stamps and other entitlements. Thus, an increase in unemployment reduces government revenue at the same time that it causes spending to rise. It is estimated that a one-percentage-point rise in the national unemployment rate increases the federal deficit automatically by about $27 billion. The converse is also true: an expanding economy will cause people to go off unemployment compensation and become taxpayers, instead of tax-consumers, once again.

For these reasons, the critics of Reaganomics should differentiate between the effects of increases in spending and those of reductions in tax rates, and should therefore differentiate between a deficit resulting from increased spending and one caused by a cut in taxes.

What, then, about the relationship between the deficit and inflation? It is obviously true that the Federal Reserve can and does monetize the federal deficit to a certain extent. However, it is also true that the Fed can monetize previously issued debt if it chooses to do so, and this is equally inflationary. As Murray Rothbard recently put it: "Every time the Fed buys a financial asset, in whatever form, money flows into the banks. The banks in turn are permitted by law to loan out about seven times that much in new money. If the Fed buys $1 billion of U.S. bonds, the banking system will create $7 billion of newly issued money. This inflationary effect will occur whether or not the budget is balanced."[18]

Thus, the question becomes empirical: is there a statistical relationship between the federal deficit and growth of the money supply? If there isn't, then inflation is purely a question of monetary policy and has nothing to do with the deficit.

A number of economists have examined the data in recent years and the consensus is that there is no statistical relationship between the deficit and money growth or between the deficit and inflation. This is not to say that monetary policy is oblivious to fiscal policy. However, increased spending leads to higher money growth and inflation, leading to higher interest rates, regardless of what the deficit happens to be.[19] (See table 1.)

As this is written in November 1981, it is difficult to predict what will happen to the Reagan economic program or the economy itself. Some supply-siders have been expressing fear that the Reagan program is becoming unraveled[20] In the wake of Budget Director David Stockman's admission that he never really thought

TABLE 1

Deficits, Inflation and Interest Rates

Calendar Year

		1971	1972	1973	1974	1975	1976	1977	1978	1979	1980
On-budget deficit	($B)	25	17	18	11	75	56	51	44	28	68
GNP	($B)	1078	1186	1326	1434	1549	1718	1918	2156	2414	2626
Deficit as % of GNP		2.3	1.4	0.6	0.8	4.8	3.3	2.7	2.0	1.2	2.6
GNP deflator		5.0	4.2	5.7	8.7	9.3	5.2	5.8	7.3	8.5	9.0
3-month T-bill rate (avg.)		4.3	4.1	7.0	7.9	5.8	5.0	5.3	7.2	10.0	11.5

Source: Department of the Treasury

supply-side economics was anything more than the old "trickle down" theory, the Reagan program must clearly appear on the defensive. On the other hand, there are already signs of success. By the fall of 1981, inflation and interest rates were dropping steadily. Although stock prices remained low, Professor Martin Feldstein argued that this was a healthy sign, indicating it was now more profitable for firms to invest in new plant and equipment than to obtain such assets through the acquisition of other companies.[21] And most forecasters were predicting a mild recession, set in motion by the economic policies of the Carter Administration.

Reagan's critics may redouble their efforts during 1982 in hopes of making the congressional elections a referendum on Reagan's economic policies, but they have nothing else to offer. There is a broad consensus that taxes and spending are too high, that the overall burden of regulation is excessive and that money growth ought to remain slow and steady. It is unlikely that we will ever return to the days of "tax tax, spend spend, elect elect."

Notes

1. On the Reagan campaign, see Rowland Evans and Robert Novak, *The Reagan Revolution* (New York: E.P. Dutton, 1981), pp. 59–83.

2. See *America's New Beginning: A Program for Economic Recovery* (Washington: The White House, February 18, 1981).

3. Quoted in Martin Schram, "Reagan the Tax Lobbyist: An Artist at Work," *The Washington Post* (August 13, 1981), p. A3.

4. Reagan was also aided by the publication of a virtual how-to manual on specific ways to implement a conservative political program. See Charles H. Heatherly, ed., *Mandate for Leadership: Policy Management in a Conservative Administration* (Washington: The Heritage Foundation, 1981). Another book widely circulated with the Reagan administration in its early days was Peter Duignan and Alvin Rabushka, eds., *The United States in the 1980s* (Stanford, CA: Hoover Institution Press, 1980).

5. Public Law 93-344, Sec. 310.

6. *Preliminary Assessment of House Committee Reconciliation Bills* (Washington: Office of Management and Budget, June 14, 1981); see also

President Reagan's address to a Joint Session of Congress, *Congressional Record* (April 28, 1981), pp. H 1546–48 (daily ed.).

7. *Congressional Record* (May 7, 1981), pp. H 1937–2056.

8. House Report 97-201, 97th Congress, 1st session.

9. *Congressional Record* (July 29, 1981), pp. H 5112–5330 (daily ed.).

10. H.R. 6201, 95th Congress, 1st session.

11. Net interest is defined as the amount by which a taxpayer's interest income exceeds his interest payments, excluding those paid on a home mortgage or in connection with a trade or business.

12. Public Law 97-34, 97th Congress, 1st session. See also Senate Report 97-176, 97th Congress, 1st session.

13. William Greider, "The Education of David Stockman," *The Atlantic Monthly* (December 1981), pp. 27–54.

14. Peter J. Ferrara, "Capital Gains: A Painless Tax Cut," H. C. Wainright & Co. *Economic and Investment Observations* (July 6, 1981); O. S. Pollock, "Revenue Effects of the 1978 Capital Gains Tax Reduction: New and Important Data," *Capital Formation* (February 1981), pp. 2–3.

15. Congressional Budget Office, *Understanding Fiscal Policy* (Washington: Congressional Budget Office, Background Paper, April 1978), p. 18.

16. See *U.S. Economic Performance in a Global Perspective* (New York: New York Stock Exchange, Office of Economic Research, February 1981).

17. Paul Craig Roberts, "The Tax Cut Will Help Savings," *Fortune* (August 24, 1981), pp. 44–45; Paul Evans, "Kemp-Roth and Saving," Federal Reserve Bank of San Francisco *Weekly Letter* (May 8, 1981); U.S. Congress, Joint Economic Committee, *Marginal Tax Rates, Saving, and Federal Government Deficits*, by Timothy Roth and Mark Policinski, Joint Committee Print (Washington: Government Printing Office, 1981).

18. Murray N. Rothbard, "P. T. Barnum Was Right," *Inquiry* (May 25, 1981), p. 20.

19. See U.S. Congress, Joint Economic Committee, *Deficits: Their Impact on Inflation and Growth*, by Robert Weintraub, Joint Committee

Print (Washington: Government Printing Office, 1981); William Niskanen, "Deficits, Government Spending, and Inflation," *Journal of Monetary Economics* (August 1978), pp. 591–602; Scott E. Hein, "Deficits and Inflation," *Federal Reserve Bank of St. Louis Review* (March 1981), pp. 3–10; David Meiselman, "Deficits, Money and the Causes of Inflation," *Wall Street Journal* (July 21, 1981); Michael Hamburger and Burton Zwick, "Deficits, Money and Inflation," *Journal of Monetary Economics* (January 1981), pp. 141–50.

20. Paul Craig Roberts, "Will Reaganomics Unravel?" *Fortune* (November 16, 1981), pp. 153–56.

21. Martin Feldstein, "The Tax Cut: Why the Market Dropped," *Wall Street Journal* (November 11, 1981), editorial page.

APPENDIX A

Excerpts from President Calvin Coolidge's Speech to the National Republican Club, New York, February 12, 1924

The first object of taxation is to secure revenue. When the taxation of large incomes is approached with that in view, the problem is to find a rate which will produce the largest returns. Experience does not show that the higher rate produces the larger revenue. Experience is all in the other way. When the surtax rate on incomes of $300,000 and over was but 10 per cent, the revenue was about the same as when it was at 65 per cent. There is no escaping the fact that when the taxation of large incomes is excessive, they tend to disappear. In 1916 there were 206 incomes of $1,000,000 or more. Then the high tax rate went into effect. The next year there were only 141, and in 1918 but 67. In 1919 the number declined to 65. In 1920 it fell to 33, and in 1921 it was further reduced to 21. I am not making any argument with the man who believes that 55 per cent ought to be taken away from the man with $1,000,000 income, or 68 per cent from a $5,000,000 income; but when it is considered that in the effort to get these amounts we are rapidly approaching the point of getting nothing at all, it is necessary to look for a more practical method. That can be done only by a reduction of the high surtaxes when viewed solely as a revenue proposition, to about 25 per cent.

I agree perfectly with those who wish to relieve the small taxpayer by getting the largest possible contribution from the people with large incomes. But if the rates on large incomes are so high that they disappear, the small taxpayer will be left to bear the entire burden. If, on the other hand, the rates are placed where they will produce the most revenue from large incomes, then the small taxpayer will be relieved. The experience of the Treasury Department and the opinion of the best experts place the rate which will collect most from the people of great wealth, thus giving the largest relief to people of moderate wealth, at not over 25 percent.

A very important social and economic question is also involved in high rates. That is the result taxation has upon national development. Our progress in that direction depends upon two factors—personal ability and surplus income. An expanding prosperity requires that the largest possible amount of surplus income should be invested in productive enterprise under the direction of the best personal ability. This will not be done if the rewards of such action are very largely taken away by taxation. If we had a tax whereby on the first working day the Government took 5 percent of your wages, on the second day 10 percent, on the third day 20 percent, on the fourth day 30 per cent, on the fifth day 50 per cent, and on the sixth day 60 per cent, how many of you would continue to work the last two days of the week? It is the same with capital. Surplus income will go into tax-exempt securities. It will refuse to take the risk incidental to embarking in business. This will raise the rate which established business will have to pay for new capital, and result in a marked increase in the cost of living. If new capital will not flow into competing enterprise the present concerns tend toward monopoly, increasing again the prices which the people must pay.

APPENDIX B

1976 Congressional Research Service Report on the Revenue Impact of Tax Reductions

August 3, 1976

TO: The Honorable Jack Kemp
FROM: Economics Division
SUBJECT: Revenue loss estimates of tax reduction legislation

This memorandum is in response to your request for the U.S. Treasury estimates of the revenue loss resulting from enactment of tax reduction legislation in 1948 and between 1962 and 1965. The following table provides estimates of loss in tax revenue receipts, exclusive of the "feedback" effect of changes in tax receipts caused by changes in income induced by fiscal policy, for the fiscal years following enactment of the tax legislation.

(In billions of dollars)
Revenue Act of 1948:

Reduction in personal income tax	5.0
Reduction in estate and gift tax	0.25
TOTAL	5.25

(Source: *U.S. Fiscal Policy 1945–1959*, A.G. Holmans, 1961, page 97.)

1962:	1963	1964	1965	1966	1967	1968
Revenue Act investment tax credit	1.1	1.4	1.6	1.9	2.1	1.3
Depreciation guidelines	1.3	1.4	1.5	1.6	1.7	1.8
TOTAL	2.4	2.8	3.1	3.5	3.8	3.1

(Source: *Meetings with Department and Agency Officials*, Hearings before Committee on Banking & Currency, 1967, p. 12.)

Revenue Act of 1964:	1964	1965	1966	1967	1968
Reduction in personal income tax	2.4	8.7	12.4	14.1	15.5
Reduction in corporate income tax		1.5	2.9	3.2	3.2
TOTAL	2.4	10.2	15.3	17.3	18.7

(Source: *Meetings with Department and Agency Officials*, p.12.)

Excise Tax Reduction Act of 1965:	1966	1967	1968
Reduction in excise taxes, net of excise tax increases of Tax Adjustment Act of 1966	1.2	2.5	2.6

(Source: *Meetings with Department and Agency Officials*, p.12.)

MORGAN FRANKEL
Economic Analyst

APPENDIX C

*The Revenue Act of 1964 and Its Effects**

Under the vigorous leadership of President Johnson, the tax-reduction bill was enacted early in 1964. At 1964 levels of income, personal income tax liabilities were cut by $6.7 billion and corporate profits tax liabilities by $1.7 billion. With further reductions in rates taking effect in 1965, the cuts in liabilities will be $11 billion for individuals and $3 billion for corporations. Withholding rates on wages and salaries were reduced from 18 percent to 14 percent in one stage in early March 1964, rather than in two stages. This meant that most of the tax reduction was immediately reflected in consumers' disposable incomes.

The Council's 1964 Annual Report estimated that a personal tax cut of nearly $9 billion would result in a direct increase of more than $8 billion in consumption. Subsequent rounds of spending and respending would add another $10 billion to consumption—producing a tax cut "multiplier" of about two. Thus, through increased consumption alone, GNP would ultimately be raised by more than $18 billion above what it would have been in the absence of the tax cut.

*From the *Economic Report of the President, January 1965* (Washington: U. S. Government Printing Office, 1965), pp. 65–66.

The evidence to date indicates that this expectation is being borne out. After rising to 7.9 percent in the second quarter of 1964, the ratio of personal saving to disposable income had fallen back to a relatively normal 7.1 percent in the third quarter, suggesting that the gains of disposable income resulting from tax reduction were already being largely spent for the purchase of consumer goods and services. (A jump in the saving rate in the fourth quarter appears to be attributable to delayed deliveries of automobiles as a result of strikes.) The tax cut directly added $7.7 billion to disposable income in 1964, and the addition was running at an annual rate of $9½ billion by the end of the year. The Council estimates that the total increase in consumer spending alone resulting from the tax cut's impact was $9 billion in 1964, and had reached an annual rate of $13 billion by the end of the year. Subsequent rounds of spending and respending will bring the full impact on consumption in 1965 and beyond.

From 1963 to 1964, GNP grew 4.5 percent after adjustment for price changes. The above calculations suggest that, in the absence of the tax cut, the growth would have been only 3.0 percent, even if it is assumed that without the tax cut all expenditures other than consumption would have been just what they in fact were.

These figures, however, underestimate the full beneficial effects of the cut. Tax policies were also prominent among the factors that helped to generate a $5.0 billion advance (current prices) in business fixed investment between the fourth quarters of 1963 and 1964. The depreciation reform and the investment credit of 1962 continued to provide added strength to capital spending. The Revenue Act of 1964 reduced the basic rates of corporation taxes and, by increasing consumer demand, gave businessmen added assurance of sustained expansion and expanded markets. This assurance was a stimulating factor, even before tax cuts added to sales or cash flow. As the tax cut raised cash flows and operating rates during the year, business investment plans were revised upward.

Since the full effects on business investment of greater sales, improved profits, and larger cash flow are accomplished only after a substantial lag, and since part of the tax cut becomes effective in 1965, much of the rise in investment stimulated by the 1964 tax cut is still ahead of us. This extra investment will have multiplied effects on total production through the route of expanded incomes and larger consumer spending.

APPENDIX D

Federal Government Receipts, 1963–68

Year	Receipts ($ in billions)	Change from Preceding Year
1963	106.6	+6.9
1964	112.7	+6.1
1965	116.8	+4.1
1966	130.9	+14.1
1967	149.6	+18.7
1968	153.7	+4.1

SOURCE: Office of Management and Budget.

APPENDIX E

Congressman Jack Kemp's Speech to the Republican National Convention, August 17, 1976

The Republican Party must move from the defense to the offense.

The time is now.

And the place is here.

We are convened not just to chart a course for our party, but one for the nation.

Yes, we are here to nominate our party's candidate for President.

And, yes, we are here to adopt a program to put the Republican Party back in control of Congress.

But the issue in 1976 is not who we are against.

It is what we are for.

If we are going to make anything of these few days together, we have to do more than just criticize the Democrats and their platform.

We have to realize that we can no longer make a political career of just opposing what the Democrats are for.

We have to put forward a vision and program of our own.

The first thing you learn in competition is that you have to believe in yourself.

You must believe you can win before you can.

If we don't think we can win we will surely lose.

This ought to be our year.

It can be.

It must be.

There is time to turn this nation of voters toward our party and our ideas.

For far too long, some Republicans have thought we could win elections by obscuring the differences between our party and the other.

This has not worked.

It's time to sharpen those differences.

History turns on ideas. Ideas rule the world.

They do have consequences and it's time to move the American people with our ideas once again.

The Republican Party has the principles and the ideas that the great body of the American people embrace.

But we must translate these principles and ideas into a plan of action that both inspires people and wins elections in this our third century.

For nearly fifty years the Democrat has ridden to political success on a horse called Spending.

More government and huge deficits are ways the Democrats have tried to satisfy divergent groups of people under one political umbrella.

It has been a successful political formula—one that captured the Congress for 40 of the past 44 years.

But while it may have been good politics, it has been disastrous economics and is threatening individual freedom.

It was bound to come to an end and the American people now know it.

It carried the seeds of its own destruction—double digit inflation, resulting in nearly double digit unemployment.

The Democrat-controlled Congresses caused these things.

Not the Republican Administrations or the Republicans in Congress.

The American people need to know this because it is they who are being crushed under these burdens of inflation and unemployment.

They need to know that not a dollar is spent, not a regulation becomes law, nor a program begins, without the concurrence of Congress.

And this is the battleground:

It's time to get Government off their backs and out of their pockets.

Let the Democrats continue to be the party of big spending.

We are the party of less spending and lower taxes.

Let the Democrats continue to be the party of more government jobs.

We are the party of private enterprise jobs.

Let the Democrats continue to be the party of inflation.

We are the party of a sound dollar.

The best and surest way to reduce the size of government is to increase and expand private enterprise.

And the best and surest way to increase and expand private enterprise is to reduce the barriers to its growth.

This is the cutting edge of our idea to reduce the burdens of government.

Let the Democrats propose spending another two hundred billion of the peoples' money.

We say if there is that much money available, why should government spend it?

Why not return it to the people through a tax cut?

When the Democrats propose spending money, we should propose giving it back to the taxpayers.

Whatever our differences, we are united as a party around the idea that the American people are being crushed by the burden of taxation and excessive regulations.

It is our job to do something about it for every working American and their families.

1976 is the year of accountability.

The leadership of Congress needs to be changed and there is only one way to do it.

That is to elect Republican congressional candidates, and by electing them we can have the new leadership and a new Congress responsive to the values, goals and needs of the American people.

There is only one way to reform Washington, and that is to reform Congress.

I ask you to pledge with me to work for a Republican Congress led by the great representative from the state of Arizona [John Rhodes], a leader who puts integrity ahead of expediency and the country ahead of politics.

Let us work for a new Congress, a new speaker, and a new vision for America.

APPENDIX F

How a Family of Four with the Median Income Fared During the Carter Administration

Year	Income	Federal Income Tax	Effective Income Tax Rate	Social Security Tax	Federal Income and Social Security Taxes	Effective Federal Tax Rate
1976	$14,925	$1,308	8.8%	$873	$2,181	14.6%
1977	15,888	1,471	9.3	929	2,400	15.1
1978	17,105	1,678	9.8	1,035	2,713	15.9
1979	19,039	1,858	9.8	1,167	3,025	15.9
1980	21,526	2,260	10.3	1,320	3,580	16.6
1981	23,593	2,641	10.8	1,569	4,210	17.8

NOTE: This table assumes that income changed as did the consumer price index and that deductable expenses are 23 percent of income. The CPI is assumed to rise by 13.0 percent in 1980 and by 9.6 percent in 1981.

SOURCE: Joint Committee on Taxation.

APPENDIX G

Estimated Increased Social Security and Inflation Tax Burden on Individuals in 1981 (1979 income levels, $ in millions)*

Expanded Income Class ($ in thousands)	Inflation Tax Increase	Social Security Tax Increase	Total Tax Increase	% Distribution Total Tax Increase	% Distribution of Present Law Social Security and Income Taxes
0–5	$ 270	$ 286	$ 556	2.2	1.0
5–10	2,010	636	2,646	10.3	6.1
10–15	2,070	852	2,922	11.4	11.7
15–20	2,272	1,009	3,281	12.8	14.9
20–30	4,501	1,946	6,447	25.2	25.0
30–50	4,302	1,664	5,966	23.3	19.1
50–100	2,363	446	2,869	11.0 ⎫	
100–200	646	77	723	2.8 ⎬	22.0
200+	214	20	234	0.9 ⎭	
Totals	$18,648	$6,936	$25,584	100.0	100.0

*The inflation tax increase in this table is the additional tax paid by individuals solely due to inflation's effect of moving taxpayers up the income-tax rate schedule and eroding the value of flat allowances. The table assumes a 13.3 percent inflation factor (as estimated for 1979 CPI) applied to 1979 income levels. The social security tax increase is the legislated increase scheduled to become effective January 1, 1981.

SOURCE: Joint Committee on Taxation; Tax Foundation calculations.

Index

Abels, Jules, 210n
Ackley, Gardner, 132
Adams, Ural, 118
Adenauer, Konrad, 191, 201n
Alchian, Armen, 132
Allen, Howard, 141, 144
American Council for Capital Formation, 92
Ames, Edward, 104n
Anderson, Benjamin M., 105n
Anderson, Martin, 52n
Anderson, Paul, 84, 94n
Archer, Bill, 81
Auletta, Ken, 59

Badillo, Herman, 67
Bartley, Robert, viii, 136n, 202n
Bastable, C.F., 15, 24n
Bentsen, Sen. Lloyd, 4, 5, 7–8
Bernstein, Barton, 165n
Blum, Walter J., 38
Blumenthal, Michael, 8–9, 153
Boskin, Michael, 7, 13n, 40n, 48, 52n, 163, 174, 179n, 180n

Bosworth, Barry P., 13n
Bradley, Tom, 141
Break, George F., 24n, 40n
Brimelow, Peter, viii
Brock, Bill, 125
Bronfenbrenner, Martin, 33, 39n, 202n
Brookings Institution, 9, 24n, 73
Brown, Gov. Jerry, 143, 207
Brown, Gov. Pat, 141
Browning, Edgar, 28, 29n
Brownlee, Oswald, 132
Brownlee, W. Elliot, Jr., 55, 67n
Bush, George, 135
Business Roundtable, 126, 142

Califano, Joseph, 49
Callaghan, James, 185, 186, 187
Cameron, Juan, 95n
Campbell, Colin, 58, 69n
Campbell, Rosemary, 58, 69n
Canada, 17, 37
Cannan, Edwin, 16, 24n
Capital Cost Recovery Act, 81

236

Carey, Hugh, 61
Carson, Gerald, 97, 104n
Carter, James Earl, 8, 49, 128, 131, 151, 153, 164, 167–78, 234
Celler, Emanuel, 106–07
Census Bureau, 51, 56, 57
Chase Econometrics, 84, 131, 132, 152
Chile, 197–99, 202n
Chin, Young D., 149n
Chrysler Corporation, 206, 208
Clark, Colin, 34, 39n
Clark, Lindley H., Jr., 94n
Clower, Robert, 132
Coalition of Northeast Government, 55
Cogan, John F., 40n, 53n
Conable, Barber, 128, 129
Congressional Budget Office, 34, 51, 57, 88, 89–91, 92–93, 117, 131
Congressional Budget and Impoundment Control Act of 1974, 88
Congressional Research Service, 118
Conservation of Human Resources Project, 66
Consumer price index, 70, 152
Consumption, 1–2, 6, 90, 114
Coolidge, Calvin, 88, 100, 101, 102, 183, 224–25
Cooper, Gershon, 39n
Copulos, Milton, 179n
Corporate tax rates, 6, 78, 79, 87, 99, 101, 110, 111, 115, 116, 209
Council of Economic Advisors, 83, 90, 92, 115, 117, 132, 141, 165, 168, 207
Crude oil tax, 169–70, 174ff, 181n

Data Resources, Inc. (DRI), 83–84, 86, 92, 117, 151, 152
Denison, Edward F., 7, 12n, 13n
Depression, 3. *See also* Great Depression.
Department of Health, Education and Welfare, 51
Dole, Robert, 134

Eckstein, Otto, 13n, 84, 86, 92, 94n, 131

Economic Stability Act of 1974, 125
Eisenhower, Dwight D., 110, 111, 112, 141, 162
Eisner, Robert, 21
Ekirch, Arthur A., 165n
Employment, 2, 19, 60, 91
Employment Act of 1946, 7
Energy Policy and Conservation Act, 174
Entin, Steve, viii, 130
Erhard, Ludwig, 191–93, 201, 201n
Estate tax, 16–17, 25n
Evans, Michael K., 13n, 84, 86, 90, 92, 94n, 120, 124n, 131, 132, 157n
Evans, Rowland, 95n, 138n, 180n
Excess profits tax, 110
Excise Tax Reduction Act of 1965, 227
Ezra, Sir Derek, 184

Fagan, Elmer, 38n
Federal Reserve Bank of Minneapolis, 10, 84, 85, 91, 94n
Federal Reserve Bank of San Francisco, 143–44
Federal Reserve Board, 2, 162, 207
Feige, Edgar, 21, 25n
Feldstein, Martin, 7, 9, 12n, 13n, 45–46, 52n, 76, 81, 82n, 152, 153, 157n
Fellner, William, 132
Ferguson, Robert, viii
Financial Accounting Standards Board, 80
First National Bank of Chicago, 61
Foley, Tom, 164
Ford, Gerald, 126, 127
Ford, Henry II, 207
Ford Motor Company, 31, 208
France, 37
Friedman, Milton, 3, 7, 12n, 132, 142, 148n, 162, 166n, 179n, 189, 190–91, 203n

Galbraith, John Kenneth, 132
Gann, Paul, 139–47
General Accounting Office, 21, 42, 65, 143

General Motors, 56, 208
Genetski, Robert J., 149n
George, Henry, 15
Gilder, George, viii
Glass, Carter, 98
Gold standard, 71
Goode, Richard, 34, 39n, 40n
Gordon, Joseph G., 52n
Government regulations, 5, 209
Grace, W. R. and Company, 155
Gramlich, Edward M., 73, 81n
Great Britain, 12n, 21, 37, 54, 182–90, 191
Great Depression, 2, 104, 160
Green, Jerry, 174, 180n
Green, William R., 100
Greenspan, Alan, 132
Gregorsky, Frank, 113n
Griffiths, Martha, 41
Gross National Product, 6, 7, 19, 20, 21, 35, 37, 45, 76, 84, 102, 114, 117, 126, 131, 134, 151, 153, 155, 177, 178, 208, 209, 228, 229
Groves, Harold M., 107
Gutmann, Peter M., 18–21, 25n

Haberler, Gottfried, 201
Hagel, Raymond C., 66
Halstead, D. Kent, 68n
Hamilton, E. J., 81n
Harberger, Arnold C., 35, 40n, 163
Harding, Warren G., 88, 99
Harnish, Reno, 210n
Harris Bank of Chicago, 4, 59, 146
Hartmann, Susan M., 113n
Hatch, Sen. Orrin, 92, 129, 130, 131
Hauser, Karl, 201n
Hausman, J. A., 37, 40n
Hay, John, 144
Hayakawa, Sen. S. I., 129, 130
Hayek, Friedrich A., 27, 30, 38n, 96n, 206, 210n
Hazlitt, Henry, 113n, 201n
Heath, Edward, 186
Heller, Walter, 115, 120, 121, 123n, 132, 133, 137n, 141, 148n, 201n
Henning, John F., 145

Hershleifer, Jack, 132
Hicks, Sir John F., 10, 13n
Higgins, Benjamin, 34, 39n
Hollings, Ernest F., 89
Holt, Marjorie, 128
Hong Kong, 194–96
Hoover, Glenn E., 25n
Hoover, Herbert, 106, 160, 161
House Budget Committee, 128, 168
Houston, David, 98
H. R. 1, 108, 110, 111, 112n, 161
H. R. 3950, 108
H. R. 4790, 110
H. R. 5899, 112
H. R. 8363, 116
House Ways and Means Committee, 99, 100, 104, 108, 110, 111–12, 116, 117, 118, 126, 128, 132, 152, 153, 175
Howe, Sir Geoffrey, 184, 187
Hudson Institute, 170
Hughes, Jonathan, 39n
Humphrey-Hawkins bill, 133

Inflation, 3, 4, 6, 7, 9, 11, 13n, 39n, 51, 70ff, 85, 86, 88, 90, 117, 121, 127, 152, 162, 170, 173, 208, 235
Interest rates, 6
Internal Revenue Service, 17, 21, 185
Investment, 5, 7, 17, 31, 86, 87, 154ff
Italy, 21, 27n, 37

Jacoby, Neil, 141–42, 148n
Japan, 24, 37, 191, 193–94, 195
Jarvis-Gann Amendment. *See* Proposition 13.
Jarvis, Howard, 139–47, 147n
Javits, Jacob, 121
Jobs Creation Act, 126, 127
Johnson, Lyndon B., 88, 117, 228
Johnson, William, 28, 29n
Joint Committee on Taxation (U.S. Congress), 72, 89, 154
Joint Economic Committee of the U.S. Congress, 4, 7–8, 11, 41, 76, 86, 92, 93, 120, 130, 178
Jones, James R., 175
Jouvenel, Bertrand de, 38n

Kadlec, Charles, 142, 148n
Kaiser, Edgar, 206
Kaiser-Frazer Corporation, 205
Kaizuku, Keimei, 202n
Kalven, Harry, 38, 40n
Kaplan, Robert S., 82n
Kemp, Cong. Jack F., vii, viii, 118, 121, 123, 125–35, 136n, 137n, 168, 226, 231. *See also* Kemp-Roth Tax Reduction Act.
Kemp-Roth Tax Reduction Act, 10, 12n, 92, 130–35, 159, 163, 209
Kendell, Jonathan, 26n
Kennecott Copper Corporation, 66
Kennedy, John F., 88, 104, 112, 114–23, 130, 141, 174
Keynesian economics. *See* John Maynard Keynes.
Keynes, John Maynard, 2–11, 11n, 52, 85, 90, 92, 94n, 110, 112, 115, 126, 131, 133, 160, 173, 178, 192, 201
Khaldun, Ibn, 14, 24
King, Gov. Edward J., 59
Kirzner, Israel M., 39n
Klein, Lawrence, 83, 117, 123n, 131
Knight, Andrew, 184–85, 189n
Knight, Frank H., 32, 39n
Knight, Michael, 69n
Knutson, Harold, 108, 110
Kolko, Gabriel, 210n
Kristol, Irving, 3–4, 12n, 133, 137n, 146, 149n

Laffer Curve. *See* Arthur B. Laffer.
Laffer, Arthur B., viii, 12n, 14, 24n, 52n, 92, 95n, 127, 131, 135n, 142, 144, 145, 148n, 149n, 170, 173, 179n, 180n, 187, 190n, 195n, 197, 199, 203n
Lance, Bert, 131
Lee, L. Douglas, 96n
Lekachman, Robert, 203n
Levin, David J., 149n
Lewis, Wilfred, Jr., 113n
Long, Sen. Russell, 87, 89, 91–92, 117, 157, 168
Lucas, Robert E., Jr., 85, 94n
Lustron Corporation, 205

Lutz, F. A., 201n
Lutz, Harley L., 28, 38n

MacArthur, Gen. Douglas, 193
McBreen, Maureen, 68n
McCracken, Paul, 132, 168, 179n
McCulloch, J. R., 27, 38n
McEvoy, John, 92
McNees, Stephen K., 94n

Magill, Roswell, 109
Mansfield, Sen. Mike, 117
Marginal tax rates, 6, 9, 10, 19, 28, 30, 33, 34, 46–47, 92, 109, 121–22, 173
Marshall Plan, 192
Mason, Noah, 112
Mathematica Policy Research, 42
Mayer, Thomas, 34, 39n
Meiselman, David, 90, 95n
Mellon, Andrew, 99–104, 108, 120, 183
Meltzer, Alan, 132
Merrill Lynch Economics, 152, 157n
Mill, John Stuart, 1–2, 11n
Miller, Judith, 13n
Miller, Preston J., 91, 95n
Millikan, Frank B., 66
Mills, Wilbur, 117
Mises, Ludwig von, 16, 31
Money supply, 2–3
Moore, Henson, 175
Moynihan, Daniel Patrick, 49, 56, 68n, 205
Musgrave, Richard A., 39n
Mushkin, Selma J., 149n
Muskie, Edmund, 92
Myrdal, Gunnar, 22, 26n, 196

National Bureau of Economic Research, 7, 84
National Journal, 55, 56, 126–27, 174
New Deal, 160–61, 163
"New" economics, 3–4, 6, 8, 12n
New York State Senate Labor Committee, 66
Northeast-Midwest Economic Advancement Coalition, 55

Novak, Robert, 95n, 138n, 180n
Nunn, Sam, 133

Okun, Arthur, 117, 123n
Olson, Janet, viii
Opinion Research Corporation, 155
Organization for Economic Cooperation and Development, 21
Oswald, Ruby, 132
Ott, Attiat F., 6, 12n
Ott, David J., 6, 12n

Pack, Janet Rothenberg, 68n
Paglin, Morton, 53n
Parkinson, C. Northrop, 39n, 183
Pascal, Anthony H., 149n
Passell, Peter, 22, 26n
Patman, Wright, 107
Paul, Ron, 128
Pechman, Joseph A., 13n, 24n, 34, 37, 38n, 39n, 40n, 120, 132, 202n
Peirce, Neil, 67n
Pellechio, Anthony J., 48, 52n
Penner, Rudolph, 76
People's Advocate, 140
Phillips, A. W., 12n
Phillips Curve, 3
Phillips, Thomas W., Jr., 106
Pine, Art, 138n, 180n
Policinski, Mark, viii
Posner, Richard A., 16, 25n, 82n
Pratt, Stanley, 155
President's Office of Management and Budget, 88, 131
Productivity, 4, 8, 9, 10, 12n, 173
Proposition 1, 140
Proposition 4, 144–45
Proposition 9, 145
Proposition 13, 132, 137n, 139–47, 153, 159, 163, 174
Proxmire, Sen. William, 205
Puerto Rico, 199–200

Rabushka, Alvin, 195, 202n
Radosh, Ronald, 165n, 210n
Ranson, R. David, 180n
Rapp, Richard, 104n

Reagan, Ronald, vii, ix, 134, 135, 140, 165
Reconstruction Finance Corporation, 205–06
Reed, Daniel, 110, 111
Reeves, Richard, 142, 148n
Revenue Act of 1921, 99
Revenue Act of 1924, 102
Revenue Act of 1926, 103
Revenue Act of 1948, 213
Revenue Act of 1964, 227, 228
Rinfret, Pierre, 84
Rivlin, Alice, 92, 131, 136n
Robbins, Lionel (Lord), 30, 32, 38n, 39n
Roberts, Paul Craig, viii, 10, 11n, 13n, 81n, 90, 94n, 95n, 126, 128, 130, 131, 133, 135n, 136n, 137n
Rohatyn, Felix, 205, 209n
Rolnick, Arthur, 91, 95n
Roosevelt, Franklin D., 106, 160
Roper Poll, 21, 26n, 132
Roepke, Wilhelm, 202n
Rosen, Harvey S., 40n
Ross, Irwin, 137n
Roth, Sen. William V., Jr., 123, 129, 132, 133, 137n, 177. *See also* Kemp-Roth Tax Reduction Act.
Rothbard, Murray N., 96n, 165n, 210n
Rousselot, John, 128, 129, 131, 169
Rowan, Hobart, 26n, 133, 137n
Rueff, Jacques, 201, 201n

Sargent, Thomas, 85
Savings, 5, 7, 16, 35, 86
Savings and Investment Act, 125–26
Say's law, 1, 2
Say, Jean Baptiste, 11, 11n
Schoeplein, Robert N., 52n
Schultze, Charles, 83, 207
Schumpeter, Joseph, 2, 11n, 15, 24n, 31, 32, 38n, 39n, 93, 96n
Schwartz, Anna, 12n
Securities and Exchange Commission, 79, 80
Securities Industry Association, 151
Senate Banking Committee, 205

Senate Budget Committee, 88, 89, 92, 132, 165

Senate Finance Committee, 56, 87, 92, 108, 110, 117, 131, 132, 134, 135, 157, 168, 170, 175, 176

Senate Select Committee on Small Business, 151

Shoup, Carl, 25n, 33, 39n, 193

Shoup Mission, 193–94

Simon, William, 179n, 207, 210n

Simons, H. C., 27, 38n

Sixteenth Amendment, 106ff

Slemrod, Joel, 76, 82n, 152, 157n

Smernoff, Barry, 170, 179n

Smith, Adam, 15, 182

Smith, Dan Thorpe, 34, 39n, 81n

Smick, Dave, viii

Social Security, 7, 19, 28, 41, 48, 82n, 170–71, 174, 179n, 186, 235

Sohmen, Egon, 202n

Special Task Force on Taxation (N.Y.), 61

Spiegelman, Robert, 49

Sprinkel, Beryl, 4

Stamp, Sir Josiah, 32, 39n

Steiger capital gains tax bill. See William Steiger.

Steiger, Cong. William, 152, 153–54, 163

Stein, Herbert, 90, 113n, 132, 165, 179n

Stigler, George, 207, 210n

Stockman, David, 50, 52n, 132

Strandlund, Carl, 205

Sunley, Emil, 132

Sweden, 22, 54, 196–97, 202n

Sweet, Stuart, viii

Tatom, John A., 12n

Tax rates, 9, 10, 14, 15–16, 22–23, 27ff, 46, 54, 60, 61, 86, 92, 97ff, 106–07, 115, 116, 120, 156, 161, 168, 173, 175, 185, 208

Tax Reform Act of 1969, 150

Tax Reform Act of 1976, 17

Tax shelters, 17, 28. See also Underground economy.

Teague, Randall, viii, 125–26

Temporary Commission on City Finances (New York), 60–61

Thatcher, Margaret, 182, 186–89

Third Concurrent Resolution on the Budget for Fiscal Year 1977, 128, 168–69

Third World, 191, 197, 200

Thompson, Bruce, viii, 130

Tobin, James, 199

Toia, Philip, 50

Tolchin, Martin, 67n, 137n

Truman, Harry, 108, 110, 161–62

Ture, Norman, viii, 13n, 38, 40n, 92, 126, 130, 132, 135n, 187

Ullman, Al, 152

Underground economy, 17–24, 25n, 26n

Unemployment, 3, 9, 12n, 19, 85, 86, 114, 117, 118, 173

Unemployment compensation, 41–46, 52n

U.S. Bureau of Labor Statistics, 60

Vanderford, D. Evans, 92, 95n

Vanik, Charles, 118, 120

Vauban, Sébastien Le Prestre, 15

Wainwright, H. C., Company, 92, 142

Wall Street Journal, viii, 22, 77, 86, 120, 126, 130, 133, 141, 142, 159, 163, 164, 172, 173, 176

Wanniski, Jude, viii, 102, 105n, 126–27, 136n, 148n, 197, 202n

Ward, Barbara, 197, 202n

Waterhouse, Price, 80

Weicker, Sen. Lowell, Jr., 135

Weidenbaum, Murray L., 210n

Weldon, H. Kent, 68n

Welfare, 41, 46–53, 56, 59

West Germany, 24, 37, 191–93

Wharton Econometric Forecasting Associates, 83, 117, 131

Wicker, Tom, 179n

Will, George, 132, 137n

Williams, Harold M., 79–80

Willes, Mark, 85
Wilson, Woodrow, 87–88
Wisconsin income tax, 54–55
World War II, 7, 33, 83, 104, 161, 183, 191, 197, 199
Wright, David McCord, 200, 203n

Yeager, Leland, 96n
Yitzhaki, Shlomo, 157n

Zarnowitz, Victor, 84, 94n
Zschau, Edwin, 151